ESSENTIALS OF
Stage Management

Peter Maccoy

Published 2004
A & C Black Publishers Ltd
37 Soho Square
London W1D 3QZ
www.acblack.com

ISBN 0-7136-6528-9

A CIP catalogue record for this book is available from the British Library

A & C Black uses paper produced with elemental chlorine-free pulp, harvested from managed sustainable forests.

Printed and bound in Great Britain
by Biddles, Kings Lynn

CONTENTS

LIST OF ILLUSTRATIONS

FOREWORD

The best stage managers are energetic, intelligent, caring, humorous, perceptive, and sensitive. Rather like you'd want your best friends to be, which isn't an accident, since one of the things a stage manager has to be is best friend to everyone involved in the show. There's a lot you have to know to be a good stage manager: nobody in the theatre has to know more about everyone else's job, so this book is to be welcomed wholeheartedly. But stage management is about more than expertise. It's about the kind of person you are: able to deal with talented, insecure, demanding colleagues; able to pour oil on troubled waters and stir them up if they become too tranquil; able to make sure everyone knows what everyone else is up to; able to make everyone feel good about each other.

I hope this book encourages a new generation of remarkable people.

Nicholas Hytner

DEDICATION

This book is dedicated to my mother, Margaret Mary St Leger Maccoy, who sadly passed away before she could see her son's name in print.

ACKNOWLEDGEMENTS

I could never have written this book without the forbearance of my family and friends, and my colleagues and students at the Central School of Speech and Drama. Their tolerant support through some difficult times has enabled this endeavour to come to fruition.

I would like to thank all the stage managers, production managers, technicians, directors, designers, performers and so forth who have taught me so much about the art of stage management.

In particular I would like to thank the following people for their help and input: David Adams, David Ayliff, Howard Bird, Daniel Bond, Tracy Cattell, Barbara Eifler, Cindy Limauro, Alastair Noonan, Keith Orton, Gail Pallin, Christine Schott, Conrad Schwartz and Jessica Turnpenny.

The *Model Technical Rider* (Appendix F) and *Risk Control: Managing the Stage* (Appendix D) are reproduced with the consent of the Association of British Theatre Technicians, 55 Farringdon Road, London, EC1M 3JB, Great Britain, Tel. +44 (0) 20 7242 9200, www.abtt.co.uk.

The *Code of Practice for Health and Safety Demonstrations for Performers and Stage Management* (Appendix B) is reproduced with the consent of the Theatre Safety Committee, a cross-industry body which monitors developments and disseminates information relating to health and safety in the theatre industry. Management organisations, unions and other industry bodies with an interest in health and safety are represented on the committee.

Four Steps to Risk Assessment (Appendix E) is adapted from free guidelines issued by the Health and Safety Committee (HSC).

Permission to reproduce material from the following publications is also gratefully acknowledged: Steven Covey, *The Seven Habits of Highly Effective People*, published by Simon and Schuster, 1999, courtesy of FranklinCovey Co, Salt Lake City, Utah, USA; Judith Taylor, *Communication at Work*, published by Kogan Page Ltd, 2001; Alan Barker, *How to Manage Meetings*, published by Kogan Page Ltd, 2002.

Finally I would like to thank my wife for putting up with me and teaching me everything I needed to know about actors but was afraid to ask!

Peter Maccoy, July 2004

INTRODUCTION

When I started teaching, after ten years as a working stage manager, I was forced, very rapidly, to examine the role. As a practitioner I had accepted the protocols, learned and practised all the shortcuts, picked up some lazy, even bad, habits and drifted into a sort of 'auto-pilot' mode of working. I was still enthused by the involvement in creating a piece of theatre, however; each working day was new and exciting; and I found the dynamics of rehearsal, the relationships between the people involved and the problems encountered endlessly fascinating.

When faced with a group of students all asking 'how?', and then 'why?', and then challenging the answer, I had to ask myself 'What is it really all about?' I was amazed at how difficult it was to explain what appeared to be obvious and, to me, automatic procedures. This has led me, over my years as a lecturer, to examine and reconsider the role and its place in contemporary theatre practice. I have encountered methods of making theatre where the 'traditional' role of the stage manager is inappropriate, yet where the process still needs to be managed. I have come into contact with practitioners, particularly from other countries, where the job of 'stage manager' is not acknowledged, yet the traditional responsibilities of the stage manager are still covered.

As a lecturer I have to recommend books on stage management and related subjects to my students and so I have had to appraise those currently available. Some of them are excellent books, yet somehow I always feel that something is missing. They set out to teach the reader 'how to do it', not a bad objective in itself. Some even tell the reader 'this is how I do it, follow my process and you'll be all right'. Yet none of them really seems to cover, or question, the reasoning behind this process.

The inexperienced stage manager can feel stranded when faced with the first day of rehearsals for a piece of devised physical theatre with no script and no design, or with 30 young people, none of whom wants to be a performer, about to embark on creating a piece of open-air community theatre. They are unable to follow the formula, it doesn't apply. There is no reassuring handbook to tell them how to do it, or even how to approach this situation.

Theatre has a certain mystique about it, and it is this that often attracts prospective stage managers. They are excited by the 'stage' but wary of the 'management'. Of course theatre is a business like any other, albeit one concerned with a creative medium, and it shares many similarities to other industries. It is bound by the same legislation as any industry and works to tight deadlines. Even at its simplest it is complex, involving a range of people with disparate skills yet, hopefully, a common goal. At times it seems to thrive on chaos, yet order needs to be found. It needs managing.

Theatre is a creative medium. If the stage manager is to be fully involved in the management of this creative process, they must have some kind of creative input. The contemporary stage manager is part of a collaborative team creating a piece of live theatre. Their sensitive and considered input to this process is crucial; they must be willing and able to contribute, well-prepared and informed. They must be prepared to be flexible, able to embrace new ways of creating theatre with an open mind and to adapt their working practice to suit the demands of each company.

To illustrate this need for flexibility, I will briefly describe my last three engagements prior to becoming a full-time lecturer. All three required a different approach. All three had their highs, and their lows.

For the first, I was company and stage manager for a prestigious theatre company taking a show out on tour around the UK. There were three in the stage management team, one of whom operated sound as well. Although we had a touring carpenter who took charge of the get-in and fit-up, it was my responsibility to supervise the get-out. The cast was large and included a couple of high-profile actors, stars of stage and screen. I had overall responsibility for about 50 people, ensuring that they were at the right place at the right time, paid the right amount, and generally happy in their work. The show was a critical failure and morale became fairly low, resulting in lack of motivation which members of the company took out on each other.

For the second, I was sole stage manager for an ambitious, though small-scale, fringe production in a studio theatre. The budget was reasonable which allowed production values to be high. I was responsible for realising the set – which included trap doors in a false stage and flown elements, finding the props, the get-in and fit-up, the get-out, keeping track of the budget and so on, as well as keeping the prompt copy in rehearsals. I was helped by the designer, the producer and a student on a work placement. During the performance I cued the show and operated sound from the control room at the back of the theatre. The sound had to be synchronised with a live musician on stage. I also had to run the scene changes. This involved leaving the control room and running through the foyer and bar area, where the interval for a different production in the main theatre was often in progress, in order to enter the studio, all to a piece of music which lasted a set number of seconds. The production won a fringe award for best comedy and subsequently toured to Singapore.

The third engagement was the launch of a new car, what is now referred to as 'industrial theatre'. I was given a budget of £25,000 and had to organise a five-minute performance involving a cast of 50, most of whom were amateurs, including a basketball team. My responsibilities involved co-ordinating the casting, which took place in a different city, negotiating contracts, organising rehearsals, transport and so forth. My budget was a fraction of the overall budget for the event, which involved state-of-the-art lighting, sound and audiovisual technology. The whole event was 'called' by another stage manager whose involvement with my section was cursory.

As you can see each project presented very different challenges, each necessitating a different approach.

What follows is an attempt to address and discuss some of these issues, to give the stage managers of tomorrow the strategies to approach any eventuality.

Peter Maccoy
April 2004

THE ROLE OF STAGE MANAGEMENT

At the heart of stage management is the management of performance, from its initial concept, through its development during the rehearsal period, to the moment of actual performance and beyond. The development of performance is a complex and dynamic process of evolution involving, even at its simplest, the collaboration of a wide range of artistes, technicians and crafts people in a constantly changing dialogue. This creative process is often intimate and exposing and requires sensitive management. Information must be accurate and concise, and must be communicated rapidly, and without prejudice.

The management of the rehearsal process and performance requires a close working relationship with the director and performers, as well as with makers and technicians. For the majority of the production team the stage management are the main point of contact with the rehearsal room and as such are responsible for recording and communicating developments to all relevant parties as this information becomes available. This closeness to the process of developing a performance places the stage management in a position that enables them to hold the widest and most accurate overview of the overall production. This may range from an insight into the personal dynamics of a company of performers to an active and creative understanding of the intentions of the director and designers. During the rehearsal period, stage management traditionally took on the role of acquiring properties and furniture, drawing on their knowledge of the production's requirements as these evolved. During performance, this knowledge enables stage management to take on a co-ordinating role, from setting up and checking the stage to controlling all technical aspects.

Theatre-making has changed radically in the last 60 years, prompted by the need to compete with TV and film, to attract a new, younger, more diverse audience, and in response to the availability of increasingly more complex technology and the accompanying regulations. The use of 'found' space for theatrical presentation is now common, and many practitioners are abandoning the traditional, custom-designed theatre building. Over this period the role, and perception, of stage management has developed from that of a service role undertaken by hopeful, or failed, performers, to a highly responsible profession.

Stage management is recognised as an integral part of the process of creating a piece of live performance. Without it, or with it done badly, the process is unlikely to be smooth, fruitful and enjoyable, and theatre-making should be all of these. The management of creativity entails more than just good administration, however; it also requires intuition, sensitivity, adaptability, resolution, intelligence and discipline. It is these qualities that are the foundation of good stage management. Good stage management should be informed by a solid grasp of the underlying principles, both of theatre-making and of management, an understanding of 'why' that will lead to 'how'.

Stage management involves the application of management techniques such as communication, time management, group dynamics, interpersonal relations, leadership skills and so on, within the context of the theatre environment. These techniques are informed by a detailed understanding of the creative process, together with text analysis and background research.

A BRIEF HISTORY

The spectacles mounted at the Hippodrome and Coliseum in Rome; Aztec sacrificial ceremonies; English medieval mystery plays; the Court theatre of the Restoration period: all these must have been managed. The Hippodrome was regularly flooded and nautical battles staged, and gladiators had to be cued on at the right time. The timing of events in the Aztec rituals was crucial; the carts needed to arrive at the right point of the procession at the right time, and the King could not be kept waiting (unless you wanted to lose your head).

Evidence exists for prompters being used in medieval pageant theatre, which was performed by illiterate amateurs on holy days. This was known as 'keeping the book' a term which has survived to the present day. During the Elizabethan period the prompter began to be referred to as the 'book-keeper' or 'book-holder'. Contemporary accounts suggest that somebody 'kept a book' for Shakespeare's company. This may have been similar to our modern understanding of a 'prompt copy', recording moves and the timing of effects as well as keeping the actual text up-to-date. How close this person's role was to that of today's stage manager, or to the prompter in opera or French theatre is, of course, not known. But we can imagine that the role was not dissimilar. The differences found between the different editions of Shakespeare's plays may well be accounted for by this.

As the custom-built playhouse developed through the Elizabethan and Jacobean periods, the role of the 'book-keeper' expanded. Their duties would have included arranging for the necessary licence to be drawn up by the Master of the Revels, copying out individual parts for the actors, noting in the book who was needed and when, marking in entrances and exits, providing a synopsis to be pinned backstage for reference during performance, noting what props and sound-effects would be required and ensuring that they happened in the right place at the right time. At this time a separate person, the stage-keeper, with different responsibilities, is also identified. They would have been responsible for the maintenance of the theatre, setting props on stage and managing the stage in performance.

It is well documented that stage managers existed in the nineteenth century in parallel with the development of the repertoire system and the rise of 'actor/managers' such as William Charles Macready. The repertoire system practised by the 'stock' companies meant that actors needed to keep many parts in their heads at any one time as they performed a different play each night. Rehearsal periods were very short, sometimes a matter of a few days, and thus the role of the prompter became crucial. The role of the 'director' or 'producer' had yet to emerge, usually being undertaken by the principal actor. Direction was sometimes referred to as 'stage management'. It is likely that the 'stage manager' and 'prompter' may have taken on some of this responsibility, particularly when rehearsing a change of cast.

In *Personal Reminiscences of Henry Irving*, Bram Stoker refers to the stage manager at the Lyceum in the 1880s, Mr Loveday. His role was primarily to organise the special effects which were an integral and important part of late Victorian theatre. Sir Henry Irving himself had worked as a stage manager with the St. James' company in the 1850s. The precise nature of this role is hard to ascertain, though we can speculate that it was probably an amalgam of the modern 'Resident Stage Manager' role, in charge of technical matters, and stage management, co-ordinating these.

The theatre of the nineteenth century became, to a large extent, the theatre of spectacle. It developed a 'star' based system, the 'actor/manager' being the centre of attention, and the more lavish the production the better they appeared. The playwright became relatively less important; classic plays, even Shakespeare, were rewritten to the advantage of the star, who stood down-stage centre in the best light, declaiming the lines, enhanced by lavish costumes and supported by lesser performers. Scenery was spectacular and not necessarily relevant to the play being performed. The technology of the age allowed scene changes and special effects to become virtually the focus of the audience's attention, and dramatic scenes, such as shipwrecks or volcanic eruptions, were inserted for effect. Stages became larger to accommodate this need for spectacle, taller fly towers were built, and mechanical stage lifts and revolves installed. To make these work the theatres needed to employ vast stage crews who would have been under the direction of the stage manager. To pay for this, and to keep up with public demand, auditoria became larger, seating up to two, even three, thousand people.

The end of the nineteenth century saw a big change in the approach to theatre, a move back towards story-telling and realism and away from pure spectacle. At this time the notion of the 'director' as we know it (then known as the 'producer') came into being. Adolphe Appia recognised that his concept of a production as a living work of art required a director — a 'managing artist', whose responsibility would be 'conducting the entire work of developing the dramatist's conception from its written form to its stage form'. He saw this as an extension to the function of the stage manager from purely 'machine minding', requiring a person who was a master of all the arts and sciences involved.

Edward Gordon Craig took this a step further, regarding the role of the stage manager as 'the highest title to be won in theatre'. He felt that one person should ideally embody the roles of the playwright, the designer, and the stage manager. In his essays *On the Art of the Theatre*, 1911, he declares that the ideal 'stage manager' must be 'capable of inventing and rehearsing a play; capable of designing and superintending the construction of both scenery and costume: of writing any necessary music: of inventing such machinery as is needed and the lighting that is to be used'. This role seems much closer to that of the 'director' that we would recognise today.

In *The Exemplary Theatre*, published in 1922, Harley Granville-Barker suggests that 'the stage manager has become to some degree an anachronism. He is still supposed to be interested in the play itself, to watch the actors, rehearse their understudies, and to be responsible for the artistic upkeep of the performances generally. But the coming into fashion of the producer has deprived him of any initiative in such matters, and nowadays he is chosen mainly for his powers of controlling the stage staff, his technical knowledge of scenery, and his ability to keep accounts. The position would be better filled by a man who frankly disinterested himself in the dramatic side of the business altogether'. Craig saw this as virtually a new role, rather than a return to the Victorian situation where the stage manager was concerned solely with the mechanics of the particular production in hand. This he regarded as part of the director's work.

So we can see that the modern concept of stage management was becoming established at the start of the twentieth century. By the Second World War we would recognise a stage management team that consisted of a stage director, a stage manager and an assistant stage manager or two. In repertory theatre the team might have included a 'student stage manager' (rather like an apprentice), and the assistant stage mangers (ASMs) would have been expected to take on small acting roles. In fact this was one of the main routes into acting as a career before the proliferation of drama schools, and the only way into stage management. This meant that the majority of acting ASMs were actually hopeful actors and not remotely interested in stage management as a career.

The stage director would have been responsible for the technical side of the production and for making sure that this ran smoothly. Once the production had opened, the stage director would be in charge of the whole production, the staff and cast, for the remainder of its run. The stage manager would usually keep the book and run the corner. The assistants would undertake a number of other duties which might include operating sound using a record player called a 'panatrope', giving calls to the actors and sometimes acting. Props setting and the operation of effects would have been undertaken by property staff under stage management supervision. A separate business manager would have dealt with front of house and box office liaison, publicity and company salaries.

During the Second World War so many people were in the armed forces that theatre managers were forced to rationalise this system. They did this by combining the roles of the business manager and stage manager. Thus was born the 'Company and Stage Manager' and the system that has remained to this day.

ROLES AND RESPONSIBILITIES

The make-up of a stage management team today will vary according to a number of factors: the scale and budget of a production, the type of organisation or type of production itself. A typical set-up in a medium scale receiving theatre in Great Britain might consist of:

- A Company & Stage Manager (CSM)
- A Deputy Stage Manager (DSM)
- Two Assistant Stage Managers (ASM) – these might be divided into a 'Technical' ASM and an 'Acting, or Understudy' ASM

The team for a large-scale 'West End' or touring musical might be made up of the following:

- A Company Manager (CM)
- A Stage Manager (SM)
- A Deputy Stage Manager
- Three Assistant Stage Managers – some shows employ up to five.

A producing, or repertory, theatre with two venues might have the following:

- A Stage Manager
- Two Deputy Stage Managers
- Three or four Assistant Stage Managers

A smallscale fringe or pub theatre production might have just one stage manager.

This list is not exhaustive. Variations will be encountered, as they will in the delegation of responsibilities which are outlined next but, while individual responsibilities will be vastly different, the underlying responsibility of stage management will remain the same.

GENERAL STAGE MANAGEMENT RESPONSIBILITIES

It is useful to consider the role of stage management as a whole, rather than assuming that different members of the team have particular responsibilities. While this may often be true, there are also many exceptions and, no matter what the make-up of the team, somebody will have to take responsibility for all of these.

Stage management ensure that all elements of the production are consistently in the right place at the right time, and meet the requirements identified in the design and direction as developed through the rehearsal process. They are there to prevent *anything* from adversely affecting a production. A performer should only ever have to worry about the performance. It is the prime responsibility of stage management to facilitate this.

A breakdown of stage management responsibilities follows. This list is not exhaustive, nor does it describe everything all stage management can expect to do every time.

- Provide support for the rehearsal process and performance
- Prepare the rehearsal space and keep it tidy and organised
- Mark up a two-dimensional representation of the set in the rehearsal room
- Maintain a presence at rehearsals whenever the director is working with the cast
- Maintain discipline within the rehearsal space and backstage
- Be responsible for Health and Safety in the rehearsal room and during performance
- Prepare and mark up the Prompt Script, recording the blocking and cue points
- Prompt, in the rehearsal room and during performance
- Call artistes for rehearsals and fittings
- Pass on information from the rehearsal room, particularly details of the production's requirements as they are raised, to the designer, technical departments etc., in the form of Rehearsal Notes
- Provide rehearsal props and furniture for the cast and director to use
- Co-ordinate communication with technical departments
- Acquire props and furniture
- Manage the stage management budget
- Participate and take minutes in production meetings
- Take overall authority backstage
- Run the technical rehearsal, acting as liaison between the technical staff backstage and the production team in the auditorium
- Run the show from the prompt corner or SM control point.
- Make back-stage and front-of-house calls
- Operate sound as required
- Place props and furniture in their correct positions both in the rehearsal room and on stage
- Prepare setting lists, running plots and cue synopsis, and keep them up-to-date
- Keep the technical, or back-stage, aspects of every performance in line with the director and designer's original intentions
- Monitor the artistic quality of the production, in line with the director and designer's original intentions, giving notes and calling rehearsals where necessary
- Prepare and circulate a show, or performance, report at the end of each performance

- Rehearse understudies
- Deal with business and financial matters, particularly concerning work contracts, hours worked, holiday allowance and cover, salaries, subsistence and travel payments, contracts with theatres
- Take responsibility for the morale and welfare of the company
- Act as the interface between the management and the company
- Liaise with marketing concerning publicity, photographs etc. and with the front-of-house staff
- Liaise with the theatres on tour
- Arrange transport and accommodation on tour
- Re-light the production in each venue on tour
- Return all props and furniture, etc., at the end of a run

STAGE MANAGEMENT ROLES

A stage management team is collectively responsible for the stage management of a production. A team may be put together to reflect the particular challenges offered by a production, and to create a balance of expertise. Individual roles within the team will usually be delegated according to ability or experience. If any member of the team is in any doubt as to whether a particular task is their responsibility, or has been undertaken by another member, they should never make the assumption that this is the case. Once a production is under way, each member of the team may make themselves familiar with each other's duties in order to provide cover if necessary.

Although there are no hard and fast rules as to the division of responsibility within the team, duties are traditionally allocated as follows.

STAGE MANAGER (SM)

The Stage Manager has overall responsibility for the team and for keeping an overview of the production process. During the rehearsal and production period the SM co-ordinates communication with technical departments, making sure all elements of the production are in the right place at the right time and correct according to the requirements identified in the design and direction. They will often take particular responsibility for co-ordinating the acquisition of props and furniture, working closely with the designer and ASMs. They will run the technical rehearsal, liaising between the DSM in the prompt corner, back-stage and the creative team in the auditorium.

During the run the SM has overall responsibility for keeping the technical, or back-stage, aspects of every performance in line with the director and designer's original concept. This includes maintaining discipline backstage. The SM may try to avoid having any specific performance duties, or keep these to a minimum. This enables them to remain free to monitor the production and to deal with emergencies when called for.

DEPUTY STAGE MANAGER (DSM)

It is usual for one member of the team to be present at rehearsals whenever the director is working with the cast. This is normally the DSM. Their responsibilities relate to their first-hand knowledge of the director's intentions, and include preparing and marking up the prompt script, recording the blocking and cue points, prompting, calling artistes for rehearsals and fittings, and preparing regular Rehearsal Notes.

During the technical and dress rehearsals and in performance, the DSM, having been responsible for the prompt copy during the rehearsal process, is the obvious person to run the show from the prompt corner or other control point. They will give cues using cue lights and/or headsets and make back-stage calls.

ASSISTANT STAGE MANAGER (ASM)

The main responsibility of the ASM is to support the rehearsal process and performance. This may include finding, or even making, props and furniture. Ideally ASMs should be present in the rehearsal room as much as possible in order to assist the DSM by taking messages/phone calls, looking after rehearsal props and furniture, assisting in runs-through of the play and so on. At the very least they should be available at the start and finish of each rehearsal, setting up and clearing up the room, and for runs of the play towards the end of the rehearsal period.

The ASM is not a dogsbody for all and sundry, making tea, feeding parking meters etc., but can reasonably be expected to run errands for the director, so long as this does not interfere with more urgent stage management duties. However the sensitive stage manager will provide tea and sympathy at appropriate moments, particularly for the director who may not be able to take breaks like the rest of the company (directors will often use breaks for important calls, meetings etc.). During the technical rehearsal and lighting plotting sessions, the ASM may offer to provide those seated at the production desk (director, lighting designer, DSM, etc.) with refreshments when appropriate, and subject to the theatre rules. They may also be required to 'walk' for lighting sessions; that is standing in roughly the same place as the actors, so that the lighting designer can light them.

Props finding is a particular skill requiring an ability to undertake detailed period research, to interpret a designer's vision, to persuade people and companies to part with objects for nothing and to go shopping effectively. Stage management often need negotiating skills to suggest alternatives to directors and designers, particularly where either Health and Safety or budget restrictions mean that they cannot achieve the ideal solution to a problem. Such alternatives need to be based on a good understanding of the script and on the artistic intentions of the creative team.

During the run of a production the ASMs are responsible for setting props, furniture etc. Depending on the degree of staffing and union organisation in the particular theatre, this can mean anything from checking the work of the staff without actually touching anything, to doing it all themselves. They can also expect to take on other performance duties, such as leading cast members off stage in a blackout: in fact anything that will make the production run smoothly. This can include operating sound.

OTHER ASSOCIATED ROLES

A number of other job titles may be encountered which relate to stage management directly. These are the people who work closely with stage management during the rehearsal process and whose roles may overlap some of the traditional roles of stage management. Of course stage management will also interact with other members of the production and theatre staff.

ACTING ASM

Acting ASMs are employed as understudies and may have small 'walk-on' roles. They can be expected to undertake other ASM duties, although the pressure of learning a part (or several) can be a hindrance.

TECHNICAL ASM

The term 'Technical ASM' may either be used to differentiate them from an acting ASM, indicating that they will not be expected to perform, or to refer to particular technical duties. Such duties might include the use of an automated control system to move scenery, such as a revolving stage in a complex production. The operator would need to be present throughout rehearsals in order to become familiar with the production. Stage managers are regularly engaged to operate shows that involve moving scenery using a hydraulic system.

COMPANY MANAGER (CM)

In larger companies a company manager is responsible for business and financial matters, and for the welfare of the company. They act as an interface between the management and the company, and are often involved in liaison with the front-of-house staff, marketing, etc. They may also be responsible for rehearsing understudies. On tour they will liaise with the theatres being visited in advance, and may be involved in arranging transport and accommodation. They may also be responsible for re-lighting the production at each venue, and for supervising the fit-up and get-out.

COMPANY AND STAGE MANAGER (CSM)

In some smaller production companies the stage manager also undertakes the duties of company manager and is known as 'company and stage manager'.

PRODUCTION STAGE MANAGER

Very large productions, particularly in the West End, may employ a production stage manager. They take on the particular responsibility for ensuring that the needs of the production, as identified by the design and rehearsal process, are being met, whilst the company manager attends to the more business and personnel aspects. The production stage manager will run the technical rehearsals and performances up to the opening night, when they hand over responsibility for the day to day running of the show to the company manager, and move on to the next production.

PRODUCTION MANAGER

The production manager is not a member of the stage management team, but works very closely with them and is often the person who employs them. They are primarily responsible for budgeting and costing and for the technical schedule. This includes engaging other members of the technical staff, arranging for the scenery to be built and transported to the theatre and so forth. The production manager will also supervise the fit-up and be present at the technical rehearsal in order to help solve any problems associated with the technical aspects of the production. Any major changes that arise during rehearsal, or major expenses, are passed on to the production manager who might then call a production meeting to discuss the implications.

TECHNICAL MANAGER

The technical manager is responsible for co-ordinating stage technology and solving technical staging problems, organising and instructing the stage crew, and liaising with the production manager, stage manager and other members of the production team in order to realise scene changes effectively. They may be called the 'master carpenter' in the West End, the 'resident stage manager' in provincial touring theatres, the 'technical stage manager' or even just the 'stage manager'. This is where confusion regarding the nature and role of stage management often arises, in particular for people who are considering a career in theatre.

PROPS BUYER

On some larger productions – musicals, opera and some producing theatres – a props buyer will be engaged to acquire props, taking this responsibility away from stage management. The props buyer will work closely with the designer and stage management and will engage makers where appropriate. Although in this situation stage management will be able to concentrate their energies on supporting the rehearsal process, they may find that they still have to become involved in either finding or making some of the props.

PROPS MAKER

Props makers will be engaged, where budget allows, to make props that cannot feasibly be found, or are beyond the making skills of the stage management. Some producing theatres will have their own props-making department, though props makers are usually freelance or work for a specialist company, and often deal with special effects as well. Stage management need to maintain close contact with the makers to ensure that all the props being made are suitable for the way that they are to be used on stage. This may change during the rehearsal process.

COSTUME SUPERVISOR

The costume supervisor works closely with the designer, co-ordinating the acquisition of costumes for a production. They will sample fabric, engage makers, and buy and hire costumes. Stage management need to have close links with the costume supervisor, organising fittings around the rehearsal schedule and availability of costume makers, organising the logistics of quick changes and making sure that props and costume are compatible.

ASSISTANT, ASSOCIATE OR STAFF DIRECTOR

Sometimes, on larger productions or in producing theatres, an assistant to the director will be employed. The responsibilities of the assistant director may vary, but they will generally be responsible for rehearsing understudies and maintaining the artistic quality of a production throughout its run. Sometimes they will undertake detailed research and may be given particular aspects of a production to direct themselves.

DRAMATURG

The role of the dramaturg is relatively new in British theatre, but is becoming more common.

Dramaturgy can be described as 'preparing the text for performance'. This may entail different things for different productions: it may mean preparing a version of a classic play, making an adaptation from a different language, creating a script from a theme or a non-theatrical text, or helping a playwright to construct a new script.

A dramaturg will normally be involved in detailed research for the production, bringing an intimate knowledge of the script to the production process. They will have gathered material that will help the rest of the production team to understand the piece better, and which will supplement and expand on the work that others will be doing. Many dramaturgs work visually, preparing imagery that will help support the text. They are often considered essential to the development of a purely visual piece of theatre, where the story is told without words.

During the development of a production they work primarily with the director but may also be a resource for actors, designers and technicians, including stage management. Throughout the rehearsal process their task is to help the production remain in line with the original vision, especially in shows where the director has many technical details to consider. Many directors will engage a dramaturg to keep an eye on the story, while they concentrate on the technical aspects and minutiae of characterisation.

The dramaturg is thus a representative for the script and its author, encouraging an appropriate interpretation, though without discouraging a non-traditional approach. They also represent the audience by making sure that the production makes sense and puts across the intended message.

PRODUCER

In commercial theatre a producer initiates a production, raises the money, engages the director and designers and senior members of the production team, negotiates contracts and finds suitable venues. The producer will ultimately be the stage management's employer. The amount of contact stage management will have with the producer will depend on the scale of the production. In a large West End production the company manager will act as interface between the producer and the company. In a small fringe production the producer and stage manager may work closely together.

GENERAL MANAGER

Producing theatres usually have a general manager, backed up by administration, who is responsible for the business and financial aspects of the theatre and its productions. They will take on many of the aspects of company management as well as responsibility for the theatre building itself. They may also be known as the theatre manager.

STAGE MANAGEMENT BEYOND THE UK
THE NORTH AMERICAN PERSPECTIVE

In the USA the system is similar to that which existed in the UK prior to the Second World War. Teams tend to be smaller, reflected in the different responsibilities expected of other production staff, and, typically, job titles have a different meaning from the UK. The following table shows equivalents based on a West End/Broadway model.

UK	USA
COMPANY MANAGER	COMPANY MANAGER
STAGE MANAGER	STAGE MANAGER or
DEPUTY STAGE MANAGER	PRODUCTION STAGE MANAGER
ASSISTANT STAGE MANAGER	ASSISTANT STAGE MANAGER
PRODUCTION STAGE MANAGER	PRODUCTION SUPERVISOR

The company manager on Broadway is equivalent to the pre-war business manager in the UK. They are not strictly speaking a member of the stage management team and are not concerned with the actual production. They represent the producer and are responsible for all contractual aspects of a production's personnel. On a show basis they are mainly concerned with front of house aspects and have little to do with the production itself, beyond liaison with the stage manager regarding financial aspects, including salary payment and travel and accommodation when on tour.

The stage manager, often called the production stage manager (PSM), works closely with the director and designers to co-ordinate the technical aspects of the production and is responsible for following its creative development and maintaining its artistic integrity. They represent the actors and crew, making sure that they know the technical requirements for running the show. They usually call the show, but are also responsible for rehearsing understudies and monitoring and maintaining the artistic health of the production. A PSM will often open a production on the book and then train up another member of the team until they can take over. At this stage they can concentrate on the aspect of their role which would be equivalent to that of an associate director, or company manager, in the UK. Once a show has opened and the director has moved on, the PSM will give appropriate acting notes to members of the cast and call rehearsals. On the larger, more technical, productions a production supervisor may be employed to take responsibility solely for the technical aspects, leaving the PSM to concentrate on the artistic side.

Assistant stage managers have a roughly equivalent role to their British counterparts, particularly when compared to the larger national and opera companies or West End musicals. On Broadway they are mainly responsible for running a side of the stage, cueing and guiding actors on and off stage and so forth, and will not actually be involved in setting props or in scene changes. That is the responsibility of the stage and props crew as agreed by the unions, although the ASMs will be responsible for creating the running paperwork, checking props presets, changes, etc. Where a crew member has to hand a prop to or take one from an actor, known as a 'hand-off', the ASM will invariably be present to ensure that it happens successfully. In smaller regional and non-union theatres, the ASM is often in charge of the props crew and may help with the props and scenery changes. During rehearsals they will spend much of their time in the rehearsal room assisting the PSM and may be given responsibility for blocking, prompting, taking and distributing notes.

There are obviously many variations on the traditional roles of stage management in the US, just as there are in the UK. The system varies between on- and off-Broadway and regional theatre, as it does between the West End, the fringe and regional theatre in the UK. While still a fairly technical role in the US, the stage manager remains responsible for maintaining the director's intention for the show once they have moved on. Although in the UK this was the responsibility of the company manager, and in some cases still is, quality control in the UK is restricted to technical matters – the British actor would not be responsive to taking notes from a stage manager.

THE EUROPEAN PERSPECTIVE

In many European countries, stage management does not exist in the same way as in the UK and US, yet performance is successfully managed. The duties associated with stage management are fulfilled by other members of the production team: assistant directors, dramaturgs, or people with very specific responsibilities such as keeping the book or prompting (as in opera).

Theatres themselves have a smaller resident technical staff whose role is often little more than maintenance. As in the USA, theatres are literally empty stage spaces with little, or no, dedicated equipment. Instead each production employs its own specialist technicians and uses its own equipment which is installed in the theatre. Technicians spend a large amount of their time in rehearsals, which are generally longer than is normal in either the UK or USA, and consequently are able to be responsible for taking their own cues. They are expected to know a production to the same depth that is expected of stage management in the UK. This means that shows do not require calling (cueing). Where a production is particularly complicated, a senior technician may call the cues using headsets.

This system is beginning to change, however. The popularity of the largescale spectacular Broadway musical, often a recreation of the original, has brought with it the North American/British system, and work in Europe for British stage managers. Reduced rehearsal time, for financial reasons, has also meant that the old system has had to be replaced in some theatres in some countries. This new system is largely modelled on its British or American equivalent.

THE STAGE MANAGER AS MANAGER

Manager! There is a word that strikes fear into the heart of stage managers everywhere, yet it forms 50% of the job title. Of course that is exactly what stage managers are – managers: managers of people, managers of places, managers of things and managers of time. The 'stage' bit refers to the location of all these elements, or at least helps to distinguish it from 'theatre' management or 'production' management. The former refers to the management of the building itself, the latter to the staging of the production. It is one of the many confusing quirks of theatre terminology that stage management deals with the management of productions and production management with the management of staging.

Before starting to examine the function of stage management in detail, it is helpful to consider it in the context of modern management theory; that is, the stage manager as manager. Many people, attracted to a career in theatre as stage managers, seem to think that it is a purely technical role. Nothing could be farther from the truth. Theatre-making is, by its very nature, a truly collaborative process involving a large group of people, all with different skills, striving together to create the perfect end-result. While individuality within the team is to be encouraged, there is little room for the loner. Like it or not, if you want to work in theatre, you will have to interact with a wide range of people and personalities. Furthermore, this collaborative process of group creativity needs to be managed if it is not to descend into chaos. Stage managers undertake this management role on a daily basis.

Many people also believe that stage management is a low-profile role; that the good stage manager should be neither seen nor heard. Of course during a performance the audience should be unaware of stage management happening. Ironically it is this perception of quiet invisibility that often attracts people to stage management as a career in the first place, yet it is not a job for the shy and retiring. The opposite is just as disastrous, however; the loud, pushy, know-it-all is not the answer either.

The good stage manager needs to maintain a confident and subtle presence, always there when needed, ready to step in and take control as necessary, sensitive to the situation and the personalities involved. They must be ready to give their opinion when called for, based both on their artistic and critical judgement and on their reading of the situation.

While theatre is a collaborative process, the degree of equality of input within each production will vary. Many people misinterpret the word 'collaborate' and take it to mean working together democratically. The *Oxford English Dictionary* defines it as 'to work jointly, especially at literary or artistic production'. At one extreme is the autocratic figurehead director; they know exactly what they want and the whole team, design included, is there to carry out their vision. Compromise is reached grudgingly and the opportunity for creative input is limited, even non-existent. At the other end is the truly egalitarian company, where all members are equal and have an equal right to creative input. This may even be expected of them. Roles become blurred and ultimately decisions may be arrived at through group discussion. The director acts like the chair of a committee and tries to maintain an artistic overview. Most theatre-making exists somewhere in the middle of these two extremes.

Stage managers need to be able to adapt to the dynamics of each group they work with. They need to be able to recognise how the theatre-making process will function with the particular group, and adapt their own working practice accordingly. One director may expect, even demand, active participation; another may require passive, yet solid, support.

An understanding of some key elements of management theory can help a stage manager to achieve this. The stage manager is a member of one large group – the production team, which includes the cast – and of several smaller subgroups, including the stage management team. Each of these groups will have a different dynamic, and the stage manager's place within them will be different. Moreover, unless they are working with exactly the same people as before, the group dynamics will be different for each engagement.

Thus an understanding of how groups work can be immensely helpful. It is useful to be able to step back from the group, to look at it objectively, and to identify which stage of its development it has reached. This can help to identify and pre-empt problems, and to offer reassurance.

It is essential to develop strategies for dealing with 'difficult' people, without prejudice. The theatre-making process involves a wide range of people with different, often flamboyant, personalities, all of whom are trying to be as creative as possible, to get their ideas adopted at the same time as appearing to collaborate fairly. It is inevitable that disagreement will occur and that sometimes these differences may be difficult, even impossible, to reconcile.

There is a misconception, held by some stage managers, that all performers, directors and designers are both difficult and stupid, and that theatre would be a much better place without any of them. Perhaps these people take the other OED definition of 'to collaborate' literally – 'to co-operate traitorously with the enemy'.

Communication is at the heart of the stage manager's portfolio of tasks. Good communication is a dynamic two-way process consisting of continuous dialogue between all interested parties. Yet it is tempting and easy to assume that once a note or message has been passed on, responsibility has been passed on with it. Giving in to this temptation may interrupt the flow of information and reduce efficiency.

The creative process often gives rise to apparent 'crises' as artistic intentions and deadlines prove to be over-ambitious. This is an inevitable and necessary part of the process and needs to be managed effectively. Such crises must be embraced and tackled by the stage manager as they arise. When the process seems to consist purely of crisis management, however, this is usually a symptom of poor management that must be addressed immediately if the real creative endeavour is to be nurtured.

MANAGEMENT THEORY
GROUP DYNAMICS

A group of people is like a living organism, adapting and evolving until it can function at its optimum potential. All groups go through a series of recognisable phases before they reach this goal – although sometimes they never reach it. Being able to recognise these phases can help the individual to understand what is happening and to offer reassurance, even to be pre-emptive in their response. To make it even more complicated, subgroups of the main group will also go through their own development, often at a different rate. Thus the stage management team will need to develop within the wider production group, as will the performers themselves. Membership of groups can fluctuate, and each addition or subtraction will alter the dynamic. Within each group the function and status of each individual will alter according to circumstance. So, for instance, the stage manager's function and status when running the technical rehearsal is very different from their function and status when sitting in a notes session after a rehearsal.

Barry Tuckman, in an article in the *Psychological Bulletin* (1965), identified four phases in the development of groups.

FORMING	STORMING	NORMING	PERFORMING

1. FORMING

In this first phase of the new group, individuals are beginning to explore the boundaries and to find out who is who. Relationships have not been formed; members are finding out about each other's attitudes, backgrounds and values and prejudices. They are keen to establish their own identities, to make an impression, even to find out where they are in the pecking order.

This can be a tense time, with people trying to make an impression that often leads to embarrassment. During this phase individuals may behave in a way that is uncharacteristic, yet that first impression, though often deceptive, is likely to be long lasting. Strong leadership is important at this stage, and rules of behaviour within the group need to be established quickly. The length of time that the 'forming' phase lasts will depend on the size and make-up of the group. A larger group made up of a wide variety of people may take longer to form than a smaller one.

Within the context of theatre this might equate to the first few meetings of the production team or, for the company, the first few days of rehearsals. In a traditional model of the theatre-making process, this coincides with the first 'read through' of the play followed by 'blocking'. The director is guiding the actors around both the text and the set. There may be some room for individualism, but it is the director who is in control. For devised work this may be the time when individuals present their own research, and workshops exploring different themes take place. All members of the group will be invited to contribute their own creative ideas, though still with the director as the focal point.

Stage management need to establish the group dynamic of their own team before this phase starts within the company as a whole. This will enable them to concentrate on helping to make it a smooth process for the company, preparing an optimum environment for the group to form in. It is worth remembering that each member will bring their own agenda to the process and that the dynamics are rarely simple. The outgoing and friendly actor may actually be compensating for shyness and a feeling that they aren't worthy of the job, while the director who is aggressive, dominant and seemingly unfriendly at the start is probably trying to establish leadership as well as covering up deep-seated insecurity. The stage manager must keep an open mind and should never try to take sides.

During this phase informal social interaction is important. In the context of the rehearsal room everyone tends to take their breaks together and socialise at the end of the day.

2. STORMING

The second phase is usually characterised by conflict. Individuals start to challenge each other's positions within the group and to push the boundaries. They are testing the ground to find out how far they can go. Value systems, beliefs and established rules may be challenged. This is a very sensitive time, when insecurities will become evident and personality clashes head towards conflict. Relationships established during the 'forming' phase may be destroyed, or at least disrupted, and allegiances shifted. Individuals within the group may try various tactical strategies, forming alliances, withdrawing, empire-building, even disruption. They will demand the right to be recognised and resist criticism or veto. Yet this phase needs to be embraced by each individual, not avoided, before the group can function effectively.

Within the context of theatre-making, this phase equates to the second stage in the rehearsal process, usually the stage at which the performers begin to establish the identity of their characters. Blocking has been completed, workshops have taken place and dominant themes have been established. The director is beginning to work with the performers on the fine detail of the script.

Interestingly this context adds a layer of complexity not normally encountered in other groups. The actor has to deal with the existence of their character within the world of the play and the particular production, and their own existence within the company. This can be an intense experience that requires sensitive handling, especially if the play is a serious drama. Some actors find it hard to differentiate between the reality of the play and their personal reality. If they are playing an unpleasant character this unpleasantness can sometimes be transferred into the way that they are perceived by the group, even the way they behave within the group. They may even take this beyond the group into their personal lives, adding further complications and levels of stress.

While they are trying to establish their identity within the group, the performers will also be learning their lines so that they can physically let go of the script. The moment that happens is both liberating and traumatic. Suddenly they have two hands unencumbered by a book, and can use them for expression and to do things physically. But they also have to remember what the playwright wrote. Was it 'but' or 'and'? They also have to remember what they did last time the scene was rehearsed, which could be a week ago. This moment will occur at different times for different performers.

An awareness of this process enables the stage manager to offer support where it is needed. Individuals may not be aware of how they are perceived by the rest of the group and can become insecure within it; they may even become ostracised. The frustration at not being able to remember lines or moves, or both, may be taken out on others. Empathy is essential: offering to go through lines, talking through the blocking, making sure that breaks are kept to.

It can also be a stressful time for the director. Performers may start to challenge their judgement and authority, often surreptitiously. They may even begin to question their own ability. This can manifest itself as an obsession with small details, or with one particular scene or performer. The performers will then feel either picked on or ignored. Either way they are likely to think that the director doesn't think that they are any good. In this situation the stage manager should be vigilant in keeping to the rehearsal schedule, pointing out what hasn't been rehearsed much and reminding the director when they are due to work on another scene. A ready supply of tissues is also useful.

It is quite common for the cast to stop socialising with the director during this period. When stage management notice that this is happening they should make a point of including the director. This is easy as there will be a lot of technical things to discuss and an informal surrounding can make this easier. The stage manager can make a point of telling the director how well they think it is all going, but may also use the opportunity to mention if an actor is feeling left out or victimised. As ever, though, stage management must avoid taking sides; if they only go out with the cast, the director may feel doubly insecure.

3. NORMING

By the third phase the group should have established a shared frame of reference based on a set of common perceptions, beliefs and values. These form the group's 'norms', which provide a practical framework within which the individual members can work together and through which the dynamic of the relationships between these individuals has been developed. The group is beginning to work as one entity with a common goal that is held by all members. This is a period of consolidation. Conflict can still take place, but 'deviant' or 'subversive' behaviour is less likely to be tolerated by the majority or cause factions to develop within the group. Miscreant members are liable to be pressurised to conform.

In the context of the rehearsal process, this might coincide with the point at which scenes are being run in their entirety and characterisations further refined and consolidated. In a devising process this might be the point where the company have agreed their creative parameters and are starting to work together to create a cohesive whole. Individual agendas become less important, group members stop protecting their own ideas and interests and start concentrating on the bigger picture.

This is an exciting and fruitful time, requiring concentration and quick thinking on the part of the stage manager. New ideas will be tried and tested, the pace will speed up. Unresolved conflicts or insecurities may still be bubbling below the surface, however, and will need watching. Any members who have not bought into the 'norm' may become sidelined and will need support if they are to be included.

4. PERFORMING

By this phase the group is fully mature and working towards its target. The whole has become greater than the sum of its parts.

This final phase equates to the last few days of the rehearsal process. The play is being 'run through', that is run from beginning to end, and the performers are beginning to spark off one another. The director can concentrate on the bigger picture, as well as continuing to refine and fine tune. This is a period of consolidation. Individual actors will begin to approach what one might call, to borrow an analogy from cooking, 'dropping consistency', that is to say the moment when they are ready to be seen in front of an audience.

See *Figure 2.1* for the four stages outlined by Tuckman. The figure relates to the rehearsal process in a rehearsal room lasting four weeks. The timescale for each stage is approximate and fluid; stages will last for different lengths of time depending on the make-up of the group. Once the production leaves the rehearsal room, the process starts again as the group becomes bigger, involving a new set of people becoming integrated; the timescales for this will again vary.

1. Forming	2. Storming	3. Norming	4. Performing
First few days **of rehearsal**	**End of 1st week** **into 2nd/3rd weeks**	**3rd week into** **4th week**	**Final days of** **rehearsal**
Introductions Read-through Workshops Blocking	Working through each scene Character work Experimentation Invention Letting go of the script Drying, needing prompting	Running scenes Off the book Developing character relationships Stagger through	Run throughs Consolidation Individual performances reach 'dropping consistency'
Characterised by: Socialising Setting up of rules and boundaries Exploration of values Establishment of leadership	**Characterised by:** Conflict Factions develop Boundaries tested Leadership challenged	**Characterised by:** Shared frame of reference Group norms (common perceptions,values and beliefs) Allocation of roles Rules of conduct Pressure to conform	**Characterised by:** Maturity Achievement of job in hand
Management: <ul><li>Establish purpose and rules of engagement</li><li>Make introductions</li><li>Define relationships</li><li>Set agenda</li></ul>	**Management:** <ul><li>Discourage argument</li><li>Encourage diverse ideas</li><li>Work through different points of view</li><li>Agree view of situation</li><li>Define problems</li><li>Define objectives</li><li>Agree behaviour</li></ul>	**Management:** <ul><li>Be wary of the 'feel good factor' and group complacency</li><li>Concentrate on opportunities for action and planning</li><li>Include any participants who may be sidelined</li><li>Challenge consensual opinions</li></ul>	**Management:** <ul><li>Minimal control necessary</li><li>Allow the group to do the work itself</li><li>Concentrate on requests for action</li><li>Allocate tasks</li><li>Set deadlines</li></ul>

Figure 2.1 Stages in group development

SUMMARY

A theatre company is a complex group, or series of groups, of individuals involved in a creative endeavour. An understanding of group dynamics can help the stage manager to prepare in advance for conflict, frenzied creative activity, and so on, by monitoring the phases as they develop. It is useful to know that during the 'storming' phase, probably in the second or third week of rehearsals, nerves may get frayed and tempers flare, insecurities may be exacerbated and individuals feel neglected. At some point somebody will be in tears in the stairwell because they can't act, their lines make no sense, the director is therefore ignoring them and the rest of the group hate them. This is a normal part of the process and the aware stage manager can lend a sympathetic ear and help the group move on.

During the 'norming' phase, stage management will have to process huge amounts of information as the performers become comfortable with their roles and start to invent and experiment. This is the most creative period but also the one in which many ideas will be changed or rejected. Knowing that this is a natural, predictable part of the process means that it should never come as a surprise to stage management. In fact, this is what theatre is all about.

During the 'performing' phase, where consolidation has become the predominant creative process, stage management must be prepared for a certain amount of their endeavour to be rejected. This is not because they have done it wrong, but because it is no longer right for the production. Knowing that this is likely to happen will enable stage management to be prepared in advance, even adjusting their work schedule to embrace it.

When things are going badly it can be helpful to step back and ask: 'Whereabouts are we in this process?' When things are going wrong within the stage management team, it is worth examining how the group has formed. It may be that earlier issues remain unresolved and are holding the group back from moving into the next phase, or maybe a common frame of reference, which takes common values and goals into account, has not been agreed. Sometimes individuals will try to highjack the process by putting personal objectives first or by manipulating the group for 'political' motives.

The formation of a group is a dynamic process; it can be volatile and it can go either way. Sometimes a group will reach the 'performing' stage very quickly, everyone gets on well and the consensus is reached with little fuss. But not all groups will reach the 'performing' phase, either becoming stuck in an earlier one or careering backwards and forwards from one step to another. Theatre productions that never quite come together successfully are almost certainly doing this because they have not reached the 'performing' phase, literally as well as in the context of group dynamics. Occasionally a company does not get beyond the 'storming' phase; the particular group of individuals just never manages to reach a consensus. This is more likely to be encountered in a truly collaborative process, where nobody is prepared to give up their own agenda or ideas. Without strong leadership, or a set of beliefs and values held in common, the process won't work.

The 'performing' phase will also be interrupted by the introduction of new members, or other changes such as new parameters. This will take the group back to the 'forming' phase, but reinvention can be very quick. Thus a company may be 'performing' successfully in the rehearsal room but will take a step back once the production arrives on stage with the actual scenery and a full quota of technicians. The technical rehearsal may take the company back to the 'norming' phase, even to 'storming', though the shared protocols are likely to make the progressions rapid. By the time dress rehearsals are under way the group will hopefully be 'performing' again.

GROUP STRUCTURE

As well as evolving through these phases, a group will develop a structure that depends on the profile of the individuals involved. Uncertainty about the behaviour of group members can be a threat to any group. The group's structure provides a 'system of solutions' which assists the group in managing the difficulties posed by unpredictable behaviour. The structure is unlikely to be fixed or permanent. It is a complex, dynamic system that operates on a range of dimensions identified by Alan Barker, in *How to Manage Meetings* (2002), as including:

1. **Status**
2. **Power**
3. **Role**
4. **Leadership**
5. **Liking**

The behaviour of individuals within the group is an indication of how they are trying to establish their place within its structure.

1. STATUS

Group members assign a value to each position within the group, either formally or socially. Formal status may be associated with the duties or rights attached to a position; the director may automatically be accorded a high formal status within a theatre company. Social status is concerned with the 'rank' of the person as perceived by the group, usually defined by the degree of respect given to that person. The experienced actor, admired by everyone, may be granted a higher social status by the group.

Status is always under threat, however; individuals can only maintain their status by maintaining the group's expectations. It is entirely dependent on the perception of others and can be reduced, even removed, rapidly. This downgrading is a powerful means for the group to exert its authority.

2. POWER

Power is the way that individuals can exert control over others. According to John French and Bertram Raven in their essay on 'The bases of social power' (1959), power can be exercised in five distinct ways.

● **Reward power** is based on the ability to grant favours
● **Coercive power** is based on the ability to mete out punishment
● **Legitimate power** is defined by recognised sets of rules or laws
● **Referent power** is associated with 'charisma' or personality
● **Expert power** is derived from specialist knowledge or skills

Different people will seek to exercise different types of power at different times.

A director with little charisma may use legitimate, reward or even coercive power to assert their authority. An assistant stage manager may use expert power to influence a group. The group may exercise its own power using the shared 'norms' established during its formation. Any challenge to these 'norms' will threaten the stability of the group and so it is in the group's interest to pressurise members to conform. The group may do this through encouragement, embarrassment, exclusion or even expulsion of individuals.

Thus the pressure to conform to group norms is very strong. This may inhibit members from voicing opinions or expressing ideas. They may hold back from challenging decisions with which they disagree. People tend to deal with this pressure either by challenging decisions and trying to bring others over to their way of thinking, by suppressing their real feelings and conforming, or by withdrawing altogether. A performer may openly challenge the director's decision and try to elicit support from the rest of the company. Alternatively they may shy away from telling a director how they really feel about a particular scene, though they may moan in private and become disenchanted.

Sometimes the group will tolerate deviant behaviour due to the high status accorded to a member; it might even change its norms accordingly. In a theatre company the group's main goal is creative. This creativity is likely to be volatile, with individuals constantly challenging the decisions being made. Status is very important here. The older, experienced, respected actor will be given higher status than the young actor straight out of university; higher even, sometimes, than the director. Yet even this can be challenged, in fact it is arguable that true creativity thrives on challenges to the perceived norms. In a stage management team, or the group that makes up a production meeting, however, there is less room for challenge. Lack of conformity here can seriously affect the work and efficiency of the group.

3. ROLE

An individual's role is the set of behaviours expected of them by the group. Charles Handy, in *Understanding Organisations* (1976), suggests that, when a person joins a group, they ask themselves three questions, the answers to which will guide them towards the role they will play:

1. What is the individual's identity within the group?
2. Where is the power located in the group?
3. What are the individual's objectives?

Meredith Belbin, in *Management Teams: Why they Succeed or Fail* (1981), identifies a number of task roles, listed over, that can be used to define individuals within a group. Using this taxonomy to locate an individual within the group structure can be enlightening. It helps to know what sort of person they are as this will help them to define their role and play to their strengths.

Belbin's task roles

- Chair/co-ordinator
- Shaper/team leader
- Plant/innovator/creative thinker
- Monitor/evaluator/critical thinker
- Company worker/implementer
- Team worker/team builder
- Finisher/detail checker/pusher
- Resource investigator/researcher outside the team
- Expert

A successful team will need a balance of all these roles; an imbalance in any direction may affect the group's ability to function at its optimal level. In the context of theatre this can easily be applied to the larger group that makes up a company.

Social roles can also be important within a group, with distinctions being drawn between aggressive, passive and assertive behaviour. Individuals within a group may take on the roles of mediator, 'devil's advocate' or 'licensed fool' amongst others.

4. LEADERSHIP

Leadership is linked to all the other dimensions, even when it is imposed on the group from outside. Leadership can be defined as 'behaviour that helps the group to achieve its preferred objectives' (Alan Barker, 2002). While it is still possible to make the classic distinction between autocratic, democratic and laissez-faire styles of leadership, current theories of leadership have moved on. Leadership is now often seen as a 'facilitative' role, allowing the group to achieve its goals, rather than a 'directive' one. It is also possible to distinguish between task leadership, focussing on the tasks to be achieved, and process leadership, focussing on nurturing good relationships within the group.

In the theatre context all these styles of leadership may be encountered, though the traditional 'autocratic' leadership style of directors is gradually being replaced by facilitative, or process lead, styles.

5. LIKING

This generally emerges spontaneously and can be a powerful influence in helping people to define their status within a group. It can also be pernicious, creating resentment and the forming of factions. Liking, or disliking, can be hard to define or articulate. Where it grows into emotional attachment it can seriously affect the dynamic of the group. The structures of like and dislike within the group may be covert and are often fluid. Individuals must rely on peripheral clues to identify them.

GROUP BEHAVIOUR

How individuals behave within a group, and the activities associated with this, can be split into three categories, each with its own characteristics, according to Alan Barker, although it is not always easy to identify these categories, or to distinguish between activities, many of which will happen unconsciously.

1. Task Behaviour – contributing to the work of the group
- Initiating: defining a problem, redefining it, making suggestions, presenting new information, proposing solutions
- Seeking information
- Giving information
- Setting standards
- Co-ordinating: relating ideas to each other, comparing information
- Building and elaborating: developing ideas, giving examples, adding detail, creating scenarios
- Summarising: restating, re-organising information, repeating, clarifying
- Evaluating: for value or relevance
- Diagnosing: seeking causes of problems
- Testing for consensus or disagreement

2. Process behaviour – assisting the group in its development
- Encouraging: responding positively, praising, accepting
- Gate-keeping: letting others contribute
- Stopping: ending a line of argument that seems unproductive or counterintuitive
- Following: listening and triggering more from others
- Redirecting: from one person to another
- Expressing group feeling
- Mediating: in moments of conflict
- Relieving tension: by suggesting a break or injecting humour

3. Non-functional behaviour – anything that hinders or prevents the group from functioning effectively or achieving its goals
- Aggression
- Blocking
- Self-confessing or sympathy seeking
- Competing
- Special pleading
- Seeking attention
- Negative or offensive humour
- Withdrawing

Looking at these in the context of theatre it is easy to see how this model fits the theatre-making process and how the role of stage management fits into the overall pattern. The make-up of the group may seem different from those encountered in business, with the emphasis placed on creativity and boundary breaking, yet there are many similarities. While the goals may be different, the way any group works together to achieve them is remarkably similar. Stage managers are involved in many aspects of both task and process behaviour. A charismatic and experienced stage manager, whom everybody likes, will be accorded high status and respect within the group. The stage manager who puts a personal agenda first in a competitive manner will threaten the effective functioning of the group.

MANAGEMENT IN PRACTICE
MANAGING GROUPS
Whilst this may seem like a complex and difficult task, the first thing to note is that any group, left to its own devices, will manage itself. Any member who wants to fulfil their responsibility and contribute positively to the achievement of the group goals must learn to work with the group rather than against it.

When considering the management of a group it is useful to ask a series of questions:
1. Is the group really a group? It may just be a collection of individuals with little relationship to each other.
2. Are there any obvious sub-groups within the group?
   The links between the individual members of each group may be stronger than within the larger group as a whole. The links between members of the stage management team are likely to be stronger than the links they have with members of the acting company and so on. This is quite normal.
3. Are there clearly identifiable task and social objectives for the group?
   Clearly defined social objectives, scheduled breaks for instance, will help the group members bond and thus make it easier for them to achieve the task objectives.
4. Is it possible to identify any individual needs that may interfere with the objectives of the group?
   'Personal' issues can play a major role in influencing a group's ability to achieve its objectives effectively. If these are recognised in advance, or before they take hold, they can be resolved.
5. What phase has the group reached in its development?
   Awareness of this process and the characteristics of each phase can help the individual make an appropriate contribution to the group's development.
6. How can an individual influence the group's structure?
   Where status or power is disproportionately influential within a group, this can pose a threat to its well-being. Rather than challenging them it is better

to work with them by channelling them towards the group's objectives.

7. What behaviour do stage management want to encourage within the group?

At any point different aspects of group behaviour will be more, or less, appropriate. The stage manager needs to be clear what behaviour is appropriate at what moment, and guide the group towards that. Non-functional behaviour should be challenged and not allowed to take hold.

Group dynamics are without doubt complicated, yet an understanding of how groups form and function, of how individuals fit into the group and of what can go wrong, is invaluable.

MANAGING INDIVIDUALS

People interact with each other on a daily basis and the relationships involved vary hugely, from the casual transaction when buying a bus ticket, through the formal way people may behave with their boss, to the informal familiarity they have with their friends and relations. These transactions are normally managed very successfully, but occasionally they do go wrong. The bus conductor may give short change, people are late for work and are shouted at by their boss, they let their friends and family down. The way that an individual deals with these situations is generally spontaneous and may depend on their 'character'. One person may shout and scream at the bus conductor, another will give them the benefit of the doubt.

Yet people are very rarely difficult by nature, though they can sometimes create difficult situations. Individuals are often demanding and it can be tempting to confuse that with being difficult. In the context of the work place any slight deviation from the social norm needs to be 'managed'. Dealing with this is part of a manager's job.

There really is no such thing as a difficult person; there are just different people who other people need to learn how to deal with. Not everybody is alike, yet people manage to be easy to get on with, or manage to get on easily with other people. It is a popular myth that directors, designers and actors are by their nature difficult and everybody else is a victim of this. Technicians and stage managers can have their moments too. They are, after all, human beings and subject to the same pressures as their colleagues. Preconceptions tend to create their own reality. When an individual joins a group thinking that a particular person is going to be 'difficult', the chances are they will appear to be so.

Of course there are individuals who appear to be difficult, who will give others a hard time, place them in awkward situations or confront them with tricky issues to overcome. But ultimately they are still people and it is important to understand what makes them tick. By understanding how people think and act the way they do, it is possible to avoid awkward situations and overcome tricky issues. Looked at from another perspective, it is the situation that is difficult and not the person.

The key to understanding how to avoid or overcome difficult situations lies in understanding how and where the blame tends to be placed. It is always easy to blame someone, or something, else but much harder to claim responsibility and fix the problem. Blame is the automatic first reaction. When someone stumbles in the street they automatically check for a hazard on which they can 'blame' the trip. Yet 'claiming', rather than 'blaming' is at the heart of good, responsible management. Before pointing the finger at the 'difficult' person it is important to look inwards. Maybe it is the 'blamer' who is actually being 'difficult', who has the problem.

In the context of the work place, or the group or team, relationships may develop in a different way than they do in a purely social situation. Some members of the team – the producer, the director, the designer – may have a vested interest in the project and this is what drives them. They may have invested many hours in it prior to the start of rehearsals and, understandably, they won't take kindly to anything getting in its way. This 'investment' may not just be in terms of time and money; it may also be in terms of their reputation. They may seem to be selfish and inwardly focused and not to care about other individuals at all. The fact is that they don't; they only care about the success of their project. When something goes wrong, or they are given bad news poorly explained and late, they may turn on the person they deem responsible.

But that is not the only reason for people appearing to be difficult. Sometimes lack of confidence creates an inner tension which will manifest itself in what seems to the observer to be 'difficult' behaviour. This is particularly true of performers, although it can also be so for directors. Nerves may be another cause. The intense actor, going through lines prior to a performance, will snap if interrupted. They will snap if their props are in the wrong place, or are different in some way. This is understandable; an interruption to their concentration may have an adverse effect on their performance.

Sometimes the nicest, friendliest people will turn if provoked. The director who goes for a drink with the stage manager at the end of each day and takes an apparent interest in their personal life may seem more like a friend than a colleague. It is very easy to become complacent in that situation, but complacency breeds inefficiency, which in turn can appear outwardly as laziness or lack of care. Poor timekeeping, poor communication and lame excuses will make people alter their attitude very quickly and precipitate a 'difficult' situation. When something goes wrong this director will make the same demands as any, yet it will seem worse.

Looked at in these terms 'difficult' behaviour doesn't seem that unreasonable.

Such situations are always avoidable in retrospect, but the effective stage manager should aim to avoid them in the first place by trying to be sensitive, strategic in their thinking and efficient. No matter how careful the planning, however, difficult situations will arise. When they do the manager must be able to take them in their stride and move on.

The theatre industry is a business like any other and the stage manager is doing a job that will contribute to the end product. It is easy to forget this. The people may be nice, the process may be fun and the end goal may be 'entertainment', but each individual still has a role to play and it must be played effectively.

When somebody snaps it is for a reason. It may be that they didn't get what they were promised, that they were told one thing when in fact something else was actually the case; in fact, they were lied to. It may be that the moment and the place were wrong. Bad news piled up until finally something had to give. Ultimately it is the stage manager's job to make sure that nothing will affect the production adversely and to know what is happening at all times. When something goes wrong the stage manager will be the person everyone turns to; they may just have to take the blame and then put it right but it is essential to understand that this should not be taken personally.

This is really the key to dealing with people in difficult situations; it is rarely personal. In fact demanding people are actually quite predictable. They may be pedantic, or obsessed with protocol, they may require all information in minute detail with every permutation outlined and explained. They may be perfectionists or workaholics. Knowing this makes it easier to deal with. For the stage manager it should be second nature, effective communication being at the heart of the role. For the pedant, the stage manager must make sure that nothing is ambiguous; for the traditionalist, protocol must be followed to the letter; and for the perfectionist, the stage manager must demonstrate that they too are striving for the perfect result, that they are an ally.

Finally it is important to be able to be wrong and to make mistakes. Mistakes are all right as long as they have been recognised, admitted, and something has been done about them. Nothing is more alarming than when a mistake happens and the person responsible either refuses to take the blame or, worse, is completely unaware.

COMMUNICATION SKILLS

Good communication is the key to effective management, whether in theatre or any other industry. Communication skills are at the heart of all management and stage management is no exception. Indeed communication is the main focus of the stage manager's role. Theatre-making is a dynamic and evolutionary process. At the centre of this process is the rehearsal room, which acts as a laboratory for experimentation. Outside the rehearsal room are a group of people either engaged in, or waiting to engage with, realising the requirements of the production. This not only includes technicians and makers, but also publicists, accountants and so forth. As the production evolves and develops, these people need to be kept up-to-date with precise and unambiguous information. In turn they need to communicate progress and problems back into the rehearsal process. The stage manager is normally the conduit for this flow of information.

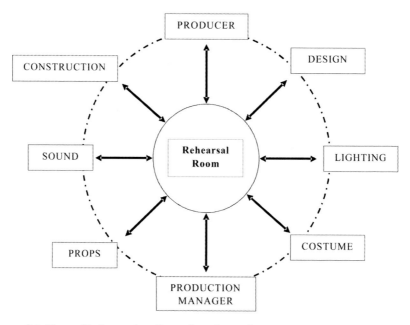

Figure 2.2 Flow of information from the rehearsal room

Figure 2.2 shows the flow of information from and to the rehearsal room, with arrows representing information flowing to different departments and feedback flowing back into the rehearsal room. The dotted line represents information flowing between departments. The conduit for information flow would normally be stage management, by means of the rehearsal notes and separate meetings. The list could also include musicians, choreographers, even theatre management; the rehearsal room would include the director, cast and stage management; and information from rehearsals might need conveying to members of the cast, even to the director.

People communicate through a variety of different means including the spoken word, the written word, non-verbal messages, drawings, graphics and numbers. They use a range of media including the telephone, e-mail, letters, memos, faxes and face-to-face meetings. The method used will depend on the situation or the type of information that needs to be conveyed or discussed. The experienced communicator will be able to choose the most appropriate and effective medium to suit the situation.

In order to be effective, communication must fulfil a number of criteria. It must be:

- **Accurate** – sending out a clear, precise and unambiguous message
- **Sensitive** – to the feelings of the recipient
- **Appropriate** – the information must be in a format that can be accessed or used effectively.

Most people tend to think that they are both good and skilled communicators, and yet it is easy to criticise the communication skills of others. Good communication requires patience, thought and commitment. As Judith Taylor shows, in *Communication at Work* (2001), it should be a two-way process undertaken in order to understand and be understood. If the process is one-way, a message containing information is conveyed but the sender does not get any feedback; they don't even know whether the message has been received, let alone understood and acted on. In order for communication to be effective there needs to be a response.

One-way message

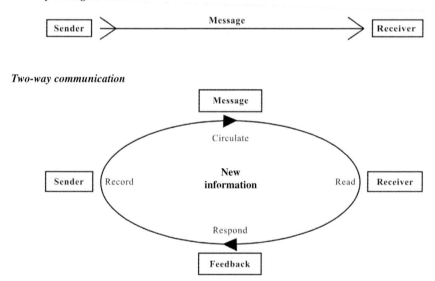

Figure 2.3 One-way message and two-way communication

Figure 2.3, based on Taylor's work, shows how, with two-way communication, the message is sent and received and a response, in the form of feedback, is elicited. This process enables the sender to know whether the message has been received and understood and to respond to any comments. If the message turns out to lack clarity, or requires further elaboration, then a new message, with clearer or updated information, can be sent and a cycle, or dialogue, ensues.

This may seem obvious, and almost automatic; it is what people do when they have a conversation. In informal, social situations, individuals give and receive feedback naturally through a variety of verbal and non-verbal methods whenever they engage in conversation. But if inadequate communication skills can create problems in a social context, this is compounded in the work environment. By identifying the key skills involved in good communication, strategies can be put in place to avoid or remedy the potential pitfalls.

ORAL COMMUNICATION

Feedback is easier and often more effective in face-to-face communication. A number of key skills are associated with this: listening, questioning, responding, summarising, assertiveness and awareness and appropriate use of body language.

LISTENING

The distinction between hearing and listening is significant. While the great majority of the population can hear clearly, most people are actually poor listeners. It is easy to get the two mixed up, yet poor listening skills can be detrimental both to effective team working and to the overall quality of the work process. The same distinction can be made between reading and comprehension. Listening and understanding are crucial factors in effective oral communication.

All sorts of obstacles can get in the way of effective listening. Background noise and activity, poor diction or a strong accent, personal situations, impatience, even over-enthusiasm, can all cause distractions which prevent people from listening properly. A good way to overcome these is to acknowledge their existence and to become an 'active listener' by taking notes, regularly checking that these are on the right track and summarising at the end. The main attributes of an active listener, based on Judith Taylor (2001), are outlined below.

	The Active Listener	The Passive Listener

Body language	Adopts positive posture
	Avoids distracting mannerisms
	Maintains reasonable eye contact
	Uses encouraging and
	    appropriate gestures
	    and facial expression
	Maintains comfortable distance.
		Looks bored or judgemental
		Doodles or fiddles
		    distractingly
		Avoids eye contact
		Shows little response
		    to what is being said

Attention	Keeps attention focused on
	    speaker with appropriate
	    prompts
		Keeps focus of comments
		    on self
		Draws focus away from
		    speaker

Accepting	Accepts speaker's ideas
	    and feelings
		Fails to accept speaker's
		    ideas and feelings

Empathy	Shows empathy with speaker	Fails to empathise

Questions	Uses 'open' questions	Uses 'closed' questions
	Probes in a helpful way	Fails to probe
Clarifies	Asks for clarification	Makes assumptions
	Checks understanding	Fails to clarify
		Fails to check understanding
Summarises	Summarises progress at intervals	Fails to summarise
	Widens range of ideas by	Narrows range of ideas
	summarising alternative options	by suggesting a
	from which to choose	single option

QUESTIONING

Many people shy away from asking questions. They think it makes then seem stupid or slow on the uptake, or gives somebody else the upper hand. Nothing could be further from the truth, though it is important to strike the right balance. Questions need to be asked in order to get or clarify information.

'If in doubt, ask,' is a good maxim, but only if used wisely. If possible, it is better to find the answer to a question without having to ask; asking unnecessary questions might appear to be a waste of someone else's time or seem to indicate lack of initiative. On the other hand it may actually save time. When dealing with complex or very specific subjects, it is a good idea to make notes before asking in order to get the answer required. There is nothing worse than coming away from a meeting and suddenly remembering something that should have been asked.

Questions fall into a number of different types that are used in different situations in order to elicit the required response. Taylor's classification of these (2001) are summarised below.

Question	Useful	Not useful
Open:		
Encourage the person to talk –	Most opening questions;	With talkative person;
'Tell me about...?'	to explore and gather information	where discipline is required
Probing:		
Vital for detail – 'Exactly how do	Checking information	Exploring emotionally
you want that to look?		charged areas
Closed:		
Narrow scope – establish specific	Probing single facts	Gaining information in areas
points or facts – 'When do you		not normally explored
want to start?'		
Reflective:		
Very powerful – repeat back	Problem solving;	Checking information and
verbatim the emotional content of	emotionally charged situations;	facts
a statement – 'You feel upset	counselling	
about the change...?'		
Leading:		
Invites the answer expected –	Gaining acceptance of your view	Gaining any information
'I expect you wished you'd		about a person
allowed more time?'		

Question	Useful	Not useful
Hypothetical: Posing a hypothetical situation for the future – 'What would you like us to do if...?'	Getting someone to think about new ideas	With someone who needs time to give a reasoned reply
Multiple: String of questions or statements	Never	Always

ASSERTIVENESS

Assertiveness is a way of interacting with people which is open and honest without being either passive or aggressive. It is an important skill, which enables the individual to state their opinions, feelings and requirements in a clear and open way, and will help in negotiations with others in order to achieve effective and mutually satisfactory outcomes. It enables the individual to stand up for their own rights whilst not violating the rights of others. Assertiveness is vital for good communication.

The assertive communicator is able to:
- disagree without unnecessary conflict
- express views and make requests confidently
- co-operate in problem-solving in order to reach a consensual outcome
- take criticism without becoming upset
- deal effectively with difficult situations and awkward people.

The aim of assertive behaviour is to achieve a mutually satisfactory result and not always to get the individual's way. Assertiveness is often confused with aggressive behaviour, which puts self first to the detriment of the needs of others. Conversely, non-assertive behaviour puts the needs of others first at all times, subjugating personal opinions or feelings.

The table below (based on Taylor, 2001) shows the advantages and disadvantages of different types of behaviour.

	AGGRESSIVE	SUBMISSIVE	ASSERTIVE
YOU DO	Try to get what you want in any way that works Often give rise to bad feelings in others Threaten, flatter, manipulate, use sarcasm or fight	Hope that you get what you want Repress your feelings Rely on others to guess what you want	Ask for what you want, directly, openly and appropriately Respect your own rights State your case confidently and without anxiety Stop emotions getting in the way
YOU DON'T	Respect the rights of others Look for situations where you both get what you want	Ask for what you want Express your feelings Upset anyone	Disregard the rights of others Expect others to guess what you want

		Get noticed	Freeze up with anxiety Send mixed messages
EFFECTS FOR YOU			
SHORT TERM	Reduces tensions – you get what YOU want	Avoids conflict Pleases others	Increased chance of your needs being met
LONG TERM	Feel guilty or ashamed Increased anger, hurt or self-pity	Growing lack of self-esteem Increased anger, hurt or self-pity Internal tensions and anxiety	Increased self-confidence Increased self-responsibility Sense of identification with others Saving in energy and reduction in stress
EFFECTS FOR OTHERS			
	They feel angry, hurt or humiliated They retaliate, openly or secretly They restrict further contact with you	They lose respect for you and feel sorry for you They feel guilt, indifference, contempt or irritation They restrict further contact with you	They feel respected They respond more positively and openly They will seek your advice or opinion
RESULT:	**WIN – LOSE**	**LOSE – WIN**	**WIN – WIN**

Assertive behaviour can be learned, and should be seen as a necessary tool rather than as an aspect of a person's character. In order to achieve this it is often necessary to challenge personal beliefs and preconceptions about the self. Someone may believe that they are very shy or that no-one ever listens to them, or that they are just the ASM. Indeed they may even believe that it is these attributes that makes them suitable to become a stage manager. These beliefs will influence their behaviour and make them passive, and thus less efficient, communicators. Individuals need to learn how to be assertive, to be active communicators, in order to undertake their role effectively.

Three simple strategies can help the individual to communicate assertively:
- **Basic assertion** This involves standing up for personal rights and stating feelings and needs openly and honestly. These should be repeated until they are listened to and taken seriously, but it is important to avoid getting side-tracked or getting into an argument. The choice of words is important; the wrong words can appear challenging to authority, even aggressive.
- **Empathy** This approach shows that the individual has listened to and understood a request, and that they may be sympathetic to it in principle. The project is being taken seriously and decisions are not being made lightly. Empathy may involve being able to say 'no' without seeming to be obstructive or threatening, in order to diffuse anger or disappointment. It can be difficult to refuse a request, or to respond with a negative answer to

a question, without feeling that the rejection is personally motivated. Stage managers need to learn how to convey negative information empathetically, without feeling negative in themselves. It can be tempting to put off giving out bad news, though that is by far the worst tactic. The longer it is left, the worse the impact, and the more difficult it becomes to address.

- **Workable compromise** Compromise is acceptable when it has been arrived at through an empathetic approach and is likely to work satisfactorily for everyone involved. A good compromise is more likely to be reached if individuals are able to demonstrate that they understand all points of view. Being able to explain why something is not possible is important; outright dismissal is obstructive and can be demotivating.

A number of practical points may help the assertive communicator.

- Posture should be upright, open and relaxed.
- The voice should be steady, with a clear tone.
- Information should be kept concise and to the point, stating exactly what is wanted or meant. It is important to remember that the person being addressed doesn't know why they are being approached; if they did they wouldn't need to be spoken to.
- Hesitation should be avoided, particularly if accompanied by 'um' or 'er' or 'you know what I mean'. This suggests a lack of confidence as a communicator or understanding of the information being conveyed.
- Apology should be avoided unless there is actually something to apologise for.
- It is legitimate to ask for further explanation of anything that has not been understood or is ambiguous. Interruption is more effective than waiting until the end; it is far more difficult to go back later and ask for the information to be repeated.
- If the answer to a question isn't available it is pointless to pretend that it is. It is better to answer honestly and offer to find out.
- Assertive behaviour is infectious. People who practise assertiveness are more likely to get a positive response from others. It shows that they have a confident, active approach to communication and to their work.

BODY LANGUAGE

Non-verbal communication is arguably the most important factor in gaining feedback during face-to-face interaction. People learn a lot about each other from body language; it puts the words being spoken into some sort of behavioural or emotional context. Everyone knows when somebody is unhappy with an outcome, even if they claim otherwise. People show their dissatisfaction by the way they stand, by the way they move and by the way they refuse to look other people in the eye.

Research in the United States in 1971, undertaken by Professor A. Mehrabian, suggested that three aspects of people's feelings are usually indicated more effectively using non-verbal signs. These are: like-dislike; status or power; and responsiveness. The research suggested that 55% of a message in these areas is communicated non-verbally (particularly through facial expression), 38% through tone of voice and a mere 7% through words alone. While this may seem simplistic, it is evident that body language plays an extremely important part in communication.

People often use body language instinctively, in the form of gestures, posture and facial expression, to enhance what they are saying. They smile when they are happy, frown when unhappy and shout when angry. Sometimes, however, these non-verbal signals belie what they are saying; there is a lack of congruence between the words and the way they are delivered. Vocal tone also plays an important part.

It is important to be aware of body language, both one's own and that of others. Understanding any sub-text will help the individual to become a much better communicator. An awareness of how they are seen by others is important; personal body language must back up what is being said, and maintaining eye contact is an essential part of this. It is no good giving out an important message if the body language indicates that it is being taken lightly.

Similarly the individual needs to learn to be aware of the non-verbal signals that other people are sending out. Even if they don't speak, the way that they react to a message will give a better picture of their true feelings. This is particularly pertinent when somebody says that everything is going well and according to schedule. If it really is, they will be able to smile and make eye contact. If it isn't and they are covering up an impending disaster, they will avoid this, shuffling about, shrugging, frowning and answering questions in barely audible monosyllables. They may even respond aggressively. Such a reaction is usually the result of embarrassment, a feeling of inadequacy, fear or lack of engagement, even complacency. This should be handled sensitively, showing empathy with the situation in order to probe further and reach a workable compromise.

OTHER FORMS OF COMMUNICATION

While face-to-face verbal communication is often the best way to give out information and receive feedback, it is not always possible or appropriate. Stage managers regularly need to write letters and memos, send faxes or e-mails and make telephone calls. Many people find these ways of communicating easier, as they involve less interpersonal interaction, but they can also slow down the feedback process and may even bypass it completely. When a message is sent out in the form of a memo, it is tempting to assume that everyone will have received and understood it. When something subsequently fails to happen, the sender is tempted to react by blaming the recipient. It is, however, the sender's responsibility; they initiated the communication cycle and should have followed it through. 'Never Assume Anything' should be written in large letters on the wall of the stage manager's office.

Sometimes the amount of information being imparted, or the number of inputs, is so large that it is impossible to take it all in. In this case it is essential to get it in written form, by making notes in a notebook or asking for it to be put into writing as a memo. This is obvious when a single person needs to give out a lot of complex information that would be impossible to take in or remember, but less so when a large number of different people give out small amounts of information independently over a short time. Imagine someone walking down a corridor lined with offices. The occupant of each office pops out to ask something to be done for them or to give a snippet of important information. At the same time other people walk down the corridor and do likewise. By the time the recipient has reached their destination they may have ten new pieces of information to digest. The chances are that they may remember the last two or three and even then are likely to get messages mixed, particularly if there is any significant lapse of time before the requested response. If they were in a hurry they will have been slowed down and this will make the effects even worse. Yet each individual encountered will have returned to their desk confident in the belief that they have played their part. They will respond with indignation when their request fails to be acted on or a task is carried out wrongly.

The stage manager can avoid this danger by always carrying a notebook and pencil so that they can jot down any information as it is received. Alternatively they can ask politely for the information to be put in a memo so that both have it in writing. Either of these is appropriate; relying on memory is not.

It is also easy, and thus tempting, to rely on just one form of communication, but to keep the cycle going, memos, letters and telephone conversations should all be followed up. For example an agreement made over the telephone should be followed up in writing. If feedback is not forthcoming, it should be sought actively. If it isn't clear whether a recipient has received and understood a message, then this should be followed up. Similarly the results of a meeting need to be summarised and documented either in the form of minutes or a simple summary of agreed actions. Either way these will serve as a reminder and future agenda setter.

WRITTEN COMMUNICATION

Being able to communicate effectively in writing is an essential skill. The stage manager needs to use the written word to communicate both internally, with other members of the production team, and externally, with suppliers and so forth. Written communication may be informal, in the form of notes, or formal, in the form of letters, memos and other documents.

As a general rule all information conveyed in written form must be:
- **Accurate** – it must state what is meant or required accurately
- **Brief** – using ten words when two will do is not helpful
- **Clear** – there must be no room for ambiguity or misinterpretation

Memos, letters, lists and tables, minutes should all conform to these rules. If they don't they are less likely to be effective, may well elicit the wrong response, and at best will result in time-consuming conversations in order to explain the information rather than clarify the outcome.

E-mail is a very effective means of communicating information quickly to large numbers of people. It should not be relied upon, however; just because an e-mail has been sent to someone doesn't mean that they have read it or even received it. Attachments are a particular problem if some recipients are unable to open them. Sending out a spreadsheet containing the Production Schedule is only useful if everybody can, and does, open it (and they usually print it out; so much for the paperless office).

The same rules apply when writing formal letters. These are business letters and may lead to a contract. A badly written letter may not get the desired response; accurate grammar and spelling as well as the correct form of address are very important. Letters asking for support or requesting a service should state the case in a businesslike and unsentimental way.

ORGANISATIONAL SKILLS

As well as interacting successfully with other people, the stage manager must also be able to manage their own work. The way in which people organise their time, the tasks that they need to undertake, and the information that they have to process, is at the centre of efficient management. It is important to be able to keep motivated by planning how best to use the given time in order to fulfil the various tasks required.

Theatre is a remarkably disciplined industry. Deadlines are often extremely tight and inflexible, while at the same time a high degree of flexibility is required to allow for continuous creative development. Theatre productions must open at a certain time on a certain date, unless they want to incur serious financial penalties. The development time is short, normally ranging from one to eight weeks. During this time scenery must be built and painted and costumes and props bought or made, and then these must be transferred to the theatre and tested before they are shown to the public. Throughout this period the creative team reserve the right to make changes, to add things, to subtract things and sometimes to change the way things are to be used. This is normal and exactly as it should be. Of course there are exceptions, large-scale productions involving complex technology are usually conceived well in advance and the set will start to be built before the rehearsals start. Yet even in this situation changes will certainly be suggested, and often allowed, up until the last minute. So theatre is not entirely like the production line in a factory or a normal business that produces a product.

TIME MANAGEMENT: DELEGATING AND PRIORITISING TASKS

The key to the successful management of personal work time lies in being able to recognise what needs to be achieved and when, what the priorities are, what one's own capabilities are, and when tasks can be delegated to other people.

Stephen R. Covey, in *The Seven Habits of Highly Effective People* (1999), identifies four main types of activity that need to be prioritised; these, summarised in *Figure 2.4* are:

1. **Important – urgent**
2. **Important – not urgent**
3 **Not important – urgent**
4. **Not important – not urgent**

		URGENT		NOT URGENT
IMPORTANT	**1.**	**Activities:** Crises Pressing Problems Deadline-driven **Results:** Stress Burnout Crisis management Always fire fighting	**2.**	**Activities:** Prevention Planning Building relationships Recognizing new opportunities Personally important **Results:** Vision, perspective Longer time-scale Balance Discipline Control Few crises
NOT IMPORTANT	**3.**	**Activities:** Interruptions Some phone calls Some mail, meetings, paper-work Popular activities Pressing matters **Results:** Short-term focus Unrealistic deadlines Importance often not obvious or immediate Boring Crisis management Reputation – chameleon character Sees goals and plans as worthless Feels victimised, out of control	**4.**	**Activities:** Time wasters Trivia Some mail Some phone calls 'Busy' work **Results:** Total irresponsibility Fired from jobs Dependent on others or institutions for basics

Figure 2.4 Time management matrix

Most people are tempted to concentrate on activities that are both important and urgent (1), or neither important nor urgent (4); *Figure 2.4* outlines the consequences of this. Time should also be dedicated to important tasks that are not particularly urgent (2), however, which may be important personally or have a longer time-scale. This can be achieved by reducing time spent on activities that may seem important but are not urgent (3) and those that are neither (4). The aim is eventually to reduce the number of important and urgent activities by achieving an ideal balance in which time is allowed for the full range.

This is a dynamic process that should be reviewed regularly; as deadlines change or approach, activities may move from being less important or urgent to a higher priority. Personal issues should also be included – paying the electricity bill or visiting the dentist may be either important, or urgent, or both.

The key skills required to achieve a balance include assertiveness, self-discipline, motivation, negotiation, prioritisation, delegation, goal-setting, recognition and reward. These apply just as much to time management within a team as they do the individual. People who are used to working by themselves on small projects often find it very hard when they become members of a team on a larger project. They may try to do everything but find that this is impossible to achieve. While one member attempts to do a lot rather badly, the rest either take advantage or become resentful; in fact it is a sign of inefficiency and usually results in sub-standard work. The team are there to share the tasks fairly and efficiently; there are no prizes for the one who does the most. Members must learn the art of delegation for the team to be truly effective.

Time is an expensive commodity; it must be used wisely. The effective manager may spend up to 30% of the time available for a project in planning how best to use it.

Finite deadlines can be identified and used as indicators. In the context of a theatre production these would include the first day of rehearsals, the get-in (load-in), the technical rehearsal, the opening night and the get-out. The tasks that will need to be achieved by each of these deadlines can then be identified and individual and team deadlines set. Some tasks will be reasonably constant (the person on the book will need to be in rehearsals every day), while others will vary (props-finding will vary on a daily basis). Each individual's particular strengths and skills can be taken into account when setting these goals.

An efficient team will try to make sure that no one member has to work harder than another. The stage manager on the book will need to be in rehearsals early in order to set up but will often feel obliged to stay late to circulate notes and rehearsal calls. These tasks should be shared out and planned into the team's daily schedule. Once the team schedule has been agreed, each individual can start to plan their own work programme.

The effective stage manager will use delegation to give authority and responsibility to other team members, while retaining accountability and overall control. By enfranchising each member to make their own decisions and take control of their own work schedules within an agreed framework, the stage manager can concentrate on other tasks, such as liaison and trouble shooting or helping out where necessary. They should be careful not to indulge in micro-management, however – organising each team member's schedule to the minute and constantly checking up on them. This can be very de-motivating and will not allow the team to operate at its optimum level.

Within the finite framework, the schedule should remain flexible in order to reflect the evolving nature of the work being undertaken. What is lower priority one day may become high priority the next. The deadline will need to be moved to account for this and the schedule adjusted.

When embarking on a project it can be tempting to start slowly; tasks often seem less urgent with six weeks to go, particularly the duller or 'easier' tasks. Individuals may be tempted to concentrate on the 'fun' tasks to begin with, or those that they feel they are particularly good at. Like any industry, some aspects of theatre can be mundane and monotonous. These are the tasks that need to be tackled from the beginning and should certainly be shared amongst the team; shared tasks will take less time and will engender a feeling of equality within the team. By getting them out of the way early on, the team will be able to move on to the more enjoyable tasks without a sense of guilt or impending panic. Left to the last minute, such activities may become overwhelming.

A daily task, or 'To Do', list can help the team and its members to manage their time more effectively. This allows changing priorities and progress to be tracked and, as a visual record of goals and of their achievement, it can help maintain a realistic perspective and provide motivation. The list can also be used to prioritise tasks. Some of these will have finite deadlines because their completion may have a knock-on effect; someone else may be waiting for the result in order to progress to the next stage. Others will be predictably lengthy and need to be started early. Yet others will become lengthy because of a number of unforeseen factors. The latter may cause the priority to change as it becomes evident that they cannot be achieved in the time allocated, and will inevitably be those that were initially identified as easy and regrettably left until last. New tasks will also arrive throughout the process. If they are urgent this will need to be reflected in the updated list of priorities

Motivation and efficiency can be optimised by planning for variety throughout the working day. The tasks that may take the longest or need to be done first are the top priority. A daily target for the ones identified as boring can be set and, when that target is reached, others that are easier, more enjoyable or challenging can be worked on as a reward. When any task becomes boring or frustrating it is important to give it a rest, to try something else, and then to return to it refreshed. Sometimes a fresh approach to a problem will be the factor that leads to its solution.

Some tasks will start to break down into smaller constituent parts as they are worked on. These should be identified and prioritised individually. This will enable the team to keep on top of progress and will make the task seem more manageable. It is good for the team's morale if at least some things can be crossed off the list every day.

STRESS MANAGEMENT

In any high-pressure job it is important for individuals to look after themselves. Theatre regularly involves people working to exacting deadlines, on challenging tasks that have uncertain outcomes, over long hours and with little tangible reward at the end. This may all take place in a poorly ventilated building with no access to daylight or fresh air. It is often tempting to work through breaks, skipping meals and eating snacks on the run, and to take work home to be completed overnight. Coupled with poor nutrition and lack of sleep, the pressures of work will inevitably lead to stress. Some stress is to be expected, and is even beneficial, but too much will lead to a drop in productivity and efficiency and may spiral into ill-health. This is all avoidable and good team management will go some way toward achieving this.

In order to minimise the effects of stress it is important to make time for some of the following:

- **Pacing** During the course of a production the pressures on an individual will vary. The production week will place high demands on each individual, yet these demands are all predictable. Long hours coupled with intense concentration, irregular meal times and lack of sleep are stressful but not unexpected. In the long term recognising the particular 'pace' of each stage of the production, and adjusting to it accordingly, is essential. Using up reserves of energy during the rehearsal period is unnecessary and may mean that they are not available when needed. In the short term the pacing needed to get through a normal eight-hour day will be very different from that needed when the day extends to twelve hours.
- **Variety** It is beneficial to try to break up the day with a range of tasks. A change of environment is helpful, especially taking breaks outside the rehearsal room, even if only for twenty minutes. Drowsiness can be overcome by getting up and doing something else, even for five minutes, particularly if it involves getting outside for some fresh air.
- **Eating properly** Take a proper break and have a balanced meal at least once a day.
- **Exercise** Regular use of a gym, playing a sport, even walking some of the way to work or joining in the physical warm-up with the cast can be helpful. Before undertaking any sort of physical work, such as moving furniture, it is essential to warm up and stretch the muscles.

- **Pampering** Allow time for the odd treat.
- **Socialising** Spend time with friends and family; they may be able to help put any work related problems into perspective.
- **Hobbies and pastimes** Allow time for these; listen to music, go to the cinema, or even watch TV. This 'out' time will aid relaxation.
- **Breathing properly** Learn how to breathe properly; yoga or meditation can help achieve this.
- **Relaxation** Learn how to use massage to release tension in the shoulders and neck. Find out if anyone else in the company knows how to give a massage, or go to a professional.

RULES AND REGULATIONS

Society has become both increasingly regulated and increasingly litigious. This has a direct impact on contemporary stage management. The rules and regulations governing live performance seem to multiply and change regularly. Stage management must work within these and ensure that everybody else does too. Health and Safety (see Appendix A) is of particular importance and stage management have a role in making sure that regulations are adhered to and that the work place is a safe and healthy one. This may seem obvious, yet theatre is traditionally an environment where risks are taken and people are expected to push the boundaries of human endeavour. Technicians have regularly been required to undertake gruelling physical work over long periods without sleep, while performers have been required to replicate abnormal actions repeatedly for long stretches of time. Remarkable feats are regularly achieved in ridiculously short periods of time with inadequate equipment. This is regarded as a sign of dedication and resourcefulness, yet it is often dangerous and is sometimes illegal; at the very best it flies in the face of received wisdom or 'good practice'.

Many of the regulations that apply to theatre work are generalised ones aimed at all industries that involve similarly demanding activities. At times these may seem to be over-restrictive in a creative environment, yet they are there to protect everyone. More confusingly, however, they are often open to interpretation and sometimes to negotiation. Legislating bodies have traditionally regarded theatres as inherently 'unsafe' places, populated by mavericks with a complete disregard for their own safety or that of others. Yet the opposite is closer to the truth. While accidents do happen, they are comparatively rare.

The rules and regulations that govern the way that people work in theatre originate at a number of different levels.

At **International** level, there are a number of agreed general rights that all people are entitled to expect. These were laid down by the United Nations under the Universal Declaration of Human Rights in 1948.

At **European** level, a number of more recent enactments have had a direct effect on theatre work. The most pertinent are the Working Time Directive

(1998), which governs the hours that can be worked, the breaks and holidays that must be taken and so forth, and the Workplace Directive, which sets a minimum standard in health and safety. In the area of theatre there are plans for European-wide legislation to be standardised, although practice in the different countries making up the EU is so varied at present that this will take a while. This move should be welcomed, with reservation, as it will make it a lot easier for theatre practitioners to work across Europe.

At **National** level, the laws of the land govern what individuals can do and how they behave. A considerable amount of legislation is directly relevant to theatre, starting with the Factories Act 1961, which governs conditions in the work place, the Theatres Act 1968, which governs public entertainment, and continuing through to the Lifting Operations and Lifting Equipment Regulations 1998 (LOLER), the Provision and Use of Work Equipment Regulations 1998 (PUWER), and the Control of Substances Hazardous to Health Regulations 2002 (COSHH) – to name but a few.

The Health and Safety Executive (HSE), issues a range of codes of practice as well as guidelines, as does the Home Office.

At **Local** level, the Theatres Act is enforced by local authorities, while other regulations come under the jurisdiction of the local fire service or police force. Very strict regulations govern the use of firearms under the Firearms Acts 1968–1997 and have been progressively tightened. Under the Theatres Act 1968, all premises used for public entertainment must obtain a licence from the local authority. Licences can be annual or occasional; annual licences apply to the premises themselves while occasional licences apply to individual productions mounted in premises not normally used for public entertainment.

At **Industry** level, unions negotiate wage agreements and standard contracts and ensure that their members are not exploited. In the UK performers, directors and stage managers are represented by the British Actors' Equity Association (Equity), while technicians are represented by the Broadcasting Entertainment Cinematograph and Theatre Union (BECTU). Trade associations act as independent forums for their members to discuss more specific issues. The Association of British Theatre Technicians (ABTT) is at the forefront of setting industry standards in technical theatre in the UK, publishing a range of guidelines, offering specialist training and helping members keep up-to-date with current legislation, while the Stage Management Association (SMA) specifically represents the interests of stage managers.

At a **Personal** level, every individual has a duty of care to their colleagues, as enshrined in the Universal Declaration of Human Rights of 1948 and in national employment legislation.

Many theatre practitioners believe that these rules and regulations get in the way of creativity and see them as a challenge, to be adapted, twisted and even avoided. Yet they actually exist to protect the individual, to help them to work more efficiently and, more importantly, to preserve their health and safety. Although the way that some regulations are enforced can seem downright absurd – somehow trapeze work seems less exciting when the artistes are wearing fall-arrest harnesses – it is often the interpretation that is at fault, rather than the rules themselves.

Viewed from a different perspective, these rules and regulations can be seen as tools that can help the practitioner to achieve safe solutions to creative problems. It is important to work openly with the enforcers rather than clandestinely against them. Chapter 9 covers in more detail the rules and regulations that particularly affect stage management.

SUMMARY

I have attempted to set stage management, and theatre, in a wider context in order to de-mystify it. Stage managers are professionals working amongst other professionals in a creative industry, and it is this creativity that defines the range of challenges that will be encountered. The tools available to deal with these challenges can be found amongst the general strategies available to a manager in any industry, and used in support of the specialist knowledge required of a theatre practitioner.

I don't believe that someone trained simply in general management techniques would find it easy to take on the stage manager's role without further training. The protocols, the terminology, the creative uncertainties, the apparent inefficiency which is an inevitable, even desirable, aspect of this creative process, might prove too confusing. I do believe, however, that the stage manager can function successfully in any other business environment.

The range of challenges offered by any production and the variety of responsibilities taken on by the average stage manager appear to be greater than those expected of most managers in most other businesses. When I described my job as a company and stage manager to a group of experienced business managers, they were aghast at the range and level of responsibility expected of one person. In their organisations such responsibility was handled by a rigidly structured hierarchy of managers, each with their own clearly defined sphere of activity and decision-making.

The successful stage manager must be good with people; they must be able to be assertive, yet to empathise with and be able to nurture, the creative process; they must be able to handle the stresses associated with this process both to themselves and to others. They must be able to make snap decisions under pressure, to delegate where necessary and to take on and learn new skills when called for. They must be efficient time keepers, yet able to change and adapt to new schedules as necessary. Above all, they must be good managers.

3 RESEARCH AND PREPARATION

Theatre is a dynamic, live art and any production will continue to develop over the course of its life-span. This development will be both directed and a natural process of evolution and will vary with every production and throughout its development. It is useful to consider the process of creating a piece of theatre as a linear progression of stages.

1. **Preparation**
2. **Rehearsal**
3. **Production**
4. **Performance**
5. **Post-production**

While these stages are not discrete – there is often a blurring of the boundaries – they form a useful guideline. The responsibilities associated with stage management will alter as a production proceeds from stage to stage. The following chapters examine the role of stage management in each of these stages in turn.

The stage manager's role begins before a production starts to be rehearsed. The degree of involvement and when it begins can depend on a number of factors: contract, budget, type of company, scale of production, etc. A contract may start on the first day of rehearsals or a week or more earlier. There is a great deal that the individual can do to prepare for a production prior to the rehearsal period, however, and this preparation is essential, both on a personal and a professional level, whether the stage manager is under contract at that point or not.

It is important for stage management (and anyone else) to be familiar with the text, score or story line of the piece, with its historical and period setting, and with how this might relate to the current context. Once familiar with the background of the piece, the next step is to relate this to the context of the actual production, that is, to take the design and style into account. Time spent in preparation is time well spent if used effectively, saving time and effort later on and, more critically, instilling confidence through familiarity with the text and context.

This period of preparation can be broken down into four inter-related tasks:
1. Initial research, including analysis of the text (this chapter)
2. Getting to know the production and its associated personnel (Chapter 4)
3. Information-processing and communicating (Chapter 4)
4. Preparing for rehearsal (Chapter 5)

INITIAL RESEARCH

It is useful for a stage manager to know a bit about the play they are going to work on in advance. This enables them to put it into the context of the production and to manage expectations. Many stage managers will do some research even before they accept a contract, sometimes even before being interviewed for a job. At the very least it is recommended to read the play, or novel if it is to be an adaptation, or listen to the music. At this stage individuals can find out whether they like the play or not, whether it is something that they are going to be able to engage with easily or whether they are going to have to work hard at this. If the play is emotionally challenging or controversial, this reaction may indicate something about the problems that may be anticipated during the production and about the sort of management that will be required. Of course a stage manager would have to feel very strongly about a play before they turned work down, but once a job has been accepted there is no going back. It must be approached with the same attitude as any production. It is no good complaining about being offended by the strong language, or by having to cook pig's offal. This should have been taken into account when the play was read for the first time.

THE THEATRE COMPANY

The stage manager should also try to find out a bit about the theatre company, the director and designer who they will be working with. Many theatre companies have informative websites and information can also be gleaned from reviews of previous productions and from articles in newspapers and magazines. This may give an insight into the company's working process, any 'house' style, whether the production is likely to be a 'traditional' one. Preparation undertaken before an interview will show that the interviewee is familiar with the company's work. This can only be an advantage – here is a stage manager who takes their job seriously, and shows an informed and intelligent interest in the project.

If the production is to be devised – that is, created from scratch through a process of workshops and rehearsals – it is even more important to find out about the company, director, etc. Stage management may be expected to make an active and creative contribution to the truly democratic collaborative process; this will come as a shock to a stage manager who is not used to it and is unprepared. Many devised productions take something as a starting point: the life of a person, a historical event, a book, a piece of music, a painting. Stage management should familiarise themselves with this subject, if they know what it will be in advance; this will make them confident in their capacity to become involved in the discussions that are likely to make up the first part of the process.

TEXT ANALYSIS

For a scripted piece, the text can be 'analysed' on several levels. At its most basic, any script will give the stage manager a good insight into the potential technical requirements of a production. Information regarding costume, furniture, props, sound, lighting and staging is all contained in the stage directions and dialogue. There is more to a script than this, however: plot, characterisation, back-story, historical context and the background of the playwright are important aspects and it is essential for stage management to get to grips with these.

It is possible to get by doing the minimum, by just by knowing what the technical requirements of a production might be, but a 'good' stage manager should be aiming for more than the minimum involvement. By undertaking in-depth text analysis supported by thorough background research, the stage manager will be able to:

- Converse intelligently with other members of the production – director, designers, cast, etc.
- Gain a good idea about the way a production might be staged, identifying potential staging problems
- Make an informed contribution to initial design meetings and subsequent production meetings
- Contribute to discussion, when required, throughout the development period
- Pre-empt, and solve, some of the problems that may become evident during the development period
- Propose creative and appropriate solutions to problems
- Make informed decisions regarding props, furniture, etc.
- Contribute creatively by giving cues that are sensitive to the dramatic and artistic aims of a piece
- Maintain self-esteem and thus status within a company. There is nothing like ignorance to make an individual feel insignificant and vulnerable, and this will affect the way they are perceived by other members of a company

ANALYSING THE TEXT

The first thing to note is that playtexts are fundamentally different from other kinds of writing. They consist primarily of dialogue between characters, interspersed with the odd stage direction which is descriptive of either location or action. Occasionally one of the characters may take the part of a narrator, setting the scene, filling in the gaps, telling the audience what has happened. Moreover each character will be bringing a different, personal perspective to the plot, often ambiguous, sometimes purposefully misleading.

By comparison a novel is packed full of descriptive information: about the characters' personalities, their personal history, detailed information about location, the weather, events that are happening elsewhere, and so forth. The novelist often invests considerable effort in setting the scene, telling the reader what they should be imagining, and the reader is able to develop a vivid personal perspective through this. The novelist can, if need be, go into microscopic detail describing the clothes that a character is wearing, the way their hair is worn, the type of rain falling against the window, the type of window itself and so on.

This device is not open to the playwright in quite the same way. The playwright must insert clues into the dialogue, clues that can then be interpreted by the director, the designer and the stage management. While the novelist can tell you in detail the facts that you need to know and feed your imagination with vivid descriptions, the playwright has to rely on your interpretation of clues in the dialogue. It is this that often makes playreading difficult; after all plays are written to be seen as well as heard, relying on the actors, through direction, to make sense of the plot and bring the characters to life.

Reading the script through thoroughly several times is a good start, annotating it with notes about plot, character, etc., as well as more the more practical aspects. But some plays can be very hard to understand just from reading, particularly those written several hundred years ago. How many people understand Shakespeare on the first reading? Even contemporary plays can be difficult. Without the benefit of the descriptive prose of a novel to set the scene, discuss the background and relationships, etc., this can be a daunting task. However there are strategies that can be followed to help to make it manageable.

Rosemary Ingham, in *From Page to Stage* (1998), recommends an approach that helps to organise and analyse a script by asking eight questions, based on the six components of drama outlined by Aristotle's Poetics. These questions may vary, increasing or decreasing in number according to the needs of the text itself. This 'interrogation' of the text can be summarised as follows:

1. **Where are they? – place**
2. **When are they? – time**
3. **Who are they? – characters**
4. **What happened before the play began? – the back-story**
5. **What is the function of each character in the play?**
6. **What kinds of dialogue do the characters speak?**
7. **What happens in the text? – the action**
8. **What is the play's theme?**

Approaching a text with the understanding that the information in it falls into these areas can make the task less daunting. Breaking this down further, there are a number of questions that can be asked under each heading. There may well be more answers, or no answers at all. The lack of an answer may, in itself, be important information that helps in the understanding of the playwright's intentions. Sometimes the answer to one question will be found once a different one has been answered, or the answer will change.

PLACE

1. What country is the play set in, what location in that country, what place within that location, what room within that place, and so on?
   Each of these has a bearing on the next. A room in a hotel in a small provincial town in Mexico may be different from that in Mexico City, or Darwin in Australia or London. The place may be familiar and comfortable to the characters or they may be in a totally alien environment.
2. How do the characters describe this place that they are in?
   Different characters may view the same location in different ways. A prisoner will have a totally different perspective on their cell than the warder, a mother on her teenager's bedroom.
3. Is there any special meaning or significance to the place they are in?
   There may be some form of nostalgic or symbolic connection. The characters' location in that place may be by design or by accident, it may be their location of choice or it may have been forced upon them. It may be a special personal place, or a place they have never visited before.

TIME

1. On what day, month, year, century, season, time of day, etc. is the action taking place?
   This is as important as the physical location. A sense of 'period' will tell you as much about the behaviour of the characters as about their appearance. The time of day, or the time of year, will affect characters in different ways. It may affect the way they behave or the way they dress, it may affect the way that they are lit.
2. What is the time-scale involved?
   Many plays take place over a distinct period of time. This can be 'real time', that is the action of the play takes place over the same timespan as the play itself, or it can be over a matter of hours, days, months, years, even centuries. Sometimes scenes may contiguous, that is they take place at the same time. Sometimes plays contain flashbacks; some even start with the conclusion and then step back to events that had an impact on this. Compiling a 'time-line' can be a useful way of organising this sequence of events. The time-line can be organised sequentially, in the order of scenes as the play is written, or temporally, in the order in which things would have happened in reality (when scenes are not in sequence time-wise). This linear structure can consist of several lines, mapping events associated with characters, or groups of characters, against each other. The time-line is a good way of making sense of a complex narrative, providing a visual map of the sequence of events in a play.
3. Do the characters have anything specific to say about their location in time?
   This may be a favourite time of day, or they may be afraid of the dark.

4. Is there any special significance to this location in time? Is it a special occasion, a national celebration, is there a major event happening in the world at the same time?

The play may be taking place the day war is declared, or peace, it may be an important birthday celebration, or the wake after a funeral.

CHARACTERS

1. How are they related?

Family relationships may be significant, but so equally will be the relationship between master and servant, school master and pupil, judge and plaintiff.

2. What are their roles in life? What jobs or professions do they have? What is their social and economic standing?

They may have advanced beyond their original background, achieving a better social or economic status. They may have married 'above', or 'beneath' them. They may have fallen on hard times.

3. What are they like?

They may be rounded complex people like you or me, or they may be caricatures, that is, representing a particular type of person in a heightened fashion. They may be nice or nasty, strong or weak, outgoing or shy, or all of these at some time. They may appear differently to different characters. The sadistic, autocratic boss may be a kind, loving father to his children.

4. What do they think of each other?

Feelings may be ambiguous, overt or covert, misdirected or misinterpreted. Characters may express different feelings about someone to different people.

5. What do they think of themselves?

They may lack self-esteem, or have an over-inflated view of themselves.

6. Under what political system do they live? What are their attitudes to this system?

They may be living under an autocratic and aggressive totalitarian government where every word has to be chosen carefully. They may be an agent of this government, or a covert opponent. They may be a member of the ruling class, or one of its subjects. They may be plotting revolution or nostalgic for an older, more stable system.

7. Which religion do they subscribe to? Is religion an important factor in their lives? What are their attitudes to other religions?

They may be a religious zealot, or a non-conformist. They may hold enormous prejudices that they believe are justified by their religion.

8. What are the prevailing attitudes to sex, family, marriage; the ethical conduct associated with the society in which they live? Do they subscribe to these, or are they rebelling against them?

The social expectations of the society they live in may be a huge influence. They may be trying to escape this, or to enforce it. Rebellion may be punished severely, even by death or incarceration. Promiscuity may be common yet covert, or celebrated.

9. Can the characters be divided into groups? Is this grouping significant? Do they behave differently in the presence of one group compared to another? Some groups, such as families, may be obvious. Others, such as sexuality or gang membership, may be secret, known only to those members. Characters may be trying to escape a group, or join another. They may alter their behaviour according to the particular group they are in at any time. That may even affect the way they dress as well as behave.

THE BACK-STORY

This requires considerable detective work. The playwright may refer to it in the opening and later stage directions but it is unlikely to be in any detail. Much of the factual information will be in the dialogue, but some clues may be found in less obvious contexts, often in what is left unsaid rather than said. The back-story may be intentionally vague; the playwright doesn't want to give too much away; but it can be immensely helpful in understanding the actions of the characters. Small snippets of information peppered throughout the play can be gathered to give you a broader understanding of each character's context. These are the clues that lend a dramatic edge to a play and help the audience to understand its denouement.

THE FUNCTION OF EACH CHARACTER

A play is a carefully crafted piece of story-telling designed to lead the audience to as predictable a conclusion as is possible, given the eminently unpredictable nature of audiences themselves. Remember that plays are about things happening. They are not about everyday life, which is generally pretty mundane, even boring, but about interruptions to the expected course of events. This applies as much to comedy as it does to drama or tragedy. Characters are created by the playwright to help communicate the meaning by driving the dramatic premise towards that conclusion. Thus each character will have a specific function within the story, even if that function is to put the audience off the scent.

1. **The protagonist**

   Every play is driven by a character with ambition; someone who wants something enough to keep the drama going to its conclusion. This 'chief personage' is known as the protagonist. Without them the play would not move forward. They are often quite outspoken and may seem larger than life.

2. **The antagonist**

   The antagonist's main function is to act as an obstacle to the protagonist, thwarting their ambition by reminding them of their shortcomings, their frailties. Sometimes they may even get in their way physically.

3. **Other principal characters**

Each of the other main characters has a function within the play, generally to thwart or support the actions of the protagonist, thus moving the drama forward. Their role may be symbolic, to act as a conscience, a role model, a figure of authority, a reminder of what could have been, or of what might be.

4. **Secondary characters**

Secondary characters may exist to highlight specific aspects of the protagonist's character and to help tell specific aspects of the story.

5. **Crowds and officials**

These often act as general tormentors or obstacles, getting in the way of the desired outcome.

DIALOGUE

When we enter into a conversation, we usually make a number of assumptions based on our prior knowledge and observations. The way people speak, their surroundings, the situation they are in, all act as signposts. In a play these assumptions have to be conveyed in a different way, through the dialogue and the limited information contained in stage directions. Of course in real life the way that we interpret these signs will vary, we may read body language differently if we come from a different culture or society, we may speak a different dialect, or even have particular prejudices. For instance, in British society wild hand gestures are rarely used and would be regarded as flamboyant, even threatening, whereas in many southern European or Afro-Caribbean cultures they would be regarded as a normal form of expression. Similarly you would be ill-advised to ask a New Yorker where you could get a fag. The signals are often confusing and sometimes knowingly ambiguous.

As already explained, playwrights have a limited set of tools at their disposal compared to novelists. In real life we will adjust our conversation to reflect common knowledge, but the playwright must tell the audience about significant events that the characters already know about. Many plays start with a description of the setting, time of day, etc. and sometimes with a series of actions but these are usually brief, rarely more than a page long, and thus cannot go into fine detail. Sometimes stage directions are used to describe an emotion, but more often they describe an action: 'A enters, B exits, gunfire off-stage'. Stage directions, while informative to the reader, are open to interpretation, and this interpretation may be third or even fourth hand by the time it reaches the audience. A word of warning is required here; it is not uncommon for stage directions to be added after a play is written, often taken from the prompt book of the first production. It is worth comparing several editions of a play to see whether they are as written by the playwright, or are a record of the first production as staged by a director and designer.

Dialogue is arguably the most important tool used by the playwright to tell the audience what they should be imagining or thinking. Dialogue is rarely comparable to the sorts of conversations we hold in real life. There is nothing random about dialogue, which is written by the playwright to give out information not just to the characters in the play but also to the audience. The characters may know what has happened earlier, even before the play starts, they may know something about each other, but the audience doesn't. This information must be conveyed to the audience via the dialogue. The style of the dialogue, the way it is written, is an important factor in understanding the playwright's intentions. A number of different styles of dialogue can be identified.

Naturalistic dialogue is often used when regional accents or dialect need to be conveyed in order to reflect the society or culture of the character. It can also be used to denote particular patterns of speech, characteristics such as a lisp, or the emotional state of a character affected by an event such as bereavement. This will tell the audience something about the background of the characters, even something about their personal characteristics. The structure of conversation is recognisable as being similar to the way that people actually speak in real life, though the content is usually more manufactured. Playwrights such as Edward Bond, Caryl Churchill and Jim Cartwright all use naturalistic dialogue in their plays.

Realistic dialogue is an extremely fluent version of the way that we actually speak. Characters speak in complete sentences and paragraphs similar to those found in descriptive prose, in a way that we simply do not encounter from day to day. Dialogue is expressed clearly using correct grammar, though colloquial expressions and slang may also be used. Playwrights such as Henrik Ibsen, Noel Coward and George Bernard Shaw all wrote using realistic dialogue.

Literary dialogue is an even more heightened version that glories in the use of language. Colourful grammatical devices such as metaphor and simile are used, with few colloquialisms or slang. Speeches are neat, concise, and well-balanced, in fact more like a prepared speech than conversation. The Restoration playwrights such as Richard Brinsley Sheridan generally wrote their comedy using a literary style.

Poetic dialogue was used by many early playwrights. Emphasis was placed on the story-telling aspect of the text; audiences went to 'hear' a play rather than to 'watch' one. Plays written in verse often contain descriptive narrative directed to the audience, giving out specific pieces of information, even setting the scene. Sometimes this information would not be familiar to other characters even though, in the context of the stage, they would be able to hear what was being said. Audiences of the time would have been familiar with and accepted this device.

Sometimes different styles of dialogue are found in the same play. From the Renaissance onwards, playwrights such as William Shakespeare often used prose as well as verse in order to differentiate between different types of character, particularly social classes. Verse was used for the upper classes and prose for the lower.

Some plays are written in a style that cannot easily be fitted into the above categories. The Absurdist dramatists of the early twentieth century wrote in a style that responded to the Dada movement in the broader arts. Playwrights such as Eugene Ionesco and Samuel Beckett are associated with this style of writing.

THE ACTION

1. What is the principal event?

   Believe it or not, most plays are about something that happens, a dramatic, tragic or humorous event, or combinations of these. They have a 'plot'. This is what makes a play interesting and, hopefully, keeps an audience's attention for its duration. The event is frequently surprising, even catastrophic. An audience is not likely to be interested in watching normal everyday life unfold, something must happen to disrupt this.

   It is useful to try to identify the major driving event, the climax towards which a play is heading. This may be quite complex, rather than simply 'A & B get married', and there may be distractions thrown in on the way.

2. How does the action work towards or support this?

   The sequence of events leading up to the climax is important. Each scene, each exit and entrance and all the action will contribute towards this. When a character makes an entrance they do so to move the plot on, to give some information or cause something to happen. When they exit the same happens.

THEME

Many plays will have an underlying theme – 'life's hard', 'all men are stupid', and so on. This may well only become apparent as the play becomes more familiar through repeated reading. Sometimes it will take actors moving about and relating to one another before this really becomes apparent. The theme may be connected to wider issues, philosophical or artistic movements, political or religious viewpoints.

BACKGROUND RESEARCH

A playtext is not just the dialogue and stage directions. Rosemary Ingham defines it as 'the sum total of the playwright's intentions and all the intellectual and aesthetic performance potential within the total written work'. That definition is taken to include both the conscious and unconscious intentions of the playwright, including any possible influences from their own life and experience. The intellectual background to the play is also important, as is any future thought that may be influenced by this. The play will also be affected by the history of the time in which it was written, while our interpretation will be influenced by our knowledge of subsequent events and our own historical perspective. This includes the standing of the play itself, or the playwright, within the history of theatre and literature. Previous interpretations of the play, the way it has been staged before, may also influence our understanding, as will the reaction of previous audiences and theatre critics. Finally we bring to a reading our own current thoughts and beliefs and this contemporary Zeitgeist (a useful but hard to translate German word, roughly meaning 'spirit of the time', but embodying much more than that) will affect our interpretation and judgement of a text. Standing through four hours of blank verse is not something we are used to in our contemporary culture, yet when Shakespeare was writing that is exactly what an audience expected. The modern interpreter of Shakespeare needs to make a production that is acceptable and interesting to a modern audience, in much the same way that the Victorian actor-manager provided the entertainment and spectacle that their audiences expected.

THE HISTORICAL CONTEXT

The context in which a play was written is an important factor which may help lead towards a better understanding. Everyone is affected by the world in which they live and the playwright is no exception. When considering the 'period' in which a play is set, or was written, it is easy to think of it purely in terms of art, architecture, furniture, clothing, etc. But it is much more than this. The politics, religious beliefs, social climate of the time all contribute to a 'period', indeed the outward trappings such as architecture and clothing may be a direct response to these.

World events, philosophical movements, literary styles, inventions, all help to define a period. Getting to grips with this 'historical' context can lead to a better understanding of a play. Most plays are set in a real world even though the story being told is fictitious. The wider events happening in that world are as important as the action of the play itself. This is true both of the time in which a play is set and the 'actual' time at which is written, which may be different.

For instance Arthur Miller's *The Crucible* is about the witch trials in Salem in 1692. When approaching this play, it is useful to know a bit about the history of that period in America, not just what things looked like, but also what people believed in and what they had been through previously. This will help lead to a better understanding of the characters and the play itself. Published in 1953, the play was intended by Miller as an allegory for events that were unfolding in America at that time. Since 1950 Senator Joe McCarthy had pursued perceived communists in public life through his chairmanship of the Senate's Permanent Committee on Investigations. Many public figures, including actors and writers, were indicted and even convicted. Anybody criticising this policy, or the American government generally, was liable to suspicion and accusations of 'red' activities. Obviously Miller could not afford to be openly critical, but he saw a parallel between these events and the witch hunts of the late seventeenth century; *The Crucible* was his response. Miller himself was subpoenaed in 1956 and convicted for contempt of Congress in 1957 for refusing to name names. His conviction was overturned a year later. Reading the play with this background knowledge can lead to a better understanding, particularly if a director and designer decide to make reference to this context in their production.

THE PLAYWRIGHT

Research into the actual playwright can be helpful. Finding out about their background may shed some light on the themes they are writing about, the issues that concern them. Reading earlier plays by the same author can give some insight into the development of their personal style and lead to a better understanding of their writing.

Sometimes playwrights take someone's life or a real event as the basis of their play, which becomes, in effect, a dramatised biography. *An Experiment with an Air Pump* (1998) by Shelagh Stephenson is an example of a play inspired by a real event. It takes as its starting-point a 1767 painting by Joseph Wright of Derby which portrays an actual historical event, a demonstration of a scientific experiment which showed that life cannot be supported in a vacuum. Others may take a novel as their inspiration, adapting it for the stage; an example is Brian Friel's *Fathers and Sons*, based on the novel by Ivan Turgenev.

With both of these the background research is made much easier. It is possible to read about the experiment, view the painting and even see the actual apparatus used as depicted in the painting. With an adaptation, reading the actual novel will give you an insight into all aspects of your text analysis, but it is also interesting, and useful to see what the playwright has left out. It is often necessary to cut characters and simplify the plot, sometimes with the loss of clarity, making the back-story more difficult to define.

DEVISED THEATRE

In devised theatre, the production is created from scratch. It may be based on a theme, a story, someone's life, a picture, almost anything, as its starting-point and generates a piece of theatre that has been created with the cast through the rehearsal process. The end-result may be a text-based script or something that is entirely visual.

A devised production can be prepared for in advance by researching the underlying theme, if that is known. This will enable an informed contribution to the process to be made, something that is often expected of stage management working in devised theatre. Knowledge of the methods that the company use to create their theatre is also useful. Many devising companies will expect everyone present in the rehearsal room to be involved in the process and to have a creative input. It is best if this does not come as a surprise!

TECHNICAL ANALYSIS

At the same time as getting to grips with analysis of the text itself, the stage manager should also look out for any technical implications. These might include the following:

- **Settings**
- **Characters**
- **Costume**
- **Furniture and properties**
- **Lighting**
- **Sound**
- **Special effects**

Stage management need to know and understand all the technical requirements implied by the text. They will certainly be concerned with finding and/or managing the props. They will cue and co-ordinate scene changes, lighting and sound. They may also be called on to operate lighting and sound, even if only in the rehearsal room. They will work closely with the costume designer and supervisor, helping to organise fittings and quick changes.

Stage directions are a major source of information regarding all of these, but dialogue must not be ignored. A lazy, or hard-pressed, stage manager may be tempted to skim through a script, noting down any mention of these technical items contained in italics in the stage directions. Yet by doing this they are likely to miss crucial pieces of information. A character may ask for a cigarette and then for a light without any mention of either in the stage directions; he or she may refer to the weather, the time of day and numerous other things that may indicate a lighting or sound effect; the topography of the set may be referred to in conversation; and so on.

Knowledge of the social background of the characters and the historical and sociological context will help with this detective work. This is one of the few times when the stage manager can make assumptions. A play such as Oscar Wilde's *The Importance of Being Earnest* is set in an 'upper' class family at a time when social behaviour was bound by a rigid set of rules. Taking tea, for instance, would have involved a ritual every bit as formal as a Japanese Tea Ceremony, involving items of crockery and cutlery beyond the obvious teapot and cups and saucers. The characters would have dressed differently at different times of day and for different occasions. The Birling family in J.B. Priestley's *An Inspector Calls* would have worn evening dress for their dinner and Priestley doesn't need to tell us that.

All this information needs to be represented in a form that will make it a useful reference. Different coloured marker pens may be used to highlight different technical aspects in the script itself, or notes jotted down on different bits of paper to start with, but the information eventually needs to be organised if it is to be of any use, and will then become a working document which will be of use to any other members of the team who may need access to it.

The same information may also be generated by other people, such as the director and designer. This could be viewed as needless repetition: why bother if somebody else is going to do the same work too? At this stage this analysis is about 'being prepared' (the motto coined by Baden-Powell for the Scout Movement could equally well apply to stage management) and managing expectation. As well as being an essential way of becoming familiar with the potential requirements of a production, it also provides a useful reference for double-checking that nothing has been missed. Two people comparing the same information are less likely to overlook something.

Documents prepared from initial readings are provisional – the information contained within them will change, probably frequently. That is the evolutionary nature of theatre. They form the foundations for the way that the stage management will order information and track changes.

The stage manager will need to identify each prop, costume, sound effect, etc. They will need to know whereabouts in the script it is mentioned, the act, scene and page number, so that it can be referred to quickly. In the case of props and costume they need to know who it concerns, that is, who is using it or wearing it. They need to know anything special about it; whether it gets eaten, torn off in a frenzy, or if it has to be identical to every other occurrence, or different. Finally it is handy to know whose responsibility it will be and when. The amount of detail that can be gone into will be invaluable later. If the car drawing up outside, in a play set in the 1930s, is mentioned later as a Rolls Royce, then that should be noted down – it may just be important.

Playwrights usually help by telling the reader, scene by scene, where the play is set. This may vary from one to many diverse locations. Stage directions are the main source of information for this but dialogue should not be ignored. Information in the stage directions may be immensely detailed, or short and to the point, like those encountered in Shakespeare's plays. When stage directions are vague the dialogue may provide useful clues.

SETTINGS

Noting down the settings scene by scene will start to give a picture of the complexity of a production. This, together with the scale of the production as indicated by the size of the budget and venue, will temper expectations. The stage manager will be able to ask 'How might this be done?' If the play has many settings and is to be produced in a small-scale theatre with a small budget, it is reasonable to assume that there will be little in the way of scenery needing complex scene changes. A large-budget production destined for a West End or Broadway theatre is likely to be a different matter. A detailed knowledge of the settings implied by the production will enable informed questions to be asked of the director and designer at the first meeting.

CHARACTERS

The characters in a play move through the settings and it is important to keep track of their movements. In a simple play with a small number of characters, this is relatively easy. Most playwrights have the foresight to tell the reader who the characters are in a character list at the beginning of a script. This is either alphabetical or, more commonly and usefully, in order of appearance. That is, the names of the characters are listed according to the point in the play where they are first encountered. Sometimes the list is in order of importance of the characters.

While this is helpful, the stage manager will need to know more than this. It is rare for all the characters to be on stage all of the time, even the protagonist. Thus it is useful to note who is in which scene. This will be helpful later when rehearsal calls need to be organised. A simple way to do this is called a 'Scene Breakdown' (see *Figure 3.1*), which simply lists the characters appearing in each scene.

THE ROSE TATTOO		
PART ONE		
ACT I Scene i pp 1–28		
VIVI	BRUNO	SALVATORE
GIUSEPPINA	PEPPINA	VIOLETTA
MARIELLA	THE STREGA	SERAFINA
ROSA	ASSUNTA	ESTELLE
ACT I Scene ii pp 28–29		
GIUSEPPINA	PEPPINA	VIOLETTA
MARIELLA	SERAFINA	ASSUNTA
Fr DE LEO		
ACT I Scene iii pp 29–32		
ASSUNTA	Fr DE LEO	DOCTOR
GIUSEPPINA	PEPPINA	VIOLETTA
MARIELLA	ESTELLE	THE STREGA
ROSA	BRUNO	
ACT I Scene iv pp 32–39		
GIUSEPPINA	PEPPINA	VIOLETTA
MARIELLA	SERAFINA	MISS YORKE
ROSA		
ACT I Scene v		
BESSIE	FLORA	SERAFINA
LEGIONAIRE		

Figure 3.1 A scene breakdown

Life is seldom that simple, however, and some plays will require a different approach. In a play with a large cast and complex plot, some characters may make exits ands entrances throughout each scene, while others may only be on stage for a fraction of a scene. In this case a simple scene breakdown would not give a particularly accurate picture of the actual shape of the play. Compiling a 'Character Plot' can be a useful way of dealing with this complexity (see *Figure 3.2*). A character plot is a spreadsheet that can be used to map the movement of characters page by page. In the example shown, crosses are used to indicate that a character is on stage. Oblique lines can be used to indicate when a character enters or exits halfway down a page. When the same characters are on stage for a few pages, these pages can be listed together.

CHARACTER PLOT Production: *The Rose Tattoo*   Venue: Playhouse Theatre

Act / Scene	I.1										I.2		I.3				I.4						I.5							I.6					
Character / Page	19	20	21	22	23	24	25	26	27	28	28	29	29	30	31	32	32	33	34	35	-	39	40	-	43	44	-	47	48	48	49	-	57	-	60
BRUNO	X	X											/	/																					
SALVATORE	X	X																																	
VIVI	X	X						/	X	X																									
GIUSEPPINA	off											X	X			/	X	X	X	X	X	X													
PEPPINA	off											X	X			/	X	X	X	X	X	X													
VIOLETTA	off											X	X	/	X	X	X	X	X	X	X	X													
MARIELLA	off											X	X	/	X	X	X	X	X	X	X	X													
STREGA	X						X										X																	/	X
SERAFINA	X	X	X	X	X	X	X	X	X	X							X	X	X	X	X	X	X	X	X	X	X	X	X	/	X	X	X	X	X
ROSA			X	X	X	X	X	X	X	X																									
ASSUNTA		X	X	X	X							X	X	X	X	X																			
ESTELLE						X	X	X	X	X																									
Fr de LEO																																			
DOCTOR												X	X	X	X	X																			
Miss YORKE																		X	X	X	X	X													
BESSIE																							X	X	X	X	X	X	X						
FLORA																							X	X	X	X	X	X	X						
LEGIONAIRE																																			
JACK																							/							X	X	X	X	X	X
SALESMAN																																			
ALVARO																																			
Girl's voice																														off			off		
Boy's voice																														off			off		

Figure 3.2 A character plot

The character plot has a number of uses. It gives a good, clear visual picture of the shape of a play. It enables a director to break up each scene into smaller entities and thus organise a more focused rehearsal schedule. Each time a character makes an entrance or exit they do so to drive the plot forward, to change what has gone before. This means that each entrance and exit defines a new section of the play that can be treated discretely. When members of the cast are to play more than one character, or cover different roles as understudies, it makes it easy to see any logistical problems. It enables the stage manager to see, at a glance, what can be rehearsed should an actor be unavailable at any point. It is also a very useful tool for the costume designer and supervisor, showing where there quick changes may be required and also giving a good indication of the number of costumes that may be needed.

COSTUME

The information contained in a script regarding costume may be highly detailed or vague. Some playwrights will specify exactly what a character is wearing; others leave it up to individual interpretation. Historical or social context can be very important here, a playwright may take for granted knowledge of the protocols regarding clothing, yet these may not be familiar to us. People no longer carry swords, unless they are military personnel undertaking ceremonial duties, but two hundred years ago ordinary people from a particular background would have done so. In a Restoration comedy such as *The Rivals* (1775), by Richard Brinsley Sheridan, most of the male characters would have worn swords in public; Sheridan doesn't write 'Acres enters wearing a sword', as that is his assumption. Stage management, as well as the director and designer, need to know this, or the costume budget may double. Moreover there may also be a knock-on effect for the cast, even for the scenic constructor. The spatial awareness of an eighteenth century character would have been different to that of a twenty-first century actor. A sword sticks out beyond a person's coat and the contemporary actor is not used to this, banging into people and things in a way that conflicts with 'period' truth. Even the simple act of making an entrance through a door will be different. The eighteenth century gentleman did not get his sword stuck in a door, the modern actor might.

Similarly, the passage of time in a play may indicate a change of clothing! The time-scale will make a big difference; changes of clothing are a good way of showing this, whether between different times of day, different times of year or even between years.

Stage management should take more than a cursory interest in costume. They will work closely with the costume designer and supervisor from the very beginning and detailed knowledge will make this easier. Costume fittings will need to be co-ordinated with the rehearsal schedule, and with a large cast and a lot of costumes this can be complex. Sometimes the props and costumes associated with a character may need to match; items such as handbags, umbrellas or jewellery may be the responsibility of stage management, and will need to fit in with a character's costume. At the very least stage management will need to know about these peripherals, to know whose responsibility they will be and to ask the right questions. Some props will have a direct impact on costume. Things that have to be kept in pockets, or just appear from a character's person, or that will soil or damage a costume, may all be spotted at this text analysis stage. The physical size and quantity of costumes may potentially have an impact on stage management. Large costumes may create congestion back-stage, they may even be too big to fit on the furniture or parts of the set. The quick changes that may have to take place off-stage will require special areas and storage for the costumes and if there are more than anticipated this may be a problem.

Supported by a good knowledge of the settings and the time-scale involved and backed up by a thorough understanding of the period context, a character plot (*Figure 3.2*) is a very handy way of keeping track of costume. Costume designers and supervisors often work from an expanded character plot in conjunction with a time-line. This enables them to plot the number of costumes that will be required and to plan quick changes. In *Figure 3.2*, the character of Serafina has potential changes in Act 1 between Scenes 1 and 2, 4 and 5, and 5 and 6. She may have a change between scenes 2 and 4, but has scene 3 to do it in.

FURNITURE AND PROPS

Furniture and props are one of the primary concerns of stage management. It is essential to compile a comprehensive list of potential items. This provisional props list (see *Figure 3.3*) will inform the approach the stage management may take towards their workload once the production moves into the development phase.

Information regarding props and furniture will be found in both the stage directions and the dialogue, but there may be also be an element of conjecture, informed by thorough research. The props list needs to contain as much information as can be gleaned from the text. Items that appear more than once should be listed separately. At a later date it may become evident that they are the same, but at this stage it is best to note down absolutely everything.

In order to save time later, it is prudent to compile a props list that has room for expansion, further notes and any more information that might be important. This is a working document and not just for the individual stage manager, as it will grow into more than just a list of the props that are going to be needed for the production. It should contain details about who uses them and when, what they have to look like, what they have to do, how many, who is going to take responsibility for what and when it will be achieved. In *Figure 3.3*, for Acts 1 and 2 of *The Importance of Being Earnest*, the props are listed in order of act, scene, then page. The prop itself is noted followed by any special requirements and who uses it. For instance, the cigarette case (p.4) is more than just that; it belongs to Jack, is brought to him by Lane and has an inscription inside. All of these things are significant and need to be noted. The bread and butter, some of which is eaten, is on a plate which is 'taken from below'. This implies that it is on something with several levels; knowledge of Edwardian tea protocol might lead the stage manager to the reasonable conclusion that there will be a cake stand or similar. The last two columns indicate how each prop is going to be achieved and by when.

LIGHTING

Information in the text concerning lighting is usually more subtle. The time of day or year may suggest a certain quality of light, exterior or interior settings, whether electricity or gas would have been used. Specific lighting effects are

PRODUCTION: *THE IMPORTANCE OF BEING EARNEST*				
Date: 6 June		Version: Provisional		
Sc/P	Item	Description/Notes	Source	Status
ACT 1				
p1	Tea Table			
	Sofa			
	Afternoon tea setting, including: Cucumber sandwiches,	In process of being set on table by Lane		
	probably on plate, served on: Salver (silver?)	All get eaten		
p2	Cups & saucers	X 3 for Algie, Gwendolen & Lady B.		
p3	Bread and butter on plate	Some eaten		
	Cake/plate stand	Inferred by 'Takes plate from below'		
	Bell	Could be small hand bell or bell pull		
p4	Cigarette case	Belongs to Jack, brought on by Lane. Inscribed inside		
	Salver, silver	Brought on by Lane		
p5	Visiting card	Belonging to Jack. Text on p.5		
		Taken from cigarette case.		
p8	Two chairs Tea – tea pot, milk jug, sugar bowl & tongs, lemon slices, tea spoons?	Jack & Gwendolen sit on them in corner		
p12	Notebook & pencil	Lady Bracknell. Taken from pocket, thus small		
p18	Pencil or pen	Algernon uses it to write on cuff		
	Railway Guide			
	Salver (as 1.1.4?)			
	Several letters in envelopes.	Bills, torn up at each perf.		
	Sherry glass with sherry	Consumed		
	Cigarettes	1 Smoked by Algernon		
	Cigarette box or case			
	Lighter or matches	Practical		
	Ashtray			
ACT 2				
p21	Basket Chairs			
	Table			
	Books, inc German Grammar	On table		
	Watering can	Cecily, practical		
p22	Diary	Cecily, written in		
	Pencil or pen	Cecily		
p23	Political Economy, & Geography books	On table, get thrown about		
	Salver	Merriman		
	Calling Card (text as p 23)			
	Same as Act 1	On salver		
p25	Scissors	Cecily, used to cut flower		
	Roses	One is cut for button-hole		
p28	Pocket watch (on chain?)	Chasuble		
p33	Box, cont.	Cecily, on table		

Figure 3.3 A provisional props list

sometimes mentioned. These may be practical, lights being switched on or off, candles lit, or more atmospheric. Clues are very often contained in the dialogue, 'What a beautiful sunset', 'I can't see a thing', and so on, as well as in the stage directions, 'The sun sets', 'Black out'. From the start of the process the stage manager on the book will find it useful to have some idea as to the potential complexity of the lighting, and in particular where cues might happen.

SOUND

Many playwrights specify sound effects that are an integral part of their play; even Shakespeare specified some sound effects. Sound can be used to denote location and events and is a useful addition to dialogue. A car drawing up off-stage can change the way the characters are behaving on stage before anybody new makes an entrance. *Figure 3.4* is a provisional 'Sound Plot' for *The Rose Tattoo*, literally a list of all the sounds mentioned in the text. As with the other elements, some sounds may only be alluded to in the dialogue.

THE ROSE TATTOO SOUND PLOT (PROVISIONAL)			
Page	EFFECT	WHERE	COMMENT
ACT 1			
Scene 1			
p21	TRUCK PASSING	USL TO USR	
	MUSIC		
p24	TRUCK PASSING	USL TO USR	
p26	GOAT BLEATING, HARNESS JINGLING & WOOD SPLINTERING	USL	
	THEN: GOAT BLEATING & HARNESS JINGLING	CIRCLING CLOCKWISE	
Scene 2			
p29	KEELING WOMEN		
Scene 3			
p32	MUSIC		
Scene 4			
p33	SHOUT & RUNNING FOOTSTEPS	WITHIN HOUSE	
p34	SCREAM & RUNNING FOOTSTEPS	WITHIN HOUSE	
	OUTCRIES FROM	WITHIN HOUSE	
p39	MUSIC		
Scene 5			
p40	PARROT		
	SCHOOL BAND		
p42	TRAIN WHISTLE		
p43	PARROT SQUAWK		
	CAR HORN		
p44	SCHOOL BAND		MARTIAL AIR
p46	SCHOOL BAND		
p47	SCHOOL BAND		THE STARS & STRIPES

Figure 3.4 A provisional sound plot

SPECIAL EFFECTS

Many plays contain technical elements that do not fit into a particular area. Such special effects might include explosions or gunshots and smoke on-stage, stage fights, people flying or falling from a height or disappearing into the stage. These may end up as the responsibility of the stage management and many have a safety implication.

DEVISED THEATRE

It is harder to prepare technically for the devising process. Some guesses may be made, depending on where the inspiration is drawn from. An image, or a novel, someone's life, or a real event may give some clues. Themes are usually chosen for their dramatic potential, which means that something interesting is likely to happen by association. Researching these may give some indication of any special technical challenge that could be expected.

Similarly the style of theatre associated with the company is important. They may have particular methods, using projection or live sound, even circus skills or large-scale puppetry. These will all have technical implications that the stage manager can prepare for.

SUMMARY

This chapter has examined how the stage manager can get to know a play; the factors that influence the way in which it may be interpreted; and what significance these may have for the stage manager as a member of the production team.

All this information – an understanding of the play, familiarity with the characters, the technical implications, a good knowledge of the historical background of the period the play is set in, when it was written and what this means in a contemporary context – can now be fed into the next stage.

The next chapter examines how this knowledge can be used to inform the stage manager's approach to the production and the other people involved in it. The stage management needs to become familiar with the actual production as proposed, or at least with the concepts that the director and designers have come up with. These can be compared with any expectations suggested by the background research and analysis and the challenges that this implies identified. Armed with their background knowledge, the stage manager will be able to ask informed questions and make an intelligent contribution to this next stage.

PREPARING FOR REHEARSALS

It is important to get off to a good start; the initial impression that a stage manager makes is likely to stay with them until the end. Set off on the wrong foot and it will be much harder to win the trust of the creative and production team. The stage manager should appear informed and interested, as well as efficient, in order to create a good first impression and to make their subsequent involvement and contribution more satisfying.

The first priority is to get to know the other people involved in the production. Initiating the formation of the production team early on will help to establish good working relationships.

A stage management team is normally employed by the producer and the production manager, possibly in conjunction with the company manager. They will usually try to put together a team of people they know who have worked well together before. While this is the ideal, in practice a team will often consist of some new members, and with a new company it is likely that no-one will have worked together before.

If they do not already know each other, individual members of the stage management team should arrange to meet in advance. It is useful to try to find out the strengths, weaknesses and interests of each member, and how these can be used most effectively. Clarifying each individual's role will help the team to work together as a single entity. This process can start immediately, as initial preparations for the production are made. An informal social get-together is a good way of doing this and is a good starting-point for any project. At this point the implications of the project itself can be discussed before they become reality.

THE CREATIVE TEAM
THE DIRECTOR
The stage manager may well already know the director, who may even have asked for them to work on the production. Nevertheless it is important to meet up with the director as far in advance as possible. The opportunity can be used to find out about their vision for the production, whether they foresee any problems with the staging, with the cast, or anything else.

If the stage manager has not worked with the director before it is useful to try to discover what part they like stage management to play in rehearsals. It is possible to find this out by asking around; other stage managers or performers will have worked with them and can be probed for information. While this can be useful, it is best to be wary. Many people carry a reputation which is unfounded, and which is more of a reflection on the people who have brushed up against them. If somebody says that a certain director is a 'nightmare' to work with it is better not to believe them. The comment may say more about their own shortcomings than those of the director.

The task must be approached with an open mind – any preconception that the director is going to be a 'nightmare' will show. A common response to such a preconception is to be belligerently defensive. This will put the director on their guard; in fact it will make the stage manager more vulnerable.

Some directors have particular requirements or idiosyncrasies. They may need a music stand on which to rest their copy of the script, or insist on drinking Earl Grey tea from a bone china cup. This may seem odd or picky, but it is important to remember that it is the stage manager's task to help create the optimum conditions for creativity to take place. Questioning or resisting these demands will have the opposite effect, and will ultimately make the job harder.

THE DESIGNERS

It is also useful to meet the set and costume, lighting and sound designers in advance. Their intentions for the design can be discussed, with a view to gaining a good understanding of the design concept and how it relates to the script.

THE DESIGN CONCEPT

Stage management will need to study ground plans and models in advance so that they have a clear and detailed idea of what the set will look like. They should try to attend any initial design meetings or production meetings and to ask any questions that will clarify their understanding of the production in terms of the relationship between the design, direction and the text.

Early on in the design process there may be a 'White Card' model meeting. At this stage the set designer will present a proposal in model form, literally constructed out of white card. The purpose of this is to address 'form' rather than colour or texture. The meeting will involve the production manager and other key members of the production team, who will discuss the technical implications of the set in relation to the proposed budget. The director and designer will have met before this to discuss and agree on their artistic response to the play. The white card model is the next stage, enabling the designer to discuss the feasibility of their proposal within the context of the production itself. The meeting will enable the production manager to make a notional costing, which will then be fed back to the designer so that any necessary changes can be made. It is unusual for stage management to be involved at this stage unless they are members of a permanent team in a producing theatre.

The designer will then produce a complete model and associated drawings, taking into account any changes that have had to be made. In the example shown, the ground plan and model is for a production of David Greig's *The Cosmonaut's Last Message*, designed by Keith Orton (see *Figure 4.1*). In this case the designer has used elements of the model box in conjunction with the ground plan to demonstrate how the set is moved from scene to scene. The model will be presented at a 'Full Model' meeting that is likely to involve more members of the production team. It is advantageous for stage management to attend this meeting.

a. Act 1 Scene 15

b. Act 1 Scene 15 on stage

c. Transition from Act 1 Scene 15 to 16

d. Act 1 Scene 16

Figure 4.1 A ground plan and model box

It is at this stage that background research starts to come into its own, where expectations can be compared with the reality of the proposed production and its parameters. The provisional lists of settings, costume, props, sound and so forth will form a good basis for discussion. The designer may also have compiled a version of the props list. These can be compared and any omissions and additions noted. Where items have been omitted this should be queried; it could be an oversight. It is tempting to take the designer's list as definitive but designers are human too and may make mistakes. By the end of this meeting there should be an updated and definitive list. *Figure 4.2* shows the second, updated, version of the props list shown in *Figure 3.3*.

The list has expanded – a number of items have been added – but it has also been rationalised and more detail added. Potential sources for some of the props

Sc/P	Item	Description/Notes	Source	Status
	**PRODUCTION:** *THE IMPORTANCE OF BEING EARNEST* **Date: 12 June 2000** **Version: 2**				
	**ACT 1 Morning-room in Algernon's flat in Half-Moon Street. The room is luxuriously and artistically furnished.**				
p1	Bookcases with:		Set	
	Books	Dressing	Make	
	Stool or chair			
	Settee	High backed		
	Window-seat with:		Set	
	Cushions			
	Lacquer Screen			
	Armchair			
	Other chair			
	Mantlepiece, on it:		Set	
	Clock			
	Candlesticks & candles x 2	Not practical		
	Table with drawer, on it:			
	Mirror			
	Cigarette box, filled with cigarettes	1 smoked		
	Ashtray			
	Bowl of flowers			
	Railway Guide	In table drawer		
	Tea Table, set with:			
	Tablecloth	In process of being set on table by Lane		
	Tray			
	4 x Cups & saucers & tea spoons			
	Cucumber sandwiches, on plate	All get eaten		
	Bread and butter on plate	Some gets eaten		
	Milk jug with milk	Practical		
	Sugar bowl with sugar & tongs			
	Bell pull			
p4	Cigarette case, on:	Belongs to Jack, brought on by Lane. Inscribed inside		
	Salver, silver	Brought on by Lane		
p5	Visiting card in cigarette case	Belonging to Jack. Text on p.5		
p8	Teapot filled with tea, on tray	Lane		
p12	Notebook & pencil	Lady Bracknell. Taken from pocket, thus small		
p18	Pencil	Algernon uses it to write on cuff		
	3 letters in envelopes, on salver (as before)	Bills, torn up at each perf.		
	Decanter of sherry & sherry glass, on salver (as before) Matches	Lane, sherry gets poured & drunk Algernon, practical		

Figure 4.2 An amended props list

and furniture can start to be identified, particularly items of furniture that are incorporated into the set or need to be made to a specific design.

The props list can be used as a basis for discussion with the designer about who is going to obtain what in the way of furniture and props. The degree of responsibility will vary with the particular designer and the needs of the production (and the management). In any case all props, furniture and set dressings will have to be approved by the designer and director.

At this stage it may become evident that the production is to be realised in a way that is far from any expectations. Shakespeare, for instance, is often staged out of period. Of course in Shakespeare's time the plays would have been staged in an Elizabethan version of the time they were set in, so there is a precedent for this. It is even possible that the play is to be staged in the round, with minimal scenery, or with no scenery at all. Very occasionally the intention is to stage the play without props at all. At this point it may seem that all the research and preparation has been in vain. Well, no, it hasn't.

Although a play may be set in a different period or use a minimalist design aesthetic, its dramatic intention will remain the same. Without serious cutting or re-writing, aspects of a play may then appear anachronistic, or even seem impossible to stage within the defined parameters. For example, *Coriolanus* involves a bloody sword fight. Set in the Elizabethan or Roman periods, this does not pose much of a problem, but one of the challenges for any director and designer wanting to update the play must be how to stage this fight. There are many options: keep it as a sword fight and hope that the audience just accept that, change it into a gun battle, and so on. This is a common problem, just how much can an audience be expected to 'suspend their disbelief'?

The stage manager should be familiar with the potential requirements of a play. In initial discussions with the director and designers this knowledge will form an agenda which leads to informed questions being asked. If they gloss over the subject of the sword fight this should be questioned. The question at the back of every stage manager's mind should be 'How are we going to do that?'

At this stage the stage management team should become familiar with all aspects of the budget that will directly affect them. This will mainly concern the budget set aside for props, but it may also take into account things like telephone calls, transport, stationery, etc., which may be   particularly relevant if stage management are not working from a base.

Thus by combining initial expectations with the actuality of the production, the stage manager will be able to form a detailed and up-to-date picture of the task ahead. At this stage it is both possible and desirable to identify any potential problems and to work out and propose solutions. By doing this the stage manager will be well prepared and able to confront all the challenges that will inevitably arise during the rehearsal period and are impossible to predict.

OTHER MEMBERS OF THE CREATIVE AND PRODUCTION TEAM

It is desirable to meet as many other associated members of the creative team as possible. These might include a musical director and choreographer if the production is a musical. Other key members of the production team also need to be met, such as the production manager, costume supervisor, props buyer, etc. They may have special requirements to prepare for the rehearsal period, such as measurements for costume and wigs, or even advance fittings.

THE COMPANY (CAST)

It is unlikely that stage management can meet before the first rehearsal but it is useful to make some form of contact in advance.

In certain circumstances, however, stage management may be required to assist with the initial casting process by helping to organise auditions. They may even be engaged well in advance of the production period solely for this purpose. Two stage managers may be required, one to look after the artistes waiting, and one to liase with the auditioning panel, introducing each artiste and reading-in as required. As auditions may take place months in advance it is entirely possible that these stage managers will not be the ones who will work on the actual production.

The stage manager is unlikely to know exactly who has been cast, however, until they receive a cast list before the rehearsals start.

AUDITIONS

Auditioning is nerve-racking for artistes, who should be treated with tact and courtesy. Timing is important so that artistes have time to relax and read over the script, but are not kept waiting too long with a lot of other people. Enough scripts need to be provided, with the parts to be read clearly marked. A comfortable waiting area is important, out of earshot of the auditions and with access to toilet and washing facilities and a public phone, and enough chairs. Providing fresh water is a nice touch. Dancers are usually called to auditions in groups and will require changing facilities. As they arrive, artistes' names, phone numbers and agents should be checked.

The director, management representatives, and perhaps the author, will be sitting in the stalls, if auditions are at a theatre, or behind a table. They will need to be provided with ashtrays (if smoking is permitted), water and coffee, as auditioning can be a long and gruelling task. Suitable stage lighting may need to be arranged in advance and the stage or audition room set up accordingly. For singing auditions, a piano will need to be tuned and positioned so that the pianist can see the singer and the music should be adequately lit.

Each artiste may need to be introduced as they come on stage, though they may be asked to do this themselves. If the stage manager is required to read in for different characters, they should attempt to do so with colour and pace, giving the artiste something to play against but without upstaging them.

PREPARING FOR REHEARSALS
CONTACTING THE COMPANY: PROCESSING AND COMMUNICATING INFORMATION

The key to forming a successful relationship with the company in the lead-up to the rehearsal period is through information. A lot of information that may be useful to the company can be compiled, collated and circulated in advance. This is particularly important if the production is going to tour. Touring schedules and lists of theatre digs should be distributed as soon as they become available, preferably in advance of the rehearsal period. This will enable the cast to start to arrange transport and accommodation before they become too preoccupied with rehearsals, and to obtain the most economical options available. Much of this information will already have been collated by the producer or theatre management, but it is always worth double-checking.

Sometimes a production will make specific requirements of the cast; they may need to wear loose clothing and appropriate footwear for a dance-oriented production, or long skirts for a period piece. If there are particular rehearsal costume requirements, these should be organised in advance. The cast will need to know whether they are expected to provide their own or whether these will be provided by the costume supervisor.

The stage manager will need to put together a list of addresses and telephone numbers of artistes and their agents, management offices, director, designers, stage management, costume supervisor, scenic studios, publicity agents and all other people relevant to the production. This is usually called a Contact Sheet. A separate 'at-a-glance' telephone list is also useful. It may be necessary to compile several versions aimed at different members of the company – not everyone needs all these details.

Contact sheets can be distributed to the people who may need to get in contact with members of the company, but it is important to be sensitive to the confidential nature of this information and for the desire of some members of the company to maintain their privacy. Under the UK Data Protection Act 1998, each individual's written permission must be sought before such details can be made more public. Performers will often request a contact sheet but it is important not to give out contact numbers to all and sundry unless those listed have given their permission. Some performers, particularly if they are well known, are very sensitive about who has their contact details; their privacy must be respected. At times the stage manager may be privy to information that might be very attractive to tabloid journalists.

It is not unusual for some artistes to have days when they are not available for rehearsals. Such non-availability should always be agreed in advance and is usually handled by an artiste's agent when negotiating a contract. Contractual obligations are usually negotiated so that artistes can honour prior contracts, such as finishing off a film shoot, matinées or even appointments with the dentist. It is important that directors are aware of any non-availability before the rehearsal period commences. Thus stage management need to find out and prepare a list of dates, as well as entering this information into a diary and/or provisional rehearsal schedule, so that they can remind the director at the appropriate moment.

THE REHEARSAL SPACE

Rehearsal spaces are usually booked well in advance, sometimes even speculatively, by the producer or theatre management, but the stage manager should not take this for granted. Few rehearsal rooms are custom-built, many are far from adequate, and strange conditions for their usage may be attached. Firstly it is necessary to make sure that a space has been booked; secondly any conditions need to be checked; and thirdly the available facilities need to be confirmed. The easiest way to find this out is to visit the space in advance and meet the caretaker. An unwary stage manager can be caught out by turning up on the first day to find that the space does not get unlocked until 10.00 am, that there is no kitchen and no telephone, that nothing can be left in the space overnight, and that every other Friday the Scouts use it from 3.00 pm. This is not a good situation to be in and is totally avoidable with a little bit of preparation.

The first thing to check is when the space is available for access; this may be different from the hours that it has been booked for. It is not uncommon for the booking costs to increase in the evening and at weekends. It is important to check this; making the assumption that stage management can arrive early and then stay an hour after rehearsals have finished could result in a financial penalty. The stage manager also needs to check how to get access to the space; whether they will be given a key or have to rely on a caretaker. Sometimes a space may not be available for a certain period. This should be checked and alternative arrangements made for that period. In the case of a musical or dance show, several rooms may be necessary and this should be double-checked.

If the rehearsal space is some distance from the company's base, then it may also be useful to have a room that can be used as an office. Without a base close by it can be difficult to administer a production during the rehearsal period by remote control from another part of town. Communication will be more difficult and the stage management team can feel removed from the process. It becomes more difficult just to 'pop' into rehearsals in between shopping trips.

There are a number of additional practical considerations that need to be taken into account, some of which are easy to overlook because they sound straightforward. Some organisations will have house rules associated with their space and the stage manager should know what these are as it will be their responsibility to sure that these are adhered to. It is not a good idea to get on the wrong side of a caretaker or anybody who can stop the company from using the space. It is particularly important to check whether smoking is permitted. Sometimes there are noise restrictions – a problem if the production is a musical.

The availability of a telephone should not be taken for granted. Access to communications is essential, without it the rehearsal room will feel cut off and the stage manager may run up a very large mobile phone bill. Many older rehearsal spaces that are not custom-built may only have a pay or card phone, or one that is shared by other users. In the first case, stage management will need to stock up on small change or phone cards and factor this into their budget. In the second, they must be clear as to how the calls are to be logged and the bill settled. In exceptional circumstances it may be prudent for the stage manager to try to persuade their management to invest in a mobile phone for the rehearsal period, although incoming calls will be an unwelcome distraction during rehearsals. The appropriate telephone number for contacting the rehearsal space should then be circulated to the company.

A power supply for sound playback and so forth may sometimes be needed. The location of power points should be checked in advance and extension leads organised if necessary.

Heating, or lack of it, may be an issue. The Factories Act 1961 defines the optimum temperature for work spaces and this includes theatres and rehearsal rooms. This is particularly important if the show involves dancers or a lot of physical activity. Working in the wrong temperature can be physically damaging, as well as pretty miserable when it is at either extreme. If heating is likely to be inadequate the stage manager may have to arrange to supplement it. In summer portable air-conditioning may need to be provided.

Sufficient furniture should be available for rehearsals, including chairs, tables and any other necessary items such as waste bins and ashtrays. If the available furniture is not adequate, then alternatives will need to be brought in for the duration. It is also important to have safe storage for props, etc., preferably lockable. If necessary a skip can be acquired.

Amenities are an important factor. The location of toilets, washing and changing facilities should be checked. Rehearsals are intensive and the company will need access to quick refreshment facilities. Even if a canteen is available, it may be worth providing alternative catering facilities if allowed. Many spaces will have a kitchen area attached, where tea and coffee can be made. If these facilities are not available, stage management will need to supply a kettle or urn, paper cups, etc. They will need to find out whether refreshments will be provided in rehearsals and who will pay for them, making necessary arrangements for tea, coffee, etc. They may even have to organise a kitty or charge for every drink, which can be an added burden. There is always one member of a company who only drinks hot water, or resents the fact that they only have one cup a day whilst other members have several. It is also important to discover the nearest place to buy milk and other supplies.

The company will appreciate it if the nearest amenities are identified in advance, such as cafés, post office and chemist. They will also need to know how to get to the rehearsal room by public transport, whether the rehearsal space has adequate (or any) parking spaces, or how easy it will be to park locally.

SCRIPTS AND THE PROMPT COPY

All members of the company should be working from the same edition of the script and this needs to be checked before rehearsals start. Different editions may have different versions of the text, different stage direction or, at the very least, different page numbers. The stage manager should check that scripts have been issued to all members of the company and production team. Scripts can then be circulated to anybody who has not got one. It is always useful to have a few spare copies handy just in case. If appropriate, scripts may need to be numbered and a checklist kept of whom they are issued to. Musical scores may have to be hired and will need to be returned to the publisher at the end of the production.

Whoever is going to be 'on the book' will need to make up a prompt copy. The Prompt Copy or Book is kept by stage management as a complete guide to, and record of, the production. It is, however, the property of the producer or management and must be surrendered at the end of a run.

The prompt copy is a dynamic document that will change daily right up to the first performance, and often beyond. The text itself must be kept up-to-date, with cuts and changes documented, and it is used to record all exits, entrances and movements made by the performers; this is known as 'blocking'. The blocking will change on a daily basis during rehearsals (sometimes minute by minute) and must be kept up-to-date. It may be referred to by the director and cast as a reminder of the previous day's or week's work and can be used to resolve confusion. It is also useful for the lighting designer, to check where and when members of the cast move so that they can plan how to use lighting effectively. All technical information should be recorded in it, so that cues can be plotted and given accurately during performance.

Everything should be set out so clearly that a new stage manager taking over the book in an emergency will have no difficulty whatsoever in understanding what is meant. It is important therefore that no private shorthand or signs be used, and that all writing should be legible.

PREPARING THE PROMPT COPY

The prompt copy must be prepared in advance of the first rehearsal so that it can be used immediately. There is no one standard way of preparing a prompt copy, but there are a number of criteria that a prompt copy has to fulfil and some tried and tested formats that work. The chosen format will depend on whether the original script is in the form of a published book, or duplicated or typed and printed specially, and on the personal preference of the stage manager who will be keeping it. They must select the method they find easiest to use.

A hard-covered ring binder that opens out flat will keep the prompt copy together and safe, although a large lever-arch type file is not advisable as it is difficult for rapid page-turning and the gap between two pages is too big. Sufficient space must be provided so that all the moves, cues and calls can be entered clearly. It is usual to keep the text on one side, with a blank sheet for recording all the details opposite it. Examples of possible configurations, using A4 text-format, with typed or photocopies pages, are shown in *Figure 4.3*.

a. Text on right

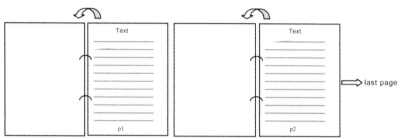

b. Text on left

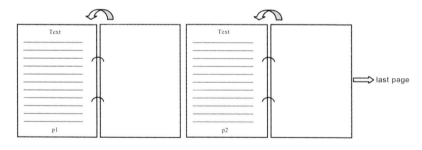

c. Reverse order (i.e. starting at the back)

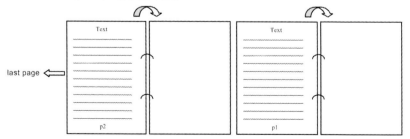

Figure 4.3 Prompt copy configurations: marking up the book

The blank sheet is used to record the 'blocking', or the movements of the characters; what props are used; where cues happen and what they are. This page is often divided up into two or three columns, as shown in *Figure 4.4*. When using a photocopied or printed text, it is best to interleave with a clean sheet of paper rather than using the back of the previous page. During the course of rehearsals, what is written on each page will change considerably and constant corrections may ultimately damage the page or become illegible. It can also be useful to keep previous versions, particularly of cue sequences.

It is acceptable to keep separate books for blocking and for running the show.

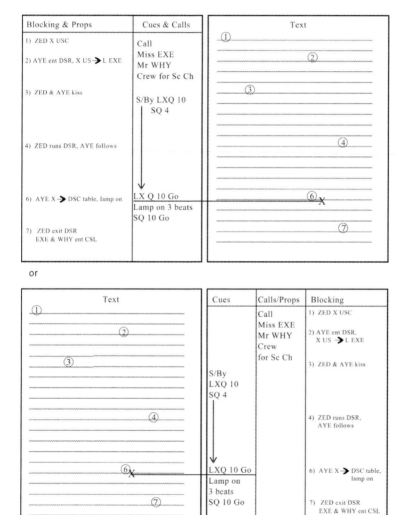

Figure 4.4 Prompt copy configurations: alternative layouts

REHEARSAL FURNITURE AND PROPS

Furniture and props are crucial to a successful rehearsal period and should be high on the stage management list of priorities. It is essential to obtain all the props on the props list and as much appropriate furniture as possible in advance of the rehearsals. Such items do not need to be accurate to the design at this stage, but they must be able to fulfil the correct function. A plastic cup is quite simply not the same as a wine glass; it behaves quite differently and is not a suitable substitute. It is tempting to take short cuts at this stage, but that is a short-sighted and lazy approach. Care and attention to detail at the start will pay dividends later on.

Any large items of rehearsal furniture, such as a piano, will need to be delivered to the rehearsal room, and a piano will need to be tuned.

Sometimes a director will request that there are no props in rehearsals for the first few days. This request must be respected, but the props should still be obtained and kept somewhere unobtrusive. This means that they can be produced on demand and will save time later on.

THE DESIGN

Although not strictly the responsibility of stage management, they should check that all relevant people have a final copy of the Ground Plan. The stage management team will need to annotate their ground plan in such a way as to assist them in marking out the set in the rehearsal room. The model box can be a useful asset in the rehearsal room, though it will also be needed by the scenic constructors and artists and may only be available for rehearsals for limited periods. This will need to be arranged in advance. At the very least it must be available for the first day of rehearsals. If it is not going to be readily available it is useful to arrange to take photographs of each setting (see *Figure 4.1*) and to display these in the rehearsal room (making sure, of course, that the rules allow things to be stuck on the wall, and that they can be left up, otherwise a display board will need to be organised). Some designers may supply story boards, which can be copied and displayed. It is also useful to make copies of all the costume drawings to add to the display. All this will serve to remind the cast and director, and stage management, what the set will look like and what they will be wearing.

STAGE MANAGEMENT BUDGET

The stage management team will need to have access to a petty cash float so that they can purchase necessary items for the rehearsal room, including props. The budget will have been agreed at an early production meeting and should include an amount for stage management administration expenses and props. Under no circumstances should any budget that has been agreed in production meetings be exceeded without first obtaining authorisation from the production manager, who is normally the overall budget holder.

The production manager will be able to release petty cash as part of this budget. The float can be topped up as necessary whenever it starts to run low but it is important to estimate how much will be needed initially. It is common for a float to have to be reconciled completely before a new one can be released, rather than just being topped up, or for banking to take place only on one particular day of the week. If that day is missed, another week will pass before cash can be obtained.

Stage management need to be familiar with the system used, and to keep track of their spending. They also need to know whether sanction has to be sought for purchases over a certain sum, what the policy is on hiring or buying, and who holds order books, before anything can be bought or ordered.

It is essential to keep accurate and readily understandable accounts, keeping copies of all expenditure. A triplicate receipt book is useful, as are petty cash vouchers, which can be used when a receipt is unobtainable.

ORGANISING THE FIRST REHEARSAL CALL

All members of a company should be present for the first rehearsal. It is usual for this to have been arranged with the cast in advance through their agents but mistakes can be made, and it is prudent for stage management to check that this has been done by making personal contact with the cast by telephone, and to make sure that they know where to go. Making verbal contact with them will also make them feel part of the process and sets stage management off on a good footing. When speaking to a member of the cast at this (or any) stage, the stage manager must try to be both friendly and businesslike, without being patronising. There will be information to give out, some of which may be repetitious or simply obvious. The stage manager needs to remember that they are checking that this information has been relayed and not just whether it has been remembered. Reminding the cast to bring pencils, a notebook, the script, and suitable clothing, may not be taken in the right vein, particularly if the actor is older and more experienced, but checking that they have actually got a copy of the script and that their contact details are correct comes over as thoughtful and efficient. The fact that stage management have bothered to contact them at all will send out the message that the team is efficient and caring. This is how stage management should be regarded.

If the location of the rehearsal room is at all out of the way, it is helpful to circulate a small sketch map of the area, details of public transport and parking facilities. In fact an information pack can be compiled and sent out to all members of the company. Any such information pack should include:

- Cast list
- Contact numbers of key personnel and places such as the rehearsal room
- Map showing location of rehearsal room including public transport and

details of parking
- Details of first rehearsal call
- Performance schedule – key dates such as the press night and curtain-up times, including matinée performances
- Tour schedule (if relevant); this should include all the above, plus a note that matinées will take place on different days and at different times at different venues, and often at the same venue
- Maps showing location of venues on tour (if relevant)
- Accommodation lists (if relevant)
- City information (particularly if touring abroad)

CAST LIST

The cast list (see *Figure 4.5*) is usually compiled by the producer or theatre management but it is always worth double-checking and updating, as individuals often get left off. All members of the company should be included. If understudies are engaged they should be added to the list against the part they are covering. In addition other key personnel should be included; all the people that the company are likely to encounter through the course of rehearsals. This might include press and publicity officers, who will be arranging interviews and photo shoots, and the senior members of the production team.

It is usual to invite all members of the production team to the first rehearsal so that they can be introduced to the cast and listen to the director's briefing. Stage management should check that all other members of the team required to attend know the time and place.

COSTUME FITTING

Sometimes costume fittings are arranged in advance of rehearsals. The stage manager will need to find out and prepare a list of any appointments for fittings for costume or wigs that have been made in advance, and check that those involved have been informed. They also need to find out whether the actors' measurements need to be taken and to arrange for this with the costume supervisor and director; the first rehearsal is often a good time for this to happen.

MARKING UP THE SET

Performers and directors need to rehearse with a representation of the set that will form their environment in the theatre. By having a full-sized plan of the set marked on the rehearsal room floor, the director and cast are able to navigate around it more easily and spot where they may encounter difficulties. The set design is usually presented as a model, a ground plan and sometimes a series of story boards or drawings. The model and ground plan will be made and drawn to a manageable scale, generally 1:50, 1:25, 1:24 (particularly in the US), or 1:20.

THE ROSE TATTOO
By Tennessee Williams
CAST (in order of appearance)

CHARACTER	PRINCIPAL	UNDERSTUDY
ASSUNTA	Mary COLGATE	Sarah FRIEND
ROSA Della ROSE	Lisa OREGANO	Harriet APPLEBY
SERAFINA Della ROSE	Julia WATLING	Fifi FIFE
ESTELLE HOHNEGARTEN	Di MORRIS	Pat WHITE
THE STREGA	Pat HASTE	Sarah FRIEND
GIUSEPPINA	Sarah FRIEND	}
PEPPINA	Fifi FIFE	} Cover each
VIOLETTA	Pat WHITE	} other
MARIELLA	Harriet APPLEBY	}
FATHER De LEO	Robert BROWN	Robin HUNTER
A DOCTOR	Robin HUNTER	Dave LORD
Miss YORKE	Pat STORY	Sarah FRIEND
FLORA	Dee SHYLOCK	Pat STORY
BESSIE	Martina TONY	Pat WHITE
LEGIONAIRE	Dave LORD	
JACK HUNTER	James CLOVER	Dave LORD
THE SALESMAN	Bob BARLEY	Robin HUNTER
ALVARO MANGIACAVALLO	Ben SCOTT	Dave LORD
SALVATORE	Donald PACKER	
VIVI	Penny FENTON	
BRUNO	Karl ALLY	

DIRECTOR	Pierre VESTIBULE
ASST. DIRECTOR	Gillian RUBY
MUSIC	Stefan EDWARDO
DESIGNER	Alison CHARLES
LIGHTING DESIGN	Marco HENCHMAN
SOUND DESIGN	Pete ADDER
VOICE COACH	June COLUMBUS
PRODUCTION MANAGER	Mike CASS
COMPANY & STAGE MANAGER	Paul McINTYRE
DEPUTY STAGE MANAGER	Kate PATTERSON
ASSISTANT STAGE MANAGERS	Deborah GIFT
	Steve WALTON
PROPERTY BUYER	Jane SALTER
COSTUME SUPERVISOR	Caroline BAILEY
RUNNING WARDROBE	Nicky BEER
WIG SUPERVISOR	Eileen HOFMEISTER
RUNNING WIGS	Peter GARDNER
SOUND OPERATOR	Rick GREEN
EXECUTIVE PRODUCER	Saul FIERSTEIN
PRESS REPRESENTATIVE	Lionel Curshaw Associates

Figure 4.5 A cast list

The model is a three-dimensional representation, while the ground plan is in effect looking down from above in two dimensions. In the rehearsal room it is usual to work on a full-size two-dimensional 'mark-up'. Sometimes, on large budget productions and in opera, three-dimensional pieces of scenery may be used as well, even the actual set.

So 'marking up' is the scaling-up of a ground plan and model box to the actual size, i.e., commonly, from 1:25 to 1:1. It is essential to the performers and director for their rehearsal process; it can also be useful for placing scenic elements in the correct position in the rehearsal room and on stage; and it may also be useful in a workshop, or wherever the scenery is being constructed or put together.

It is usual to mark up the set in the rehearsal room for the first rehearsal. That way everyone can relate the tape marks on the floor to the model box and pictures on the wall. If there are several sets involved, this can be explained, and the cast can even be walked through the mark-up. Sometimes a director will ask that the mark-up is left until later, particularly if the rehearsal process is to begin with a workshop. Working without the mark up will give a degree of freedom to begin with. Either way, a mark-up takes time, which must be allowed for, and people. With experience it is just about possible for one person to mark up a set, but two is better and three ideal. If it can be done in advance of the first rehearsal, that is an advantage and worth checking, otherwise the stage management may have to arrive at 8.00 am for a 10.00 am start, or persuade the director to start the rehearsal later. A clear space without people milling about and getting in the way is essential.

If there is to going to be a frequent change of rehearsal room or if the marks will have to be removed daily, it is a good plan to mark up on a stage cloth, so long as it is anchored securely. This is not, however, suitable for dancers. The alternatives are time-consuming, using either lengths of cloth tape or string or, if lucky, leaving dots of PVC tape at each corner. It is important to check in advance whether the mark-up can be left down. If rehearsals are in a sports hall, for instance, the mark-up will be competing with basketball pitches and badminton courts which may well get used as such in the evening and at weekends. In such cases it is unlikely that the mark-up can be left down. Even when it can, stage management should always be prepared for it to be damaged over a weekend; so much activity is likely to kick up some of the tape.

Before examining the technicalities of actually doing a mark-up it is worth considering a number of standard features that may be found on a good ground plan. Most theatres will have a blank ground plan that designers will use each time they design for a new production. Computer-aided design (CAD) has made it possible for this to be stored on a computer and to be printed at any scale. Designers will generally start with their model and transfer dimensions from this onto their plan. They may also execute a set of 'working drawings' –

that is, technical drawings of scenic elements to scale.

ORIENTATION

The theatre space can be divided into quadrants like a graph, to be used as datum lines. The centre line is a longitudinal reference which divides the stage, or acting area, into two equal halves. In a theatre with a proscenium arch, it is midway within the proscenium and at right angles to it and divides the acting area in half. On an open stage it is at right angles to the front of the stage, dividing the stage in half. It provides a useful reference for marking up and can be useful for performers, particularly in a dance show. When embarking on a mark up it is advisable to mark the centre line first.

The centre line is usually marked on a ground plan as a dashed line and abbreviated as CL. Sometimes it may be permanently marked on a stage by studs US and DS.

The setting line is an arbitrary line at right angles to the centre line and forms a useful longitudinal reference, or datum line. It is useful reference for marking up. In a proscenium arch theatre it signifies the furthest down-stage that scenery can be set before it interferes with the smooth operation of the house curtain or iron, and may even correspond to the tab line. As with the centre line, the setting line may be marked on a ground plan as a dashed line, and abbreviated as SL (not to be confused with Stage Left). See *Figure 4.6* for the centre and setting lines in proscenium arch theatres.

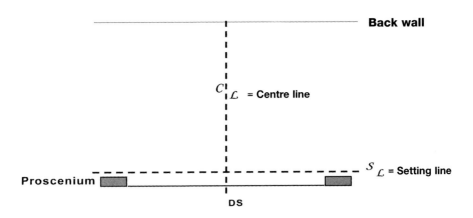

Figure 4.6 Centre and setting lines for a proscenium arch theatre

In theatres without a proscenium, the setting line may be marked on a ground plan as a convenient reference at right angles to the centre line and may coincide with the edge of the stage or acting area, the scenery, or whichever is the most logical.

In order to mark the centre line, the centre of a wall, the proscenium opening, or the front of the acting area must be found first, by measuring it, dividing it in half, and marking the middle point. Next a line needs to be drawn at a right angle to this; this can be done using trigonometry, that is, by using bisecting arcs or triangulation.

a. Finding the centre line in relation to Line A

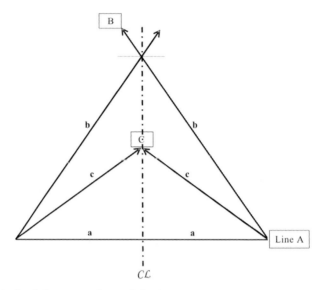

b. Finding the centre line in in a proscenium arch theatre

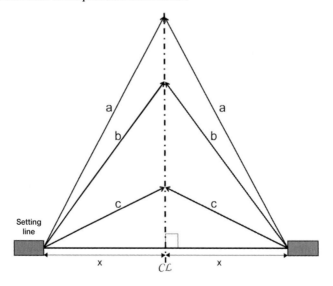

Figure 4.7 Finding the centre line

In *Figure 4.7* the centre line is at right angles, or perpendicular, to Line A. Line A might represent the front of a stage or the distance across the proscenium arch opening. The centre line is equidistant (a) from each end of Line A. The other lines, B and C, start at either end of Line A and meet at the same distances (b) and (c). The points where they meet also coincide with the centre line. As long as these measurements are taken from the same points and are equal, they will enable a perpendicular line to be drawn.

In a studio or theatre without a proscenium arch the principle is the same, that is, the centre line is at right-angles to the front of the stage or acting area, dividing it in half. It may be tempting to use the rear wall of the theatre, as this represents a tangible feature, but theatre spaces are rarely symmetrical and the rear wall is often not parallel to the front of the stage. When working from a ground plan, it is important to work to the same centre line as the designer. The setting line is more arbitrary in a studio theatre, yet forms a useful reference or datum line from which to take measurements. As long as it is at right-angles to the centre line, it is reasonable to use the front of the acting area or the front of the audience seating (see *Figure 4.8 on next page*).

When dealing with 'theatre in the round', that is, where the audience are seated all around the acting area, both the centre and setting lines become arbitrary, although still useful for reference for the mark-up. If the designer has used a centre line, then that should be used, otherwise it is best taken from the point of view of the person who will be on the book.

ACCURACY AND SCALE

That's the easy bit. Before looking at marking up the set itself, it is worth taking a number of other considerations into account. First, a couple of points concerning the issue of accuracy are worth discussing; the first is technical, the second psychological.

When embarking on their first few mark-ups, the novice will inevitably find that at least one piece of scenery or part of the stage is several centimetres (a few inches) or more out. This is not something to worry about unduly; it is only to be expected and, with a bit judicious tweaking, is easily corrected. At the end of the day, and to court controversy, it actually doesn't matter much, though that isn't an excuse for not trying.

The most common scale used for drawing ground plans in theatre is 1:25, though 1:20 may still be encountered and 1:24 is used in the USA. These are inherently inaccurate, as *Figure 4.9* demonstrates. At a scale of 1:25, the width of a line drawn with a 0.5 mm drawing pen actually represents 12.5 mm or nearly half an inch. That means that when making a drawing the designer is working to an actual tolerance of $\pm$ 25 mm (1 inch) between two points, which is then compounded to a tolerance of $\pm$ 50 mm (approx 2 inches) when measurements are taken off the plan and transferred to a mark-up. This is a very

i. End on

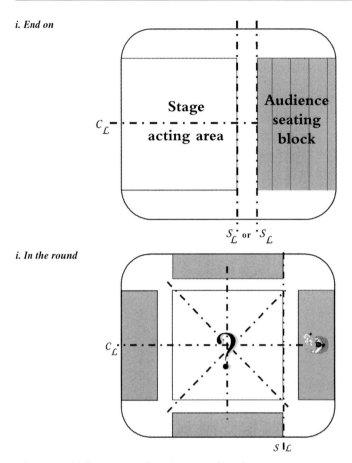

i. In the round

Figure 4.8 The centre line in a studio theatre

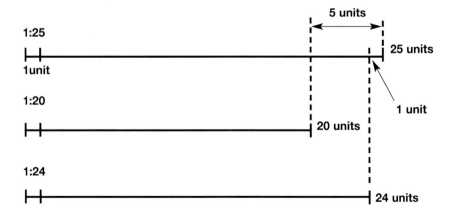

Figure 4.9 Scale

high degree of inaccuracy. To look at it another way, it is hard to know from which side of a 0.5 mm line to take a measurement, let alone to actually do it with any accuracy.

Yet a completely accurate mark-up in the rehearsal room actually does not matter that much. One of the most common reactions from a performer when they arrive on the actual set on the actual stage is 'It seemed much bigger in the rehearsal room'. This isn't a damning criticism of the stage manager's marking up ability because it is, in fact, absolutely true. It did seem bigger in the rehearsal room by about 50 cm (1' 6") all round and for a very good reason. In the rehearsal room the set is a two-dimensional mark-up on the floor. Features are represented by lengths of coloured PVC tape. Without actual walls physically there, the performers will work right up to them and sometimes even through them. When they arrive on stage they encounter physical barriers that they aren't used to. They may have worked with their feet hanging over the representation of the edge of the stage on the mark-up; on stage that becomes a 3-metre (9-foot) drop into an orchestra pit (with or without musicians). The performers will treat that with more respect and move further up-stage. They will also try not to bump into the scenery. So the physical space really is reduced.

In the rehearsal room the mark-up is a representation of the real thing, purely a guide to help the cast and director. A few centimetres inaccuracy will usually not cause much upset, although of course there are times when pinpoint accuracy is required, in particular when scenic elements have to be placed accurately on the stage.

It is essential to be sure of the scale being used, particularly if the production is touring from Europe to the US. 1:24 and 1:25 may seem similar, but over a whole ground plan the difference becomes huge (see *Figure 4.9*). Sets, or individual pieces of scenery, have been built by scaling up, using 1:25 measurements from a 1:20 drawing. The consequences can be both catastrophic and embarrassing; the set, quite simply, will not fit in the theatre. For example a 50 mm line represents 1 metre at a scale of 1:20, 1.25 metres at 1:25 and 1.2 metres at 1:24. The width of a stage of 10 metres is represented by 400 mm at 1:25. This would represent a width of 8 metres if measured using 1:20 or 9.6 metres using 1:24.

When taking measurements it is important to use the correct units. In Europe metres, centimetres and millimetres are used. Engineers and scenic constructors use millimetres as the standard unit and stage management should follow their lead. A measurement of 'one metre sixty' could mean 1,060 millimetres or 160 centimetres (which is in fact 1600 millimetres). A misunderstanding here could lead to an inaccuracy of 540 mm, over half a meter or twenty inches.

Some designers also use 1:50 for their models and ground plans; it is easier to transport the model of a large theatre at this scale and the ground plan will fit a smaller sheet of paper. It is impossible to take any accurate measurements at this scale, however, and so any mark-up can only be approximate.

There are a number of things that the stage manager, and the designer, can do to make working with scale more accurate. Many designers will actually write measurements on their plans, usually indicating the dimension of each piece of scenery (see *Figure 4.10*). If computer-aided design (CAD) is used for the drawings, life is made easier still as the CAD programme can automatically add the dimensions on the plan, and these will be accurate.

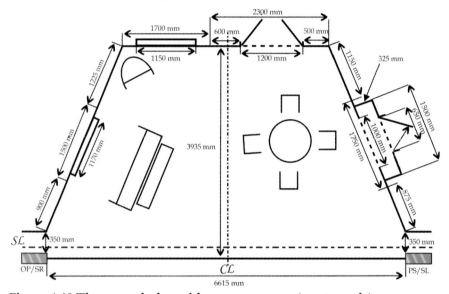

Figure 4.10 The ground plan with measurements (not to scale)

If the designer does not add measurements, it is useful to check if any discrepancies are encountered. Designers will often design to standard sizes, for instance doors (even old ones) come in standard sizes, or work to round numbers, and anything that deviates from these may look out of proportion, even on a stage. If, for example, the measurements of a door seem to be unusual, it is a good idea to query them – does the designer really want the door to be 686 mm wide? The answer, in this case, might be 'Yes', as that is a standard size and is equivalent to 27 inches or 2 foot 3 inches. Of course the same measurement might have been taken as 698 or 674 mm, in which case the answer would have been a 'No'. However sometimes measurements will turn out to be unusual, simply to fit on the stage!

As well as sticking to architectural conventions, designers may also design to 'stock' sizes, either of materials or standard scenic elements. Thus rostra (deck) may be designed in multiples of 2440 x 1220 mm (8' x 4') as these are the dimensions of standard steel framed decking that can be bought or hired, as well as of the sheets of plywood that are used to cover them. Anything that does not fit within these dimensions may need to be specially constructed, thus adding to the cost. The same applies to flats which may be covered in plywood sheets. A flat that is just slightly wider than the stock sheet width may require twice as many sheets to cover it, thus resulting in wastage and a higher cost. It is always worth querying; the drawing or measurements may be inaccurate, but the answer may be 'Yes, that dimension is intentional'.

Designers will also use a number of conventions to represent scenic elements on their plans; the common ones are shown in *Figure 4.11*. It is worth noting, however, that, although these are commonly used, they are not nationally or internationally standardised. Steps are being taken to try to standardise theatre drawing conventions, particularly for CAD, but these have yet to be accepted by the theatre design community at large.

THE MARK-UP

There are two ways to mark up a set. The first employs the same method used to find the centre line, the triangulation method; the second uses the centre and setting lines (or front of the stage) as datum lines. Both are equally valid.

The following essential items are needed for a mark-up; see *Figure 4.12*:

- The ground plan
- A scale ruler with the correct scale marked on it
- A 0.5 mm drawing pencil
- Craft knife
- PVC tape in a variety of colours – tape that is 12 mm in width is best. It is more flexible than the standard 25 mm sort, which is useful for marking curves, and is less likely to be used as insulating tape by the electricians.
- 30 metre (100 foot) cloth tape measures – at least one, two are better. Cloth tapes are better than steel ones as they are stronger and flexible. With the distances involved it is easy for someone to tread on a tape laid out across the floor. This will not harm the cloth tape but will break a steel one.

The following are also useful:

- Retractable steel tape measure – useful for measuring short distances or right angles
- Chalk line (also known as a 'snap line')
- Chalk – the old-fashioned sort that works on polished floors
- Calculator
- 18 inch, 2 foot or 50 cm ruler
- Hammer and nails
- Model box, or photographs of the set

When taking measurements from the ground plan, a scale rule which has the scale the plan is drawn in marked on it can be used. At 1:25 the rule is graduated

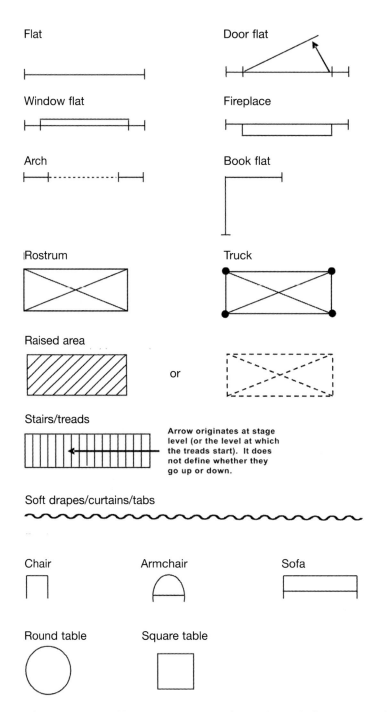

Figure 4.11 Marking up – commonly used symbols on ground plans

in units of 0.8 mm, which is equivalent to 20 mm at 1:1 (thus adding another layer of inaccuracy, as it is impossible to take an accurate measurement between 0 and 20 mm). It is also possible to use an ordinary ruler and a calculator (or mental arithmetic). To do this measurements are taken in millimetres and multiplied by the scale. Thus, on a 1:25 ground plan, a measurement of 133 mm represents 3325 mm.

One of the drawbacks of a scale rule is that it is only 300 mm in length (using 1:25 = 7500 mm). As most stage spaces are deeper and wider than 7.5 metres, this makes taking accurate measurements slightly more difficult. The problem can be overcome by using an 18 inch ruler or longer, either by drawing lines on the plan and then taking measurements with the scale rule or by using the calculator.

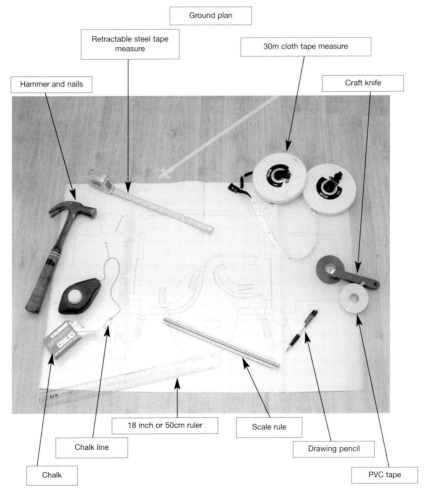

Figure 4.12 Ground plan with marking-up equipment

THE TRIANGULATION METHOD

For the triangulation method, two points need to be identified on the ground plan from which all the measurements will be taken. In a proscenium theatre the corners of the proscenium arch may be used as these are, by definition, equidistant from the centre line. The width of the proscenium opening is rarely a nice round number, however, and thus can be difficult to transfer into a rehearsal room (it is difficult to mark the mid-point of 8673 mm, for instance). It is, however, acceptable to take two points that are still equidistant from the centre line but are a round number and thus easier to measure and mark, say 3 metres (or 9 feet) (see *Figure 4.13*).

In a theatre without a proscenium the same principle stands, taking either the front of the stage or acting area, or the edge of the seating (as in *Figure 4.8*). It can be tempting to use one of the walls in a studio theatre, but this is only really feasible if the wall itself needs to be marked up in the space. Theoretically measurements taken from any two points on the plan will give an accurate mark-up.

In *Figure 4.13* the two reference points are 3 metres from the centre line. A is 3450 mm from the OP reference point and 5900 mm from PS, while point B is 6800 mm from OP and 1875 mm from PS. These co-ordinates give unique definitions for these two points; no other points can have those measurements from those two reference points.

In order to make the process faster and more efficient, some preparation can be done in advance. The number of measurements necessary can be decided in advance and each point labelled and marked on the plan. These can then be transferred into a table which will form an easy reference for the mark-up. For each point there will be two measurements, one from OP and one from PS. It is not necessary to triangulate every single point on the set. In *Figure 4.14* the four points are actually as many as are needed. All the other features, doorways, windows, the fireplace, can be measured from each of those four points. Thus the double doors USL are 500 mm from point C and are 1200 mm wide. As the wall between B and C is a straight line, this is easy to measure and mark.

These measurements can then be transferred from the table to the rehearsal room floor using the same principles and the equipment detailed above.

The first step is to mark out the front of the stage, or equivalent. The next step is to measure and mark the centre of this, followed by the two reference points from which all measurements have been taken. These two points will then form the reference points for the mark-up. From these the centre line can be constructed. The centre line does not always need to be permanent, in which case the chalk line can be used to mark this temporarily.

Having established the two reference points, each measurement can be transferred from the table prepared in advance to the floor, using the two cloth tape measures. Two people will be needed to do this and preferably three. If

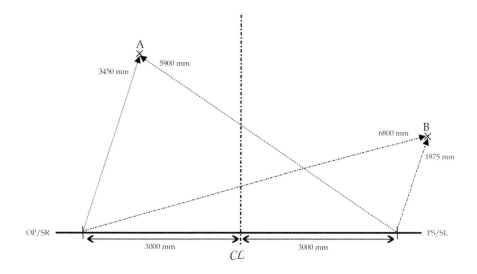

Figure 4.13 Marking up using the triangulation method

there are only two, one should keep the end of the tape on the appropriate reference point, while the other measures off the correct distance by drawing a large arc on the floor with a piece of chalk in roughly the right area. It is useful to refer to the ground plan when doing this. A second arc can then be drawn using the opposite reference point. The point where these two coincide will represent the same point on the ground plan. It is then advisable to mark this point with 'X', using PVC tape as this is more permanent. If three people are involved then two can keep the ends of one of the two tapes on each of the reference points, while the third marks where the two tapes intersect. In a space where it is possible to nail into the floor, a nail can be attached at each reference point and the ends of the tapes placed over them. It is then possible for one person to do the mark-up.

Once all the points have been marked on the floor they can be joined up using PVC tape. At this juncture it is useful to refer to the model box to check that it looks right. Doors and windows can then be marked in as outlined above. It is also worth checking that the measurements between each point are reasonably accurate. They almost certainly won't be and so adjustments can be made.

When marking up it is useful to mark permanent features of the theatre, such as the front of the stage and the proscenium arch, in one colour of PVC tape and the set in a different colour. If the production involves several sets, or a set that moves to different positions, each set or position will need to be marked in a different colour.

Laying down PVC tape is an art in itself. PVC tape stretches. When running it out over a reasonable distance it will stretch quite a lot. If it is stuck down immediately its effective stickiness will be reduced; that is, the ratio of adhesive to surface area will be less. This means that it is likely to come unstuck in a few days, particularly if there is a lot of activity on the mark-up. There is nothing more depressing than arriving to set up for rehearsal one morning and finding that the mark-up is nothing more than a few pieces of stray tape and has to be put down again in fifteen minutes. A complex mark-up can take three people a couple of hours. To minimise this, the tape should be allowed to go slack and literally laid on the floor before it is stuck down. Rather than grovelling on the floor on their hands and knees using their fingers to ensure 100% adhesion, stage managers have developed the 'stage management shuffle', a way of walking along the tape toe-to-heel with a stamping motion, which seems to be effective. This is also where the craft knife comes in. Tearing the tape, or using teeth, also stretches it and reduces its adhesive properties. Using a craft knife to cut it neatly will prevent this. It also looks better.

THE CENTRE AND SETTING LINE METHOD

This method appears to be simpler and is thus favoured by many, yet has its pitfalls. Measurements are made from the setting line, or front of the stage, and from the centre line (see *Figure 4.14*). As with triangulation, each point on the mark-up has a unique set of co-ordinates, up-stage from the setting line and either stage right or stage left. Preparation is equally important here, drawing up a table of measurements in advance, and the tools remain the same. When taking measurements from the ground plan a set square can be useful as they must be at right angles to either datum line.

i. Principles (not to scale)

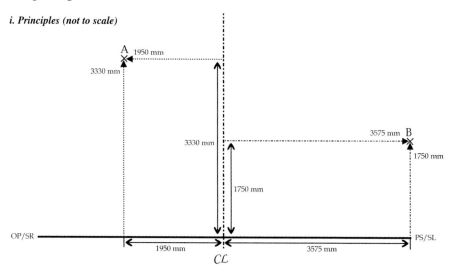

ii. Practice (not to scale)

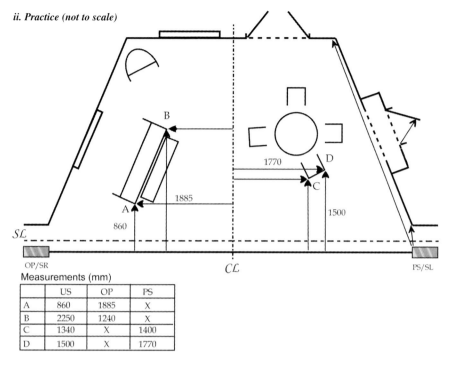

Measurements (mm)

	US	OP	PS
A	860	1885	X
B	2250	1240	X
C	1340	X	1400
D	1500	X	1770

Figure 4.14 Marking up using the centre and setting lines or upstage/offstage co-ordinates

When transferring from the plan to the rehearsal room floor, it is simple to run a cloth tape up the centre line and mark off each measurement from the front. The distances to stage right or left from each of these points can then be measured off and each point marked.

Problems can arise when the measurements to left or right stretch to metres. The measurement must be at exactly 90 degrees to the centre line. Over 100 mm, a half degree discrepancy will make the point off by 0.85 mm. Not much, but over 1 metre it becomes 8.5 cm and over 10 metres an embarrassing 0.85 metres. It is arguably impossible to place a tape measure accurately at a right angle by eye, and protractors are not manufactured that are big enough for the dimensions of a stage.

The solution is then to measure along the setting line and triangulate between each of those points and the centre line points. This is actually one step more than triangulation; it will take longer and is therefore less efficient, but this method is without doubt appropriate in some circumstances. During the course of rehearsals the placing of furniture on the set needs to be recorded. Using this method is fast and as efficient as required and can be actioned effectively and quickly by one person. The position of furniture will need to be reproduced in the theatre, but will certainly change once the scenery, lighting and cast are brought together. Accuracy is less of an issue; speed is paramount.

THE REHEARSAL SPACE

This may seem straightforward enough so far, but there is one more variable that will affect the way the mark-up is handled. Ideally the rehearsal room will be large enough to fit the whole of the set in, with extra space for people to sit. It is useful to be able to provide a distance of at least 2 metres (6 feet) between the front of the acting area and where the director will sit. This allows the director to have a reasonable view of the whole area (see *Figure 4.15*). If possible the entrance to the room should be kept behind the director so that people arriving in the room do not create a distraction.

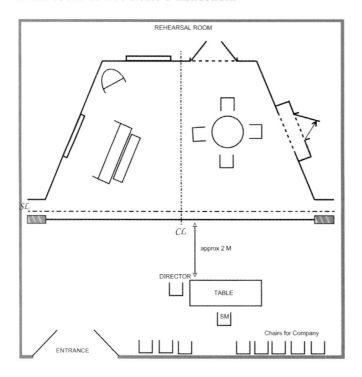

Figure 4.15 Ideal orientation in the rehearsal room

Unless the theatre company has specially designed rehearsal spaces, the chances are that the rehearsal room was, or is, a church hall, gymnasium or similar and that it is either an awkward shape or smaller than the stage space. This means that the set will quite simply not fit into it completely and decisions need to be made as to what to leave out. A number of options will need to be considered and a suitable decision made (see *Figure 4.16*):

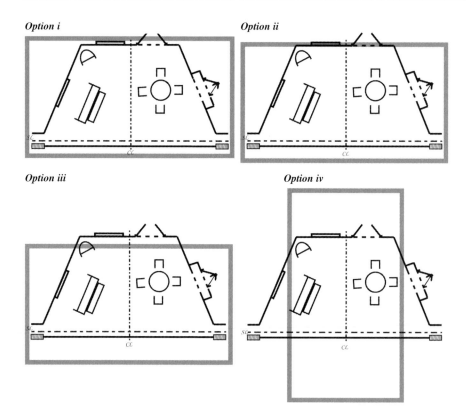

Option i   *Option ii*

Option iii   *Option iv*

Figure 4.16 Fitting the mark-up into a smaller space

i)   Include all the walls of the set, but leave no room at the back and little for the director at the front of the stage.

ii) Allow a little bit more room at the front for the director, and just manage to fit in the rear wall.

iii) Allow plenty of room for the director, but cut off the whole rear part of the set

iv) Allow the complete depth of the set to be included, but miss off both the SR and SL extremities of the set.

This may seem to be an extreme example but is a dilemma that may be encountered. In this case option ii would seem to be the most sensible solution, using the wall of the room as the back wall of the set. Before making this decision, however, it is a good idea to consult the director; leaving out the space behind the back wall could be a problem if a lot of action happens in that area.

Other complications may be encountered. When a single set has several different positions, particularly on a revolving stage, the mark-up can become confusing. It is simply impossible for the cast and director to work on what just becomes a jumble of coloured tape. In *Figure 4.17* the set consists of a representation of a house on a revolve, which can move to as many different positions as are wanted. Even with just four (*Figure 4.17 i – iv*), the end result becomes confusing (*Figure 4.17 v*). Imagine the work involved if the director decides that one of the positions needs altering (especially if it is the one that was marked first).

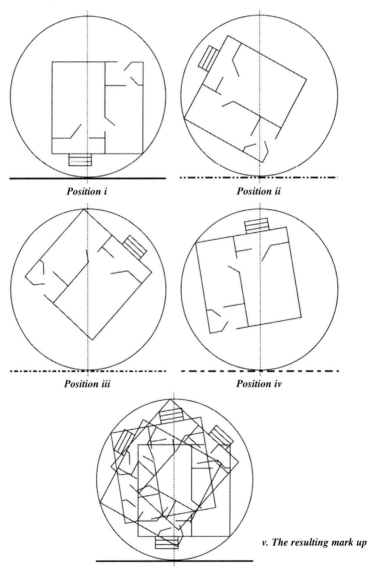

Figure 4.17 Marking up a set on a revolve: the problem

The solution is to mark the set just once and then mark the front of the stage (and centre line) in relation to its position. For each scene the director and stage management will need to move to the appropriately marked position (see *Figure 4.18*).

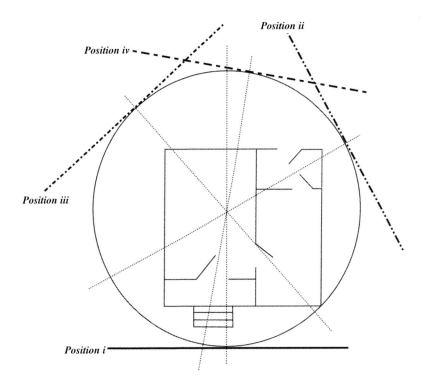

Position ii

Position iv

Position iii

Position i

Figure 4.18 Marking up a set on a revolve: the solution

SUMMARY

The set is marked up, the rehearsal props have been acquired, the prompt copy prepared, the cast contacted. The next stage is to start rehearsing and to see the production evolve and develop into maturity.

THE REHEARSAL PERIOD

The purpose of rehearsal is for the cast and director to define and identify both the emotional and the physical journey through a text, and then to refine and consolidate this. This process may involve a great deal of experimentation, often leading down false avenues before the true path is discovered.

As a rough guide it is useful to think of the traditional rehearsal process as being divided into four distinct phases, each defined by the type of activity involved. These might be identified as:

1. Introductions
2. Blocking
3. Working
4. Running

While rehearsals should always be prepared for and organised in the same way, each of these phases will offer different challenges for stage management. With devised or non-text-based theatre, the process will have a different shape. The Blocking phase may become the third element and will typically be shorter; it may even disappear altogether.

PHASE 1: INTRODUCTIONS
– THE FIRST REHEARSAL

The first day of rehearsals will be different from all others. This is the first time that all the company will have met together and is often the only time that many of the peripheral members, such as the production manager or lighting designer, will meet with the whole company before the technical rehearsal. Arrangements for the first rehearsal need to be organised in advance after discussion with the director and producer. The stage manager will need to find out what form they would like the first day of rehearsals to take, and how they would like the rehearsal room arranged.

It is usual for the day to start with a short informal social gathering; it is not unheard-of for food and drink to be provided (even champagne), quite possibly organised by stage management. This may be followed by introductions, the giving out of important information, such as the smoking policy in the rehearsal room, and a presentation about the intended interpretation of the text and staging concept by the director and designer. This will include a model box presentation.

The stage management team should arrange to be at the rehearsal room early in order to set up, and then meet and greet the company as they arrive. If it has not been possible to mark up in advance, then extra time will need to be allowed for this to be done. When the director arrives, it is important to explain how the set has been marked out.

For the first rehearsal, the room may have to be set up in a special way; it is best to consult with the director about this. Chairs might be set in a circle, or in a semi-circle facing a table and chairs for the creative team. There should always be enough litter bins prominently placed and, if allowed, ashtrays.

The model box will need to be displayed on a table in such a way that everyone can see it, and it may require suitable lighting. Costume and set drawings may need to be attached to a wall or display board. If recorded music is to be played, appropriate equipment will be needed. If music is involved, a piano needs to be in tune and placed in a position where the cast can see the pianist.

The following items will be needed for the first, and subsequent, rehearsal days:
1. Marking-up equipment (see Chapter 4)
2. Pencils – an ample supply, preferably with rubbers; the cast always ask for them, although excessive demand should be discouraged (they will never be seen again)
3. Scrap paper
4. Pencil sharpener
5. Rubber (eraser)
6. Stop-watch
7. First Aid kit
8. Change for telephone (if necessary) and tea/coffee machine (if appropriate)
9. Notebook
10. A sufficient supply of tea, coffee, milk, sugar; teacups, teaspoons, kettle, etc. (if appropriate)
11. Spare scripts
12. The prompt copy (see Chapter 4)
13. An extension lead

This is a crucial period for establishing working relationships and for working out who in the company may need special attention. It is also the time at which the Stage Manager can establish their authority, and it should be they who call the meeting to order and start the introductions.

As the artistes arrive, stage management should introduce themselves and also introduce other members of the cast and staff to each other. It is important to know who everyone is. This is a good time for checking that all contact addresses and telephone numbers are correct.

Formal introductions may involve the whole company sitting in a circle, introducing themselves and saying what they do. Sometimes there may be some form of activity such as a warm-up exercise, and stage management should be prepared to be involved in this. The director and designers and other members of the creative team may then talk about their artistic interpretation of the text and describe the setting, using the model box, and costume designs. This may also involve their presenting some of their initial background research.

The second part of the day may involve a 'read-through' or a 'play-through' if it is a musical (in fact the first day is often referred to as the 'Read-through'). This involves the cast sitting in a circle reading their parts. During the read-through each act and scene should be timed, as this will give a very good indication as to the actual length of the play. Stage management should also add in any sound effects indicated in the stage directions and even be prepared to read stage directions in detail, and/or read in a part when a member of the cast is not available.

For this part of the day, it is as well to have spare scripts available as people do forget their own, together with a liberal supply of soft pencils so that the cast can make notes in their scripts. Musical scores are generally hired and have to be returned at the end of the run without graffiti, so pencils are the only option. Any cuts or alterations to the script that the director may announce during the read-through should be marked in the prompt copy, and then circulated as a separate memo to all members of the company later. This ensures that no one has missed, or misunderstood, the changes.

It has become increasingly common, however, for directors not to read through the play with the cast, but instead either to start rehearsing the play straight away or to start with a workshop. The latter may last several days before the actual text is touched. Many directors reason that the cast may begin to 'act' at the read-through and start to develop their characters. Funny voices may be used, cockney for servants and suchlike, which may not be appropriate for the production. The director will then have to devote part of the rehearsal period to undoing inappropriate characterisations rather than developing a fresh interpretation.

Workshops may be appropriate where a particular, and unfamiliar, society needs to be explored before the text can be fully appreciated. For instance, a play by Lope de Vega may benefit from an exploration of Spanish society in the sixteenth century, with which the company are unlikely to be familiar. Similarly a workshop on verse reading may precede rehearsals for a Shakespeare play or other play written in verse.

Some directors will start with character work and text analysis for the first few days before they start putting a physical shape to the play. This involves the cast in examining their characters in detail and discussing the relationships between them. Sometimes they will be asked to undertake some historical or social research which they will then bring back to the rehearsal room.

In musical theatre the introductory phase may include an intensive period in which the cast work on the musical numbers with the musical director.

The first phase can last anything from a morning to several weeks, depending on the type of production and the working practice of the director or company in question.

DEVISED THEATRE
The creation of a devised piece from scratch will usually begin with a workshop to explore ideas and themes; indeed the whole rehearsal process may take on the feel of a workshop, particularly if the piece is to be purely physical in nature. It is common for a workshop phase to take place before the main rehearsal period begins, sometimes with a gap of several weeks. This allows the creative team to discover and explore themes during the workshop and then to go away and develop both a structure and a design aesthetic.

PHASE 2: BLOCKING

Directors traditionally start rehearsing by 'blocking' a play, which involves working through the play scene by scene deciding where and how the characters are going to move. Blocking gives a physical shape to the play, a rough framework for the performers to start to explore the physical dimensions of the relationships between their characters and with the environment formed by the set. Some directors have even been known to work this out in advance and mark it in their scripts.

The process of 'blocking' will normally take several days, depending on the actual length of the play and the number of characters. The cast will usually be expected to read from their scripts and should make notes of their moves. During this phase the stage manager on the book will normally mark down all the moves in the prompt copy. This process is also known as 'blocking' and the recorded moves are referred to as 'the blocking'.

Some directors dispense with this phase altogether, however, preferring to move straight into the third, 'Working', phase and allowing the physical shape of the play to evolve out of an exploration of the emotional relationships between characters. This has become an increasingly popular way of working. Occasionally a director will ask stage management not to write down the blocking until the very end of the process.

DEVISED THEATRE
When a production is being devised the process is slightly different, as there may be no script to work on at the start. In fact the rehearsal process is about creating the production from scratch rather than interpreting a text. This may include all aspects of design, as the physical shape and look of the production is developed throughout the rehearsal process. If the final piece is to be text-based, the script will evolve alongside the physical dimension. With this way of working, the

'blocking' becomes an integral part of the working process rather than a separate phase. Sometimes a devised production will develop without any set 'blocking', the performers instead using improvisation techniques to explore the agreed themes.

RECORDING MOVES: BLOCKING

All moves should be recorded in the prompt copy which will have been made up to allow for this (see Chapter 4). This 'blocking' has a number of uses. During the early stages of rehearsal the director and cast may not return to a scene for several days, and may not be able to remember what happened when the scene was 'blocked' originally. With all the moves written in the prompt copy the stage manager will be able to remind them; the 'blocking' acts as a useful reference. However the stage manager must be prepared for it to change, even for it to be ignored completely. This is a normal and essential part of the rehearsal process.

Later on during rehearsals the blocking will form a useful reference for the lighting designer, who will need to know whereabouts on the stage different members of the cast will be moving and when. If understudies are involved, the blocking becomes their guide, and stage management will often be involved in running understudy rehearsals, telling them where and when to move.

The blocking may also be a useful tool for pre-empting logistical problems on the set, particularly when a large cast has to negotiate a set which involves automated scenery, or where space offstage is tight. It is useful for the technical staff and wardrobe to know where exits and entrances are being made so that scene changes and quick changes can be co-ordinated efficiently and congestion avoided.

Blocking is an acquired art that gets easier with practice and experience. It is tempting, when starting out, to record every single small move that every performer makes. This is not necessary, but it is hard to know where to draw the line. As a simple guide all moves that are directed should be recorded, together with any moves that may provoke another action. Moves that are part of an actor's characterisation, such as a nervous tic, do not need to be recorded unless they have been directed to happen at a specific point; more usually such moves will happen at random. Sometimes they will become set, that is the actor will always do something at the same time and this may, for instance, be used to initiate a lighting cue. In that case the actor needs to know that this move has a wider implication, so that they can make sure that they always repeat it at the same point. The danger with this is that a different actor taking over the role will develop the character differently and is unlikely to take on similar character traits unless actually directed to do so. It can also be tempting to record too little.

There are no set rules that apply to recording the blocking, but there are a number of conventions that will be expected. 'Blocking' needs to be recorded using a simple shorthand system that can be understood by anybody. The aim of shorthand should be to make it quicker to record the moves. Complicated systems developed by an individual rarely work for anyone other than that individual, even when a key is provided. Blocking is a way of communicating information; it should be accurate, brief and clear.

Character names should be used rather than the actors' names, so that anyone following the 'blocking' will not have to know who is playing which part. Names may be abbreviated to the first three letters, thus Hamlet becomes HAM. A move across the stage is referred to as 'crossing' which can be abbreviated to 'X'. Other commonly used shorthand abbreviations are detailed (see *Figure 5.1*).

ENT	= Enters		↺ = Circles up	
EX	= Exits			
X	= Crosses, or moves across stage		↻ = Circles down	
⟶	= Direction of move			
↓	= Sits		**In the text**	
↑	= Rises		// or ⌢ = Pause	

Figure 5.1 Common abbreviations used in 'blocking'

Other items of set, furniture or props can be abbreviated, but a key should be provided, for instance 'SL Ch' might refer to a chair on stage left and 'tab' to a table.

The following move 'Hamlet enters from centre stage right, moves to the stage left chair and sits' could be abbreviated as: HAM ent CSR, X → SL Ch ↓

When recording the blocking, it can be useful to divide the stage into sectors in order to help define where the actors are moving to. The stage is normally divided into nine sectors (see *Figure 5.2*).

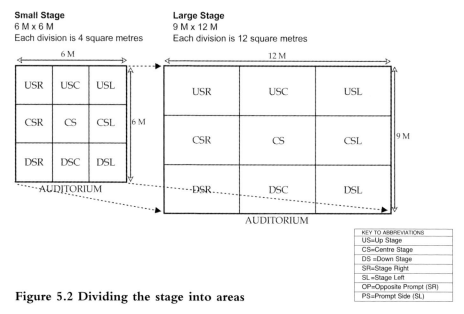

Figure 5.2 Dividing the stage into areas

KEY TO ABBREVIATIONS
US=Up Stage
CS=Centre Stage
DS =Down Stage
SR=Stage Right
SL =Stage Left
OP=Opposite Prompt (SR)
PS=Prompt Side (SL)

As the stage gets bigger, however, each of these sectors will increase in size accordingly. If they get too big they cease to be particularly useful. For instance, if an actor moves to DSR on a small stage, this might define an area only a few metres square, and a metre or so in either direction will make little difference to the actor's perceived position. On a large stage, however, the actor can be several metres in either direction and still be DSR; this does make a difference and a more exact way of defining the actor's position needs to be found. Increasing the number of divisions can help, but the way each of these extra divisions is described needs to be unambiguous. In the example shown (see *Figure 5.3*), they are described as being either right or left of centre.

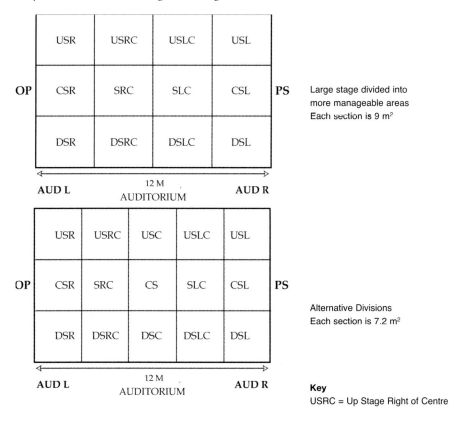

Figure 5.3 Alternative divisions for a larger stage

If the production is being staged in the round, it is necessary to find a way of describing the areas of the stage when terms such up-stage and stage left no longer make sense. The clock face or points of the compass may be used for this (see *Figure 5.4*). It can also be helpful to label each entrance that will be used by the performers and to use these as reference points.

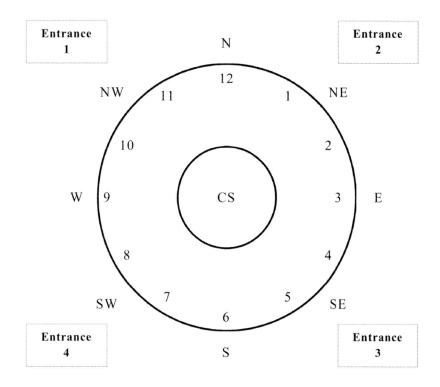

Figure 5.4 Stage divisions for theatre in the round

The stage manager responsible for blocking should always sit in the same place. This is particularly important if the production is in the round, where the director will move around the acting area as they direct. It can be tempting to follow them, but this will make blocking very difficult to execute or follow.

When moves become more complex than simply from A to B, or involve several characters moving at the same time, diagrams may be used (see *Figure 5.5*). The blocking on p. 117 could be recorded as in *Figure 5.5i*.

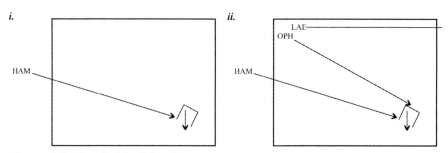

Figure 5.5 Simple blocking diagrams

A more complex piece of blocking involving three characters moving might be:
HAM ent CSR, X → SL Ch ↓
OPH X → US of SL Ch
LAE X → USR, ex

This would be represented diagrammatically as in *Figure 5.5ii*. The character's name indicates the position from which they move, the arrow shows where they will end up.

As well as the actual movement itself, the blocking must also record the point in the text at which each move is made. In a prompt copy it is usual to write the blocking on a blank sheet of paper opposite the point in the text at which it occurs. The point in the text is then indicated using a symbol, such as a number in a circle, which is duplicated next to the piece of blocking (see *Figure 5.6*). It is the uniqueness of the symbols used that is important and not the fact that they are numbers; each point in the text must be able to be related to the appropriate move. It would be perfectly acceptable to use Egyptian hieroglyphs.

In Figure *5.6i* the numbers in the text relate to the corresponding moves as recorded in the original blocking. In *Figure 5.6ii* the 'blocking' has changed. Move ① occurs several words latter, move ③ has disappeared altogether, move ⑥ has changed and a new move ⑧ has been added before move ⑥. This demonstrates that the numerical sequence is not important, the numbers are simply acting as markers. It would be a waste of time to renumber these during a blocking session and might actually lead to confusion.

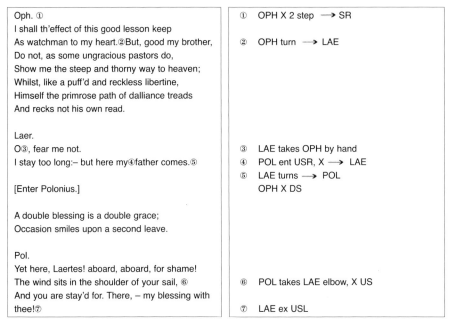

| Oph. ①
I shall th'effect of this good lesson keep
As watchman to my heart.②But, good my brother,
Do not, as some ungracious pastors do,
Show me the steep and thorny way to heaven;
Whilst, like a puff'd and reckless libertine,
Himself the primrose path of dalliance treads
And recks not his own read.

Laer.
O③, fear me not.
I stay too long:– but here my④father comes.⑤

[Enter Polonius.]

A double blessing is a double grace;
Occasion smiles upon a second leave.

Pol.
Yet here, Laertes! aboard, aboard, for shame!
The wind sits in the shoulder of your sail, ⑥
And you are stay'd for. There, – my blessing with
thee!⑦ | ①   OPH X 2 step   → SR

②   OPH turn   → LAE

③   LAE takes OPH by hand
④   POL ent USR, X → LAE
⑤   LAE turns → POL
     OPH X DS

⑥   POL takes LAE elbow, X US

⑦   LAE ex USL |

Figure 5.6i Blocking: recording moves against the text, original version

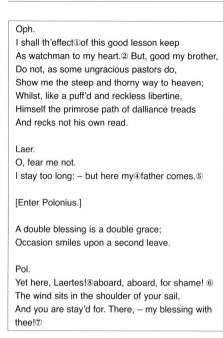

| Oph.
I shall th'effect①of this good lesson keep
As watchman to my heart.② But, good my brother,
Do not, as some ungracious pastors do,
Show me the steep and thorny way to heaven;
Whilst, like a puff'd and reckless libertine,
Himself the primrose path of dalliance treads
And recks not his own read.

Laer.
O, fear me not.
I stay too long: – but here my④father comes.⑤

[Enter Polonius.]

A double blessing is a double grace;
Occasion smiles upon a second leave.

Pol.
Yet here, Laertes!⑧aboard, aboard, for shame! ⑥
The wind sits in the shoulder of your sail,
And you are stay'd for. There, – my blessing with
thee!⑦ | ①   OPH X 2 steps ⟶ SR

②   OPH turns ⟶ LAE

④   POL ent USR, X ⟶ R LAE
⑤   LAE turns ⟶ POL
      OPH X DS

⑧   OPH X ⟶ DSL
⑥   LAE X US

⑦   LAE ex USL |

Figure 5.6ii Second version with adjustments

In situations where a character has to reach a particular position by a particular point in the text, numbers can be used to indicate that point.

⑧ POL X ⟶ OPH ⑨ ⟶ DSL ⑩

This indicates that Polonius makes a move reaching Ophelia at ⑨ and arriving DSL by ⑩.

An even more complex move involving several people moving around the stage is shown in *Figure 5.7*. In this Jim enters as Henry leaves the stage ②. Jim stops at the fireplace and looks at the clock ③. As Sue enters SR, Jim moves to the chair DS of the table, Sue meets him on the way at ⑥.

Some stage managers like to start each page of blocking with a small diagram of the set on which they can record the positions of each character at that point. This helps them to keep track of exactly where everyone is at regular stages, a task that can be difficult with a large cast.

When a production involves a large number of characters, as with an opera or musical, it is not always necessary to block each character individually all the time. The movements of chorus members can be blocked en masse, for instance 'CHOR A X USL, CHOR B X USR'. Similarly, individual moves in a dance number do not have to be recorded by the stage manager; the choreographer or dance captain will take care of that. The stage manager needs to know when people move and where they go to, but not usually what they do on the way or how they get there. Dance notation, also known as choreology, is complex and no stage manager would be expected to learn it, even those who work in ballet. It can take several years' training to learn a notation system such as the Laban method.

① HEN ↑ ex SL ②

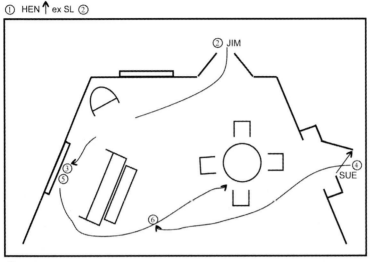

③ JIM looks @ clock
⑦ SUE X → chair SR of table↓

Figure 5.7 Complex blocking

Some productions will involve a staged fight. This may be directed by a specialist fight director, who will leave nothing to chance. Safety is of paramount importance here and it is useful for the stage manager to keep a detailed record of the moves. However this does not make it essential for stage management to learn fight notation. The fight director will block the fights and record the moves so that they can be re-rehearsed if necessary. Many fight directors use their own recording method, though sword fighting generally uses the same terminology as competition fencing.

During the initial blocking phase, complex moves involving many characters are reasonably easy to record. As the process develops, however, it also speeds up and it can sometimes be difficult to write it all down. In this situation it is acceptable for the stage manager to ask the director for some time to do this. If it is important, the director is likely to agree; if they do not, then they will have acknowledged that recording the moves accurately is not a priority at this point.

The most important thing to remember about blocking is that someone else may have to use it to rehearse understudies or a replacement cast member. The lighting designer may also rely on the blocking for their initial design ideas, and for the plotting session.

PHASE 3: WORKING

Once the play has been blocked, the director and cast can start to work on it in detail scene by scene. Starting again at the beginning, the initial blocking will be re-visited and worked on; it will change, and it will change again and again until it 'feels' right. The stage manager on the book must keep on top of this. Small sections may be worked on many times, while others just seem to fit into place. It may be several days before the scenes are revisited and both cast and director will inevitably have forgotten what they did in the original blocking session. Thus the accuracy of the blocking in the book is crucial. Accurately recorded blocking will enable the stage manager to steer the cast through their moves and to correct them when they go astray, even when they insist that they did it differently before.

The process of rehearsing is a dynamic one that involves experimentation and evolutionary change. Each time a scene is re-visited the moves may change from the way they were originally executed, as recorded in the blocking. Unless otherwise requested, the blocking must be kept up-to-date to record this. The stage manager must be able, and prepared, at all times to remind the cast what the last version rehearsed looked like. This may involve having to erase and rewrite movements many times. With experience it is possible to simplify this, developing a sixth sense for what is pure experimentation and what is likely to become a set move for the time being.

Working through the play is the most exciting and demanding time for all involved; this is the phase where the production really begins to take shape. However a number of problems may be associated with this process. Sticking points in interpretation for both cast and director may become evident and solutions will need to be found. It can be an emotional time, and both cast and director will need looking after. Performers need to find out what their characters are feeling and develop the relationships between them; sometimes it can be hard not to extend this beyond the rehearsal room. It may also be a frustrating process, as the right emotional journey seems just out of reach. This frustration may become manifest in short temper, often directed at the most accessible person – the stage manager or other cast member. It is essential to rise above this, as it is rarely personal, by being sensitive to the situation and by trying to pre-empt and diffuse apparent tension in advance. Rudeness is not acceptable, however, and should be dealt with firmly.

It is during this phase that tensions within a company will also become evident. At some point the cast may stop trusting the director, shunning their company during breaks and after rehearsals. Directors need support through this and it is the job of stage management to offer this. Stage management should remain sensitive to this changing dynamic, but preserve their neutrality at all times. They are likely to be canvassed for opinion on the capability, even sanity, of the director; at no time should they reveal their actual opinion, but if they detect real signs of unrest or impending mutiny, they have a responsibility to warn the director, who may be oblivious to the problem.

Sometimes these grievances are legitimate, though the cause is invariably unintentional and the result of misunderstanding. Performers will worry about their performance, especially as it is being developed through rehearsals. They are often insecure and will worry both about a perceived lack of rehearsal and/or too much rehearsal. At a certain point during the 'Working' phase this insecurity may become manifest – simply put, they will start to think that they can't do it, either because the director has only rehearsed their scenes once, or because he has concentrated on their scenes to the exclusion of all others. The assumption is that the director thinks they are so bad that either he has abandoned hope of getting a decent performance and so stopped rehearsing, or they need more rehearsing than anyone else. While either may be the case, it is more likely that the director is either completely happy with the actor's performance, or is struggling to find their own way into a particular scene. In this situation the stage manager can find out what is actually happening by raising it with the director directly or through general conversation about progress. It is not inappropriate to tell the director about a cast member's worries, particularly if their mind is on a totally different, and to them more important, problem. Reassurance can then be offered.

At a particular point during the 'Working' phase the cast will have learned their lines and will feel confident enough to rehearse without a copy of the script in their hands. This is known as 'being off the book' and the point at which it happens may be dictated, or at least requested, by the director. Being 'off the book' is both liberating and, initially, frustrating. For the first time the actors can use both hands and eyes and can develop and refine the physicality of their characters and the relationships between them. However they also have to remember their lines without a script to refer to, at the same time as having to remember what they are feeling and where they are moving. At this stage they may start to get words wrong and to paraphrase the text; that is, to get the gist of the meaning without actually saying the exact written words. This must be dealt with before lines become consolidated and difficult to unlearn. An actor will learn lines both by understanding the motivation behind what their character is saying and through repetition. During the initial learning phase motivation will be the dominant stimulus. Once the lines have been learned, they will become consolidated through repetition. If the wrong words are allowed to be repeated it will be these that become set. Stage management can help during this process in several ways. They will certainly be required to prompt, that is, to call out a line when an actor forgets it. They may need to interrupt, to put the dialogue back on track when it goes wrong. They can note down all the mistakes that are made and then go through these at the end of rehearsals. They can also offer to go through lines with individual members of the cast at times when they are not rehearsing.

If there are still many changes being made once the cast have started to rehearse without scripts, it may be necessary for another member of the team to prompt while the stage manager on the book concentrates on the blocking.

At this stage pauses should also be marked in the script, to differentiate them from points where an actor has dried and thus avoid unnecessary prompts, particularly when a substitute is on the book (see *Figure 5.1*). By marking pauses, uncalled for prompts can be avoided; the actor hasn't dried, they have just paused. Sometimes an actor will put in a new pause, however, which may lead to confusion.

This is arguably the most creative period. New ideas will be explored and props and costumes will be added or subtracted. Without the encumbrance of a script the cast suddenly have two hands with which to experiment; they will try out different actions, which may involve the props and costume, even the set, being used in ways for which they were not originally designed. Some of these actions may become set, others rejected. Stage management must keep on top of these developments, relaying relevant information to the rest of the production team on a daily basis. A stand-in for every new prop will be needed in rehearsal as soon as possible, and the feasibility of implementing the requested changes will need to be discussed and confirmed.

REHEARSAL NOTES

Information from the rehearsal room is normally circulated via formal 'Rehearsal Notes'. These enable stage management to keep in touch with all other departments, passing on information concerning any changes or additional requirements immediately.

Before requests or information are passed on they should always be double-checked with the director at the end of each rehearsal. It is not uncommon for a director to discuss something with a member of the cast during the day but to have little intention of actually letting it happen. Performers will frequently start to enhance their characterisation by adding things; pipes, walking sticks, hats, handbags. While some of these will stay, many others will be experimented with and then rejected. With the director's agreement, it is reasonable to hold off on some requests until they have become concrete, though rehearsal stand-ins should always be provided. This helps to avoid unnecessary expenditure and misdirected effort. When time and budget are at a premium, it is important not to waste them looking for props that turn out not to be needed.

Rehearsal notes should always be circulated to the director, designers, production manager, technical manager and stage manager, as well as to individual departments. They should always be followed up verbally, to check that they have been understood and are going to be acted on.

As well as changes to the props and costumes, there will also be notes that concern all other departments, sound, lighting, construction, etc. Sometimes the implications of decisions taken in rehearsals are not always obvious; it is important to remember that changes specific to one area may impact on other departments, and stage management need to be on their toes to spot who may be affected by what. For instance the decision to block a fight so that the actors involved roll around on the floor might appear unworthy of a note, yet it could affect costume, construction, scenic art and even props. Detailed knowledge of the design will help; if the costumes are made of silk and the floor is roughly textured, there could be a problem requiring a rethink of both floor and costumes.

The information needs to be comprehensive. In the example shown (see *Figure 5.8*), Props note 2 is not just for a chair to be added – the chair has specific requirements, it is used to reach a shelf and it has to fit in a corner. Some notes may also affect other departments. LX note 1 which refers to the standard lamp could also be relevant to props and stage management. In such a case it might be prudent to draw attention to LX note 1 under the Props heading, but it is not always possible to spot all the ramifications at the time. It is better if all recipients read all notes and pass on any further information they think relevant.

Timings should be included for information, as well as any alterations to the script. If large cuts are made in the text this may have a knock-on effect, particularly for costume changes (see *Figure 5.8 Costume note 1*). Potential problems with quick changes, such as a character exiting up stage and then re-entering from the rear of the auditorium in a completely different costume twenty seconds later, should be drawn to the director's attention and discussed. If alterations to the script are comprehensive they can be circulated separately; all members of the production team need to work from the same text. The cast also need to know about all script changes; these can be displayed either inside or outside the rehearsal room and drawn to the cast's attention.

As well as rehearsal notes, stage management will also need to carry out risk assessments on anything that happens during rehearsals that could be hazardous (see Chapter 9). This includes any requirement for smoking and the use of live flame such as lighted candles. A 'Smoking Plot' may be compiled, detailing where a cigarette is lit, the action while it is being smoke and where it is extinguished. These risk assessments and the smoking plot will form part of the information forwarded to the Local Authority so that a license can be granted.

DEVISED THEATRE
Rehearsal notes are not always necessary. In a company where the production team is small and stage management have a more hands-on involvement in other areas, and where the team as a whole is more involved with the rehearsal process, regular notes become less necessary as information can be passed on and discussed first-hand. This might particularly apply to a devised production

where the whole team is involved in the devising process. However it is important, in this situation, to keep a record of decisions made and a digest, published daily, can be useful. When a larger production is being devised, rehearsal notes become an even more crucial way of keeping everyone informed.

REHEARSAL NOTES	
Production: *The Rose Tattoo*	
Date: 6 June	**No: 7**

General/SM
1. Timings for 'stagger' through:
   Act 1 – 49.5 mins   Act 2 – 32 mins   Act 3 – 29.5 mins   Total: 1 hr 51 mins
2. We may put the interval in Act 2.
3. The truck must be absolutely silent when it moves as it does so during dialogue.
4. The DSM & truck operator may need to have monitors, or to be operating the show from a position with a clear view of the truck as it moves. Is this possible?

Production/Set
1. The screen door needs to swing shut by degrees once Serafina lets it go as described on p. 71.
2. Is it possible to cut the pillar in the centre of the room?
3. In addition to the high shelf over the front door please could there be shelving on the wall to the left of the front door (the wall the phone is on)?
4. A 'silent' wind machine to billow the curtains in Act 3 Scene 3. It needs to be off stage DR.

Props
1. The Madonna needs to be placed quite high up on the wall.
2. A 2nd chair for the parlour which Serafina uses to reach the wine on the high shelf. It needs to fit in the corner by the back window, up stage of the front door.
3. The corks in the wine bottles should be ordinary corks, not champagne style corks.
4. The women will bring 'pom-pom' chrysanthemums to Serafina in Act 1 Scene 2.
5. An open bottle of wine in Act 3 Scene 1.
6. Are there going to be, or could there be, curtains on the windows?
7. The parrot must be a real one but silent! It should not be too small.

LX
1. The standard lamp needs to be practical. It will get knocked over in the fight sequence.
2. The lights in the Sicilian Cart need to be wired up to a battery to make them practical.

Sound/Music
1. The following Q's should be a combination of live & recorded FX:
2. Act 2 Sc 1 p 75 – Youthful cry
3. Act 2 Sc 1 p 82 – Distant cry of children
4. Act 3 Sc 1 p 88 – Wild distant cry of children.
5. The sound of the sewing machine will need to be amplified for Act 1 Sc 2

Costume
1. The interval may be in Act 2. This would mean a quick change for Miss Watling & Mr Scott between Act 2 Scene 1 & Act 3 Scene 1.
2. We will see Alvaro's jacket being torn during the fight with the Salesman, p.69. It should be that the back centre seam comes apart.
3. Mr. Clover would like to have his hair cut ASAP.

Signed: *"Deputy Stage Manager"*

CC: Director / Designers / MD / Production Manager / SM / Production HoD's

Figure 5.8 Rehearsal notes

PHASE 4: RUNNING

Towards the end of the rehearsal period the director will start running the play in its entirety, or scene by scene. It is at this point that the stage manager on the book needs maximum support from the rest of the team – help with resetting furniture and props for scene changes, prompting, possibly even special effects or sound operation. It is also at this stage, once the actors are off the book, that they will start demanding, and should be given, the actual props.

Members of the creative team, such as the lighting and sound designers, will wish to be invited to runs as soon as possible. This will give them a better insight into the artistic requirements of the production. It is important to check with the director, however, before issuing invitations, and the Company should always be informed in advance of the presence of strange faces in rehearsal, so that they are not unnerved.

Runs, whether of individual scenes, acts or the whole play, enable the director to see the way it is shaping up in its entirety. They also allow the cast to find their emotional journey and physical pace. Runs will be interspersed with notes sessions, which the stage manager on the book should attend, and the continued working of the bits that are not quite right. This phase is about consolidation and refinement.

PROMPTING

In the later stages of rehearsals the stage manager should check with the actors individually about how they want to be prompted. Many actors would rather struggle through than be interrupted, unless they actually ask for a prompt. The director should be included in these decisions. It is also important to check whether the run should be interrupted if the cast veer radically from the written text. This policy will vary from run to run depending on what the director wants to achieve. If the purpose is to look at the physical shape of the play, then prompting or interrupting might interfere with this, and the stage manager should make notes in the prompt copy so that any mistakes can be drawn to the cast's attention at the end. If the purpose is to concentrate on the meaning, then prompting and interrupting paraphrases or mistakes becomes essential. During runs it is sometimes necessary for one member of the stage management team to concentrate on prompting while another checks the blocking.

Generally, but not always, an actor can be relied on to ask for a prompt, by shouting 'line' or 'prompt', but they may just stop, shout 'What?', or even swear through frustration.

The stage manager should prompt by calling out the next line loudly and clearly and, of course, promptly. If the actor is still attempting to get themselves out of trouble, or simply cursing their memory, the prompt must be loud enough to interrupt and attract their attention. It is important to give a line rather than just a word and to continue with it until the actor picks up their cue. If Hamlet were to dry after 'To be or not to be', the prompt would be 'That is the question' and not just 'That'. A single word can easily be missed and will have to be repeated. If they have dried in the middle of a phrase then it is useful to start from the beginning of that phrase rather than from where they left off.

MANAGING REHEARSALS

Stage management need to arrive at the rehearsal room in good time for each rehearsal, in order to do the mark-up and to set up furniture and props. Props should be set as close as possible to where they will be set on stage, in relation to entrances, etc. Setting up for the day's rehearsals in good time will allow stage management to talk to the director and cast as they arrive. This is a good time for the team to meet and to clarify any rehearsal notes that need further discussion and to pass on messages. Helping the person on the book set up will also free up some of their time so that they can prepare themselves for the day's rehearsal.

Before the rehearsal the cast need to be shown where their props have been set and what the substitute items of furniture and props represent in reality; it may be necessary to label these accordingly. As the actual props and furniture arrive in the rehearsal room, the cast should be shown them before they get to use them and, if necessary, shown how they work and allowed to practise with them. If someone prefers their props to be set in a particular way, then that should be noted down so that it can be reproduced.

The stage manager is responsible for calling the rehearsal to order once all the cast have arrived and, in collaboration with the director, for starting it off. Once the rehearsal has started they must ensure that absolute quiet is kept in the rehearsal room. During the course of the rehearsal, they should keep an eye on the rehearsal schedule and remind the director if it is time to move on. This may be ignored. They are also responsible for calling official breaks as allowed for in the contract and for stopping the rehearsal at the end of the day. Enough time should be allowed for the rehearsal room to be tidied and props put away.

Ideally there should be at least two members of the stage management team in rehearsal at all times. One will be on the book, the other will deal with props, answer the telephone, etc. When a scene needs to be reset, it should be the stage management who do this and not the cast. who will have other things to think about.

At the end of the rehearsal day it is useful for the whole team to help clear up, check on any notes that have arisen, type out the call and contact the company with the next day's schedule.

REHEARSAL SCHEDULE

It is useful to have a basic outline for the rehearsal schedule. This may be skeletal or in minute detail, every director works differently, and however detailed the schedule for the rehearsal period may be, it can be expected to change.

On a daily basis, a rehearsal call should be worked out for the next day before the end of each day's rehearsals. This may be a condition of some union-approved contracts. Some directors will go into the call in great detail, scheduling a time for literally every section of the play, while others would rather have all the cast present all the time so that they can work on any bits they like. The latter is generally unpopular with performers, particularly if they are not actually in every scene, even if the play is being directed so that they are always on stage. Some directors even expect stage management to work out rehearsal calls for them.

With a complex production involving a large cast, a character plot (see *Figure 3.2*) is a useful tool for organising the rehearsal call. It can be used to prevent members of the cast being called unnecessarily if they are not in the beginning of a scene and is particularly helpful if someone is not available at a particular time; it is easy to see, at a glance, which sections of the play can be rehearsed without a particular character being present.

Once the following day's rehearsal call has been worked out with the director, the company need to be informed. Cast members who are present once the call has been finalised can be informed before they leave, whilst others will need to be contacted by telephone. Some actors will call stage management to find out when they will be needed.

The rehearsal call must contain all relevant information, namely:
- The name of the production
- The date of the call
- The location
- The time of each call
- What scene or section is to be rehearsed
- Who is needed

Nothing should be left to chance.

A copy of the call should be posted in, or outside, the rehearsal room so that individual members of the cast can check when they are needed.

There are a number of conventions that will normally be expected in a rehearsal call. Company members are called by their family names, not their characters' name, prefixed by either 'Miss' or 'Mr'. The list should be alphabetical with female members listed first; this may seem old-fashioned and reactionary, and exceptions will be encountered, but it is important to check before using a less formal or more contemporary system as offence may be taken. The tradition refers back to a time, not so long ago, when all artistes would have been addressed as 'Miss' or 'Mr' at all times and the familiar use of first names would not have been permitted at all. Some high-profile artistes still expect this form of address.

When all the cast are needed for a rehearsal call, they do not need to be listed individually but as 'Full Company'. Similarly if the call is for the full company except for several individuals it can be written as 'Full Company, less *the names of those not required*. When those not called are needed later they can be asked 'To join'. Using such shortcuts will make compiling a call involving a large company much easier. A rehearsal call is a formal means of communication, however; it must be unambiguous and convey all the necessary information. If a cast member misses a call because they misunderstood it, it is the call and its compiler who are at fault. Meal breaks and finish times must be included on the call, but should be posted as 'approximate', thus giving the opportunity for flexibility. *Figure 5.9* shows three examples of the same call. In *Fig 5.9i* the two activities, rehearsals and voice tuition, are integrated into the same list, while in *Fig 5.9ii* they are separated. These calls can be related directly to the character plot (*Figure 3.2*).

THE ROSE TATTOO				
REHEARSAL CALL				
DATE:	**MONDAY 2ND MAY**			
TIME	COMPANY		CALL	LOCATION
10:00 a.m.	Miss Appleby Miss Haste Miss Watling	Miss Fife Miss Friend Miss White	Act 1 Scene 1 p.19 Opening sequence	Old Church Hall
11:00	To Join: Miss Colgate Less: Miss Appleby Miss Haste Miss White	Miss Oregano Miss Fife Miss Friend	Act 1 Scene 1 pp 20 & 21	Old Church Hall
12:00 p.m.	Miss Oregano Miss Watling	Miss Morse	Act 1 Scene 1 pp 22 – 24	Old Church Hall
12:30	To Join: Miss Haste			Old Church Hall
1:00	**LUNCH BREAK (approx)**			
2:00	Miss Appleby Miss Colgate Miss Friend Miss Watling	Miss Fife Miss Haste Miss Oregano Miss White	Work through Act 1 Scene 1	Old Church Hall
2:00	Mr. Brown		Voice Tuition	Music Room
2:45	Mr Hunter		Voice Tuition	Music Room
3:00	To Join: Mr Brown Less: Miss Haste	 Miss Oregano	Act 1 Sc 2	Old Church Hall
3:30	Miss Colgate Mr Brown	 Mr Hunter	Act 1 Sc 3 pp 29/30	Old Church Hall
3:30	Miss Oregano		Voice Tuition	Music Room
4:00	To Join: Miss Appleby Miss Friend	 Miss Fife Miss White	Act 1 Sc 3 pp 30/31	Old Church Hall
4:15	To Join: Miss Morse		Act 1 Sc 3 p 31	Old Church Hall
4:15	Miss Watling		Voice Tuition	Music Room
5:00	**CALL TO END (approx)**			

Figure 5.9i A rehearsal call

THE ROSE TATTOO			
REHEARSAL CALL			
DATE: MONDAY 2ND MAY			
LOCATION: OLD CHURCH HALL			
TIME	COMPANY		CALL
10:00 a.m.	Miss Appleby Miss Haste Miss Watling	Miss Fife Miss Friend Miss White	Act 1 Scene 1 p.19 Opening sequence
11:00	To Join: Miss Colgate	Miss Oregano	Act 1 Scene 1 pp 20 & 21
	Less: Miss Appleby Miss Haste Miss White	Miss Fife Miss Friend	
12:00 p.m.	Miss Oregano Miss Watling	Miss Morse	Act 1 Scene 1 pp 22 – 24
12:30	To Join: Miss Haste		
1:00	**LUNCH BREAK (approx)**		
2:00	Miss Appleby Miss Colgate Miss Friend Miss Watling	Miss Fife Miss Haste Miss Oregano Miss White	Work through Act 1 Scene 1
3:00	To Join: Mr Brown		Act 1 Sc 2
	Less: Miss Haste	Miss Oregano	
3:30	Miss Colgate Mr Brown	Mr Hunter	Act 1 Sc 3 pp 29/30
4:00	To Join: Miss Appleby Miss Friend	Miss Fife Miss White	Act 1 Sc 3 pp30/31
4:15	To Join: Miss Morse		Act 1 Sc 3 p 31
4:30	To Join: Miss Haste	Miss Oregano	Act 1 Sc 3 p 32
5:00	**CALL TO END (approx)**		
VOICE TUITION			
Location:	Music Room		
2:00	Mr. Brown		
2:45	Mr Hunter		
3:30	Miss Oregano		
4:15 – 5:00	Miss Watling		

Figure 5.9ii Alternative layout of rehearsal call

During the rehearsal the person on the book needs to have a clear list of the day's rehearsal call to hand, so that they can check that the artistes called are there and that it is running to schedule. If anyone is missing they should be traced before they are needed. The lateness or non-appearance of a performer

THE ROSE TATTOO
REHEARSAL CALL
DATE: MONDAY 2ND MAY

Location:	**Old Church Hall**		
10:00 a.m.	**Act 1 Scene 1 p.19 Opening sequence**		
	Miss Appleby	Miss Fife	Miss Haste
	Miss Friend	Miss Watling	Miss White
11:00	**Act 1 Scene 1 pp 20 & 21**		
	To Join:	Less:	
	Miss Colgate	Miss Appleby	Miss Fife
	Miss Oregano	Miss Friend	Miss Haste
		Miss White	
12:00 p.m	**Act 1 Scene 1 pp 22 – 24**		
	Miss Oregano	Miss Morse	Miss Watling
12:30	To Join:		
	Miss Haste		
1:00	**LUNCH BREAK (approx)**		
2:00	**Work through Act 1 Scene 1**		
	Miss Appleby	Miss Colgate	Miss Fife
	Miss Friend	Miss Haste	Miss Oregano
	Miss Watling	Miss White	
3:00	**Act 1 Sc 2**		
	To Join:	Less:	
	Mr Brown	Miss Haste	
		Miss Oregano	
3:30	**Act 1 Sc 3 pp 29/30**		
	Miss Colgate	Mr Brown	Mr Hunter
4:00	**Act 1 Sc 3 pp 30/31**		
	To Join:		
	Miss Appleby	Miss Friend	Miss Fife
	Miss White		
4:15	**Act 1 Sc 3 p 31**		
	To Join:		
	Miss Morse		
4:30	**Act 1 Sc 3 p 32**		
	To Join:		
	Miss Haste	Miss Oregano	
5:00	**CALL TO END (approx)**		

Figure 5.9iii Alternative layout of rehearsal call

can have a devastating effect on rehearsals. Other cast members and the director are kept waiting and there is often nothing else that they can do. Rakhmanov's reproach to Kostya from the first chapter of Stanislavski's *An Actor Prepares* neatly summarises the effect:

'We have been sitting here waiting, our nerves on edge, angry and [you are] late. We all came here full of enthusiasm for the work waiting to be done, and now, thanks to you, the mood has been destroyed. To arouse a desire to create is difficult; to kill a desire is extremely easy. If I interfere with my own work, it is my own affair, but what right have I to hold up the work of the whole group?

The actor, no less than the soldier, must be subject to iron discipline.'

Incidentally, this applies equally to stage managers and all other participants in the creative production process.

No rehearsal schedule is perfect and individual sessions regularly overshoot. It is actually quite hard to estimate how long is needed for each section to be rehearsed in detail, and this means that some of the cast may be kept hanging around. This is potentially disruptive, as they get bored, so the stage manager should try to prevent this from happening. If a scene is obviously going to overrun and that is spotted early enough, the stage manager should consult with the director and agree to reschedule. They can then make sure that members of the cast are not kept waiting around. It may sometimes even be possible to contact them before they leave home. For instance, if an actor is called for a rehearsal at 4:00 that is scheduled to finish at 5:00, but by lunchtime it is plainly obvious that that scene will not be reached, it may be acceptable, with the director's agreement, to call them and tell them not to come in. This is good for morale; it would be a waste of their time to come in just to sit around for an hour and then go home.

Productions such as musicals may involve a complex rehearsal process with different activities happening at the same time. The director may rehearse a scene with some principal characters while the choreographer works with the chorus in a different room, a pianist works with other members of the cast individually and the assistant director rehearses understudies. There may be separate fight calls, dialect coaching, in fact whatever is necessary. All of these will need to be worked into the schedule by the stage manager.

The stage manager needs to be familiar with the terms of the particular contract under which they and the cast are employed, as various requirements regarding the number of hours worked, breaks taken, etc., have to be observed. This means that the stage manager must be firm with the director concerning breaks and the hours that can be spent rehearsing, allowing time for the rehearsal space to be set up and cleared up. Issues relating to overtime should always be checked with the management.

The stage manager may be required to keep a detailed record of the hours that are worked by individual members of the company. This may form the basis for the way that rehearsal calls are worked out.

COSTUME FITTINGS

Another important aspect of the production that requires scheduling throughout the rehearsal period is the costume fittings (see *Figure 5.10*). These inevitably come at the most intensive part of the rehearsal period and need sensitive handling, as they often involve busy people travelling long distances. They invariably take longer than has been estimated and it is always advisable to allow extra time for every fitting. Fittings should be organised with the costume supervisor and designer well in advance and with the full involvement of the director. Sometimes the director will be required, or want, to be present.

THE ROSE TATTOO	
COSTUME FITTINGS	
Date: Monday 2nd May	
LOCATION: Church Hall Annexe	
TIME	COMPANY
10:00 a.m.	Miss Colgate
10:40	Miss Morse
11:10	Miss Appleby
11:40	Miss Haste
12:20 p.m.	Miss Fife
LOCATION: Classic Costumes – please allow 1 hour to travel from rehearsal room	
3:00 p.m.	Mr Lord
3:30	Mr Clover
4:00	Mr Barley
4:30	Mr Scott

Figure 5.10: A costume fitting call

Costume fittings often take place away from the rehearsal room or theatre, at the costumiers themselves, particularly if the costumes are being hired rather than made. If that is the case travel time and breaks should always be allowed, especially if the actor is to rehearse either before or after the fitting. Fittings can sometimes involve shopping trips with the designer.

PUBLICITY

During the rehearsal period a production photographer may be invited to take informal photographs for the programme of the cast rehearsing for a day. The company must be informed of this in advance so that they are not taken by surprise and can make proper preparations. In an industry where physical appearance and image are important, individuals may not appreciate being photographed without make-up and wearing scruffy clothes.

Publicity agents may arrange for journalists to sit in on rehearsals and to interview members of the company. Sometimes a television company will make a documentary about a new production or simply film extracts for an arts or news programme. This should never be arranged without the consent of the director and company, and it must be at their convenience. If demands are made at short notice it can be extremely disruptive; television directors will often try to take over and interrupt the flow of the rehearsals. The stage manager will need to be firm, the crew are there as guests and, unless otherwise agreed, must fit in with the rehearsal schedule.

The company will also be required to provide short biographies and photographs for the programme. They are usually asked to provide these at the start, even when they sign their contracts, but this often fails to happen, and the stage manager may need to chase them for these so that the programme can be assembled. Towards the end of the rehearsal period, programme proofs will be circulated and will need to be checked by each member of the company including the director and designers. In fact any member of the production team who is to be credited will need to check that their name has been spelled correctly. It will often fall to the stage manager to organise this.

PROPS

Throughout the rehearsal period props will be added or removed and the way they are being used will change. The Props List (see Chapter 8) must be kept up-to-date and there should only ever be one version in circulation. Rehearsal props must be provided and the actual props should normally be introduced into the rehearsals as soon as possible.

If there are any props that are fragile or perishable (or indeed destroyed in the course of the action), a secure supply of replacements needs to be organised. There should always be spares of any china and glass.

By the final, running, phase the cast should be working with all the actual props and furniture, apart from any that have been added at the last minute and are still to be acquired. There are a number of exceptions to this rule.

- The budget may only allow for some props to be hired for the duration of the performance and not for the rehearsal period.
- Props that are eaten, smoked or broken as part of the action may be rationed. It may be too expensive to allow them to be used at every rehearsal, in which case they should be restricted to rehearsals called solely for that purpose and for final runs of the play in the rehearsal room.
- Some props are too fragile or valuable to release into the rehearsal process until the very end. When in the rehearsal room they will need to be looked after carefully.
- For Health and Safety reasons, firearms that fire blanks may not be compatible with the rehearsal space and may only be licensed for use in the theatre space.

Any of these should be discussed with the director in advance and the cast informed.

Props must be set in the same position for each rehearsal, as most actors like things to be set in exactly the same way each time and even a minor change can be upsetting. This is particularly important for those set on-stage, but props set off-stage should also be set in the same position every time, preferably as close to their actual setting as possible. It can be helpful to mark the table used for props in the rehearsal room with tape making a space for each prop; this also helps when checking props and, if done on a soft cover, can be easily transferred from the rehearsal room. Small props used by the cast that can fit into pockets need to be retrieved at the end of each rehearsal session.

Running the rehearsal room as if it were the performance space will help the stage manager to work out and acquire the necessary number of props tables and to make any special requests, such as shelving that may need to be built into the set backstage.

By the final week of the rehearsal period, a detailed setting list for all the props and furniture used in the production should have been compiled. The setting list should enable stage management to set every single prop in exactly the right place both in the rehearsal space and on the set when the production moves into the theatre. It must be accurate and easy to understand.

THE PROMPT COPY

Throughout the rehearsal period the Prompt Copy must be kept up-to-date as a complete, and accurate, guide to the production. This includes the text itself as well as the blocking, which must show the moves as they have been finalised at the end of each day's rehearsal. The setting and movement of props and furniture, scene changes, and every cue and call, must be added as they become evident.

Everything should be set out so clearly that a new stage manager taking over the book in an emergency will have no difficulty whatsoever in understanding what is meant. It must be legible and any shorthand used must be easy to interpret.

The stage manager on the book should try to enter cue points as they become evident. Some of these will have been obvious from the very beginning but many will be added throughout as the production develops. It is helpful to arrange a meeting with the director, lighting and sound designers and technical manager to discuss cue sequences in advance, though this is not always feasible. With complex technical productions, the sequence of events in a scene change may be critical and as the stage manager on the book will be in control, they need to have prior information concerning this.

These discussions will also enable the stage manager to work out and request the number of cue lights and headsets that will be needed and where these should be positioned. They may also need to check whether a CCTV and monitor are available if there is a restricted view of the stage and to make alternative plans if they are not.

PLOTS AND CUE SHEETS

By the end of the rehearsal period stage management should have compiled a comprehensive setting list for all the props and furniture (see Chapter 8) and cue sheets and plots for themselves and the appropriate technical departments (see Chapter 6 and *Figure 6.10*). Depending on the way a production is to be staffed, lighting and sound cue synopses are likely to be the province of the lighting and sound designers, though the stage manager on the book will need to have a copy and it is best if they have been involved in discussions earlier.

A Master Plot which amalgamates the cues for each staging element should be compiled. This will enable the technical manager to see everything that happens in sequence and thus to work out the logistics of staffing the production. Separate plots should also be prepared for the stage staff and fly crew, and any other specific scenic elements such as a revolve (turntable) or traps. These should detail the sequence of actions for each scene change and any other cues. If the production involves complex staging technology, the technical manager may have been involved in working out the sequence of technical actions in advance with the designer and production manager. The stage manager on the book will also need to be involved in this, as it is they who will be calling the cues.

The information contained in these plots must clearly define each sequence of actions so that the technicians can carry these out successfully. At this stage it is not usually possible to put together cue sheets for each individual, though it is an advantage if this can be worked out prior to the technical rehearsal. The plots compiled in rehearsal are provisional and will change once the production arrives on the stage.

PRODUCTION MEETINGS

The Production Meeting is the principal forum for communication for all aspects of the production. It should be used to assess progress, to pass on information between departments, to raise issues and concerns regarding the production process and to agree action points. Ideally a production meeting should not last for more than 45 minutes.

Production meetings are normally attended by the production manager, all heads of department, the creative team (director, designer, lighting designer, sound designer, costume designer) and representatives of the stage management team, including the person on the book. All departments should be represented at these meetings, though the production manager will often act as the representative for any contractors such as the scenic constructors.

The meeting is usually chaired by the production manager, who is responsible for keeping discussion relevant and useful. Production meetings are a formal means of communication and, as such, should be run efficiently and seriously. An agenda may be prepared in advance and distributed at the start of the meeting, and should include standing items relating to each department. One member of the group should be nominated to take down the minutes.

Following any apologies, a meeting will usually start by looking back over the previous meeting's minutes to check on progress regarding the agreed action points. Each department may then be asked individually to report on:

- Progress
- Issues or concerns
- Information which may affect other departments

During this discussion any action points need to be agreed and clearly highlighted in the minutes. If at this point issues arise that may require complex discussion between two or three departments, a separate meeting should be arranged and a time and date agreed and recorded in the minutes. The meeting should not be used for showing new props or costumes to the designer and director, nor for discussing fine detail. Nor should it be used to report back on something that could have been done earlier. Waiting for the production meeting, delaying by even a day, can have serious consequences for other people.

The meeting may also be used to table production schedules and for these to be discussed and approved. However it is better if these have been circulated in advance.

Once each department has reported, any other agenda items can be discussed and an opportunity given for individuals to raise issues under any other business. The time and date of the next meeting should be agreed at the end.

Following the meeting the minutes should be produced promptly, with clearly highlighted action points, and circulated to each department.

Production meetings may be held regularly or as required, and may be called at short notice if an important issue needs to be brought to the attention of the whole team and discussed.

It is important to note that production meetings form one part of a complex communications system, one where the whole production team are brought together. Other meetings between smaller groups of individuals should happen as required throughout the process.

TOURING INFORMATION

If the production is to tour, the company will need to be given the chance to find accommodation well in advance, particularly if there is more than one theatre in the town being visited or it is a popular tourist spot in midsummer. Most venues will supply a 'digs' list and this can be circulated to the cast as soon as it is available. It is also good practice to put together information packs for each town, including maps, train times and the performance schedule.

Foreign tours will be arranged well in advance, including transport and accommodation. The stage manager will need to check that airline tickets are booked in the correct name. Many artistes work under a stage name which is not the same as the one on their passport. A ticket booked in their stage name will cause an annoying, and avoidable, hold-up at the airport and may incur extra expense. It is also worth double-checking visa requirements, especially if some of the company hold foreign passports. This is particularly easy to forget when touring in European Union countries.

SUMMARY

By the end of the rehearsal period, the cast and stage management should be ready to move on to the stage. The props and costumes will have been acquired; the cast will have rehearsed as far as they can. They are now ready to bring all elements of the production together on the set.

THE PRODUCTION PERIOD

The production period starts with the 'get-in' ('load-in' in the US) and 'fit-up' and continues until the opening night. The level of involvement of stage management in the early stages will depend on the scale of the production and the size of the team. No matter what the scale, however, it is usual for the production period to start while the director and cast are still working in the rehearsal room.

The scenery will have been constructed and painted during the rehearsal period and will then be transported to the performance venue. This may be a matter of simply moving it from a workshop onto the stage, or transporting it across the country in a fleet of trucks. By this stage too the sound will have been recorded and the lighting rig designed, and any necessary equipment ordered and transported to the venue.

PRODUCTION SCHEDULE

A production schedule is normally prepared by the production manager in conjunction with all heads of departments including the director, designers and stage manager. The schedule is an attempt to estimate the time required for each element of the production to be prepared on the stage. It will enable the production manager and heads of department to work out who will be needed when and for how long. The schedule needs to be realistic but should also be flexible, with contingency time planned in. Illustrated is an example of a typical schedule for a medium-scale touring production (see *Figure 6.1*). The ideal schedule would allow time for each of the following as appropriate:

1. Get in set, lighting and sound equipment
2. Rig lighting and sound equipment
3. Rig flown scenery
4. Erect set on stage
5. Paint stage
6. Focus lights (dark time)
7. Plot lights (dark time) including programming moving lights
8. Rig communications equipment – cue lights, head sets & CCTV
9. Plot sound (quiet time)
10. Plot automation
11. Get in props, furniture and costume
12. Set up props, furniture and quick change facilities
13. Rehearse scene changes
14. Cast orientation and familiarise with Health and Safety issues

15. Licensing inspection
16. Technical rehearsal
17. Dress rehearsals
18. Acting notes time
19. Technical notes time
20. Photo call
21. Touch up paint call

THE ROSE TATTOO			
PLAYHOUSE THEATRE			
PRODUCTION SCHEDULE			
Sunday 21st April			
09:00	Get-in & commence fit-up	12 stage	4 LX
13:00	LUNCH		
14:00	Continue above		
19:00	SUPPER		
20:00	Continue above / Focus FOH if possible		
23:00	FINISH		
Monday 22nd April			
09:00	Continue Focus / fit-up	6 Stage	4 LX
12:00	Stage Management set up on stage	Stage Management	
12:30	Local Authority Inspection		
13:00	LUNCH		
14:00	Continue Focus		
15:00	Plot Lighting		
17:00	SUPPER / Dressers called / Sound plot (quiet time)	3 Dressers	2 Sound
18:00	Company on stage to start Technical Rehearsal	Show Crew	
22:30	Company break / Technical work as required		
23:00	Technical work to finish		
	Touch up paint call	1 Stage	1 LX
24:00	Painters to finish		
Tuesday 23rd April			
09:00	Technical work as required	3 Stage / 2 LX as called	
11:00	Company on stage to continue Technical Rehearsal	Show crew	
13:00	LUNCH		
14:15	Continue Technical Rehearsal		
17:30	Press Photo Call		
18:30	SUPPER		
19:45	DRESS REHEARSAL		
Wednesday 24th April			
09:00	Technical work as required	3 Stage / 2 LX as called	
13:00	LUNCH		
14:00	DRESS REHEARSAL	Show crew	
16:30	Company Notes		
18:00	Company Break/Crew reset		
!8:30	Crew break		
19:45	PERFORMANCE 1		
Provisional Show Crew:	3 Stage	3 Dressers	
	1 Stage LX	1 Board operator	

Figure 6.1 A production schedule

The length of time allowed for each activity will vary. On a very complex production using automated scenery, the plotting and rehearsing of scene changes may take several days without the cast being present. It is not uncommon nowadays for the initial programming to take place well in advance of the fit-up. The automated elements will be set up in a workshop, where they can be programmed and any problems sorted out before they are moved to the venue. Three-dimensional animated computer simulations may be used.

The schedule will need to be reviewed on a daily basis and adjusted accordingly. Problems will inevitably be encountered and departments will need to reach a compromise if they are to be solved effectively.

TRANSITION FROM REHEARSAL ROOM TO STAGE

The move from the rehearsal room to the stage needs to be well managed. Stage management must check that all members of the company know the time of their first call at the theatre and, if they have been rehearsing elsewhere, how to get there. This is particularly important if the production is opening on tour. The stage manager can put together and circulate a Company Production Schedule (see *Figure 6.2*) which just details the calls relevant to the acting company.

On a tour the stage manager will need to have an address and telephone number where each member of the company can be contacted. It is also useful to publish the times of trains in advance and to put together an information pack similar to the one circulated before the start of rehearsals. If members of the cast intend to travel together by car this should be checked with the management. An accident involving principals as well as their understudies could jeopardise the show's opening.

All props should be packed up carefully to prevent breakage. If the props list is large and the setting complex, an inventory showing what is packed where will be useful. In fact it is helpful to pack away props according to where they are set. Transport will need to be arranged for the props and furniture.

The final positions of the furniture should be checked and measured so that they can be reset in the correct position on the stage itself.

Finally, before leaving the rehearsal room, it is important to check that nothing at all has been left behind. Tape marks must be completely removed from the floor and the space left as clean and tidy as possible.

THE GET-IN AND FIT-UP

Stage management will be involved either directly or indirectly with the get-in. Unless the production is small they are unlikely to be called on to help unload the set or to put it up, although the company manager may be in charge of the get-in on tour. On larger productions the get-in may take several weeks, commencing well before the company are ready to move from the rehearsal room.

THE ROSE TATTOO		
PLAYHOUSE THEATRE		
PRODUCTION SCHEDULE		
Monday 22nd April		
5:30 pm	Company called for Technical Rehearsal	Full Company
6:00	Stage orientation & Health & Safety briefing	
6:30	Start Technical Rehearsal	
10:30	Company break	
Tuesday 23rd April		
10:30 am	Company called	Full Company
11:00	Continue Technical Rehearsal	
1:00 pm	LUNCH	
2:15	Continue Technical Rehearsal	
5:30	Press Photo Call	as called
6:30	SUPPER	
7:10	Half-hour Call	
7:45	DRESS REHEARSAL	
10:45	Company to break	
Wednesday 24th April		
1:25 pm	Half-hour Call	Full Company
2:00	DRESS REHEARSAL	
4:30	Company Notes	
6:00	Company to break	
6:30	Crew break	
7:10	Half-hour Call	
7:45	PERFORMANCE 1	
Thursday 25th April		
AM	Rehearsals on stage	as called
PM	Rehearsals on stage	as called
5:30 pm	Company to break	
7:10 pm	Half-hour Call	Full Company
7:45 pm	PERFORMANCE 2	
Friday 26th April		
1:55 pm	Half-hour Call	Full Company
2:30 pm	MATINEE – PERFORMANCE 3	
7:25 pm	Half-hour Call	
8:00 pm	PERFORMANCE 4	
Saturday 27th April		
4:25 pm	Half-hour Call	Full Company
5:00 pm	MATINEE – PERFORMANCE 5	
7:25 pm	Half-hour Call	
8:00 pm	PERFORMANCE 6	
WEEK 2 & 3		
Rehearsals – as called throughout the week		

Evening Performances:		Matinee Performances:	
Monday to Thursday	7:45 pm	Thursday	2:30 pm
Friday & Saturday	8:00 pm	Saturday	5:00 pm

Figure 6.2 A company production schedule

Stage management may be needed early in the fit-up to mark up the stage, particularly if the positioning of some scenic elements has only been finalised during rehearsals. With a production involving several settings the position of the scenic elements, including trucks and revolves, will need to be marked in a different colour for each scene. Once the set is in place the positions of the furniture also need marking. In the US this is referred to as 'spiking'.

When putting down marks it is usual to use small L-shaped pieces of tape on the US corners, or back legs, of the object being marked. If the marks will be used in a scene change, normally under low lighting conditions, they should be positioned so that the person looking for them can set the object to them easily. Items of furniture with three or more legs only need two marks. Marks should be kept as inconspicuous as possible; the marks required for a production involving a lot of furniture can destroy the illusion of a beautifully painted floor. Yet they must be able to be seen by the crew during scene changes; bodies milling around in a semi-dark lighting state peering at the floor and shuffling bits of furniture about look equally bad. Luminous tape may be used as a solution and can now be found in several colours, though even this is not invisible when the lights are up.

During the fit-up it is a good idea for stage management to make regular checks on progress. This will help to spot any potential problems early on, particularly if any changes in the schedule are likely to affect the director and cast. Time can be usefully spent becoming familiar with the areas backstage, checking that props tables and quick-change areas are being set in the right places, and that there is enough room.

ARRIVAL OF STAGE MANAGEMENT AT THE THEATRE

The first task on arriving at a strange venue is to become familiar with the layout of the building, the dressing rooms, the toilet facilities, etc., and where to get refreshments.

The Company Production Schedule and performance times should be posted on the notice board, and details of approximate running times, taken at the final run-through, given to the theatre management and stage door keeper.

Stage management should try to get to know the local staff and learn their names as soon as they can, starting with the heads of departments. Any communication should initially be through the heads of department. Later on, as other members of the staff become familiar, it may be more appropriate to deal directly with them, but without seeming to go behind the boss's back.

The stage manager on the book should try to meet the fly crew and lighting board operator. They will become familiar during the technical rehearsal, but only as disembodied voices from above or over cans. It will be embarrassing if they aren't recognised the next time they meet in person.

Dressing rooms must also be allocated. This can be done in advance if accurate information has been sent by the theatre, but is often better left until each room can be surveyed in person. The Dressing Room List is a high priority. The wardrobe department must be able to place costumes in the correct rooms and the stage door keeper direct the company members to their rooms as they arrive.

A Dressing Room List (see *Figure 6.3*) should be posted on the company notice board and copies circulated to the stage door keeper, wardrobe and wig departments, the director, designers and theatre management. If radio microphones (mics) are to be used, the sound department will also need a copy. Each dressing room will need a card or label with the names of the occupants. These should always be typed.

THE PLAYHOUSE	
THE *ROSE TATTOO* COMPANY	
DRESSING ROOM LIST	
STAGE RIGHT	
STAGE LEVEL	
DRESSING ROOM 1	
Miss WATLING	
FIRST FLOOR	
DRESSING ROOM 2	DRESSING ROOM 3
Miss APPLEBY	Mr BROWN
Miss FIFE	Mr HUNTER
Miss OREGANO	Mr BARLEY
Miss WHITE	
SECOND FLOOR	
DRESSING ROOM 4	WARDROBE
WIGS & MAKE UP	
STAGE LEFT	
STAGE LEVEL	
DRESSING ROOM A	DRESSING ROOM B
Mr SCOTT	Miss HASTE
FIRST FLOOR	
DRESSING ROOM 5	DRESSING ROOM 6
COMPANY OFFICE	Miss COLGATE
	Miss FRIEND
SECOND FLOOR	
DRESSING ROOM 7	DRESSING ROOM 8
Master ALLY	Miss FENTON
Master PACKER	
CROSSOVER	
STAGE LEVEL	
DRESSING ROOM 9	DRESSING ROOM 10
Miss MORSE	Mr BARLEY
Miss SHYLOCK	Mr LORD
Miss STORY	
Miss TONY	

Figure 6.3 A dressing room list

DRESSING ROOM ALLOCATION

The allocation of dressing rooms is governed by a complex set of protocols and is not as obvious and easy as it might appear. A number of factors need to be taken into consideration when making the allocation dressing rooms. If in any doubt, the management or producer and director should be consulted before finalising the allocation.

These factors include:

1. Billing

An authoritative order of precedence for the company will need to be obtained from the management. The principal performer, or 'Name', will expect the room with the best facilities, normally the Number One or 'star' dressing room. Where there is more than one 'name', then their status may need to be considered. This is often indicated through their billing, which is the way each individual's name appears in the programme, on posters and outside the theatre. Status is denoted by the position of the name on the poster and by the size of lettering. A name above the title of the play denotes the highest status. This is particularly important with commercial theatre productions, though may not be an issue at all with younger or less 'star' orientated companies; but getting the precedence wrong can make life very difficult.

2. Contractual agreement

The above issue is often resolved through contractual negotiation at an early stage, particularly when stars are of equal status. Sometimes other performers will have a dressing-room clause written into their contracts, such as not sharing, access to a shower, etc. Whoever is in charge of room allocation will need to know this in order to avoid heated phone calls from irate agents.

Sometimes these requirements cannot be accommodated; there may not be the right number of rooms. In this case the problem should be explained in advance and a compromise negotiated.

3. Age

Many actors continue to perform well past normal retirement age. Older performers will appreciate being assigned to a dressing room at stage-level so that they do not have to negotiate a lot of stairs. If there is a large age gap between members of the company it is best to try to keep members of a similar age together. Although age is rarely an issue between performers, the intensity of the process can make generational differences an issue in the dressing room. A middle-aged performer may form close friendships with younger members of the company, yet still feel intimidated by their youth in the intimacy of the dressing room. This can be as simple as needing to sleep in between a matinée and evening performance while the younger members would rather chat or listen to music.

4. Disability
Any performer who has a mobility problem or who is visually impaired will appreciate being placed in a room that is easy to reach from the stage.

5. Gender
Female and male artistes will expect to be in separate rooms. In exceptional circumstances, if there is only one dressing room available, they can be asked to share but should be warned in advance.

6. Personality and compatibility
Stage management will get to know who gets on with whom through the course of the rehearsal process, although this can change during a long run. If possible, smokers should not be asked to share with non-smokers, noisy people with quiet ones, very young with very old and so on. However taking the requests of individuals into account can cause problems.
If someone asks to share with someone else it is important to make sure that both are agreeable. If one would rather not share with the other then the situation will need to be handled with a great deal of tact.

7. Costume
It is helpful to put performers with large heavy costumes, or a lot of elaborate changes, close to the stage or at least at stage-level. Bulky costumes take up space, however, and this may mean that fewer people can share a room. The wardrobe department will be able to offer advice regarding the space needed to store costumes in the dressing room.

8. Children
The rules governing child performers are very strict, depending on their age, as outlined in the Children and Young Persons Act, 1963 and the Children (Performances) Regulations, 1968, 1998 and 2000. Generally boys and girls have to be assigned separate rooms and neither can share with adults. They must also have exclusive use of their own toilet facilities. Each Local Authority will be able to supply guidelines in advance and will need to make an inspection in order to grant a licence.

9. Other factors
It is important to be sensitive to individual requirements. For instance, a

performer playing a part which requires elaborate body make-up will need access to a shower. One of the rooms may need to be set aside as a Company office, and there may be other departments such as Wigs who will need their own space.

PROPS AND FURNITURE

For stage management the main responsibility during the get-in will concern the props and furniture that have been moved from the rehearsal room, and other sources, to the theatre. Initially these will need to be stored somewhere safe; boxes of props and bulky furniture will get in the way of the scenery and lighting equipment as it is being rigged, and are in danger of getting broken. The technical manager, resident stage manager or master carpenter will be able to suggest a suitable space where stage management can unpack, check props and undertake repairs, washing-up, etc., out of everyone's way. If there is a property master, they will take this responsibility over from stage management but will need a thorough briefing.

Later, when the fit-up is nearly complete, props tables can be set in the wings as required and suitable 'working light' arranged. The lighting department will normally be able to provide subdued blue lighting for the back-stage area, but this must be checked in advance. Unless the production is on such a scale that it has a very large number of props, it is unusual for stage management to be allocated dedicated stage time for setting up the props on stage, though this can be requested as part of the schedule. The lighting plotting session is often a good time to do this, as long as other duties are not compromised.

QUICK CHANGE ROOMS

Requirements for temporary private spaces in the offstage areas for quick changes should have been established with the theatre in advance, because permission from the licensing authority may need to be sought. The actual setting-up may need tactful persistence, as three busy departments are involved: stage for the masking, props for chairs, table, mirror, etc., and electrics for light. The wardrobe department will be able to offer advice on the amount of space needed.

CUE SHEETS AND PLOTS

These need to be circulated to the heads of department, who can then assign tasks to individual members of staff. The technical manager will require a master plot of all cues that are relevant to the stage and fly staff, so that they have an overview of exactly what happens when and in what order. This will also need to be broken down into separate elements such as Flies, Trucks, Revolve and Stage, as necessary.

Cue sheets and plots must be clear and up-to-date. If there is sufficient time the stage manager should try to brief the technicians, who are unlikely to be familiar with the show, particularly if it is a touring production. This briefing will ensure a more efficient and speedier technical rehearsal and is essential once a production has moved on to the next venue on a tour.

LIGHTING REHEARSAL/PLOTTING

Once the set has been put up and the lighting rigged and focused, the next stage is to plot the lighting cues. This involves setting levels for each lantern for each lighting change and recording these on the lighting desk, and can be achieved in several different ways.

1. The lighting rehearsal

Time may be set aside in the schedule for a formal lighting rehearsal. A production desk will be set up in the auditorium and the lighting desk moved onto it so that the creative team can sit together and communicate easily. This gives the lighting designer a place to spread out the lighting plan and other associated paper work. Many lighting designers now use laptop computers and these can also be set up. The production desk will remain in place until after the technical rehearsal. During this the lighting designer, set designer and director will go through the show setting up a lighting state for each lighting cue. The stage manager on the book needs to attend, sitting next to the lighting designer and director, so that they can become familiar with each lighting state and discuss how the cues relate to the other elements. Each cue should be plotted in the Prompt Copy, together with simplified notes of what happens in each cue.

Other members of the team should be on stand-by on stage for 'walking'. This involves standing on the set in the same places as the actors and walking around the space, so that the lighting designer can see how well they are lit and patch up any holes or dark spots in the lighting. Whoever is walking should wear dark clothing, preferably black, unless some of the costumes are white, in which case the lighting designer will also need to see how these look under the lights.

While walking for lighting, the stage manager will be asked to move around the stage always facing front. As well as referring to up- and down-stage, stage left and right or PS and OP and centre stage, directions will also be given in terms of moving 'on' or 'off'. This refers to the direction in which to move rather than actually leaving or entering the space (though it can also refer to that); see *Figure 6.4*. Understanding the nuances of direction on stage will be useful throughout the process, when resetting furniture and so forth.

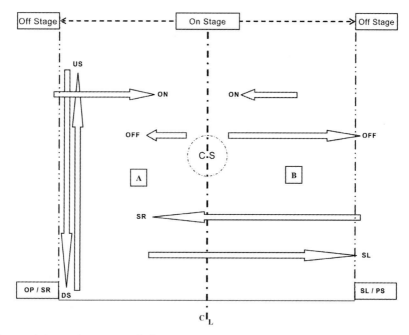

Figure 6.4 Moving around the stage

The lighting rehearsal also gives stage management the opportunity to set props backstage, as there is unlikely to be other technical work happening at the same time. Furniture can be marked if it has not already been done; some of it will almost certainly change position and need to be re-marked.

In addition the 'working lights' required back-stage can be checked and added where necessary. This can affect the overall lighting; the designer will not want blue light flooding onto the stage from the wings during a black-out. Many theatres will have an integrated system which allows working lights to be switched from white to blue, but these often need to be supplemented.

2. Plotting session

The current trend is for productions to be lit during the technical and dress rehearsals. In the hands of an experienced technician, the new generation of computerised lighting boards are very quick to programme. In order to achieve this, however, a plotting session may be organised at the end of the focus, enabling the lighting designer to set up basic lighting states without the director present.

During the technical rehearsal, the lighting designer will show their proposed states for each cue to the director and adjust them accordingly. This saves time before the technical, though not necessarily during it, and is particularly useful if a large number of moving lights are used, as these take quite a long time to programme initially.

Software such as 'WYSIWYG' can also be used to programme lights even prior to the production week. This enables the designer to simulate lighting effects in a three-dimensional and animated representation of the set. Lighting states can be set up and saved and then transferred to the lighting board.

For stage management this approach has a number of disadvantages. For example, it reduces the time that they will have to set up props and furniture and to put cues into the prompt copy. If there is to be no lighting rehearsal, it is even more important for the stage manager on the book to gain a clear picture of the positions of the lighting cues in advance of the Production Week.

Whichever method of lighting the production is to be used, the stage manager should meet with the director and designers to discuss cues in advance.

SCENE CHANGE REHEARSALS OR DRY TECHNICAL REHEARSALS

Whenever possible it is desirable to schedule in a scene change rehearsal which does not involve the company, particularly when dealing with large scene changes involving the co-ordination of several departments and potentially dangerous equipment. It also means that the crew will start the technical rehearsal with more than just a cue sheet, and this will speed things up; scene change rehearsals are usually the first things to be cancelled, however, when time gets tight.

Large and highly technological productions involving automation may have a number of days scheduled for a 'dry' technical rehearsal when all the cues are programmed and rehearsed without the presence of the cast. The stage manager on the book needs to be present for this. If this lasts for several days the cast will still need to rehearse in a rehearsal room. This will need to be covered by other members of the stage management team who will be able to use the opportunity to become more familiar with the production.

The 'dry' tech will be followed by a 'technical dress' rehearsal where the actors and their costumes are introduced into the formula.

LOCAL AUTHORITY LICENSING INSPECTION

At some point during the production period representatives of the Local Authority licensing department (see Chapters 2 and 9) may want to make an inspection. They will check specifically that the set and any electrical installations are safe and that the correct provisions have been made for special effects such as pyrotechnics, smoke, flame and smoking. They will want to be shown how any moving or automated scenery is operated and what provision has been made for the safe handling of firearms, and may want to set fire to items that could be flammable. The risk assessments that should have been forwarded to them in advance will form the basis for their inspection, but they will be on the lookout for anything else. The more information that they receive in advance the more likely they are to approve a licence; in fact they may forego a visit and grant the licence purely on the strength of the documentation. At the end of the visit they may grant a licence, signing a form which approves the production and allows it to go ahead.

The terms of the licence may allow the special effects tested but stipulate further action or restrictions. These are legally binding and must be adhered to. If any effects are added after the inspection, the Authority must be informed and an addendum to the licence granted before they can go ahead. The stage manager should be present at the inspection, along with the technical and production managers. It is they who will be responsible for making sure that the terms of the licence are adhered to.

It is worth noting Local Authority inspectors can, and do, make spot checks during the run of a production, and if they find that the letter of the licence is not being followed they have the authority to call a show to a halt, close it down and even take the company to court.

PROMPT DESK, CUE LIGHTS AND HEADSETS

The main priority for the stage manager on the book is to become familiar with the prompt desk from which they will be calling the show. They need to check visibility from the prompt desk and that cue lights and headsets are in the correct positions and working properly.

Prompt desks are generally situated in the prompt corner, which is either Prompt Side or Opposite Prompt; if the latter, it is known as a 'Bastard Prompt'. In some more modern theatres the prompt desk is situated at the rear of the auditorium, in a room or 'box' with the lighting board. In some theatres it is possible to move the prompt desk into the auditorium so that it can be operated from the production desk. This gives the stage manager on the book closer contact with the director, though they lose contact with the performers and other stage management back-stage.

Wherever the prompt desk is situated, visibility is often compromised, particularly by the scenery. If a clear view of the whole set is required, CCTV may be installed using a camera at the rear of the auditorium or suspended from one of the lighting base front of house. Infra-red cameras will allow the stage manager to see the stage reasonably clearly during the low lighting states or the black-outs often associated with scene changes. Many theatres have CCTV permanently installed but it is always worth checking in advance.

In opera houses and on musical productions, a separate camera may be needed for the conductor. The prompt desk will need a monitor so that the stage manager can see the conductor, and other monitors may be placed strategically back-stage so that the company can see the conductor when they are off-stage, especially if they are singing in the wings. Monitors may also be placed in the auditorium, often on the front of the circle. This is particularly necessary if the conductor and orchestra are not situated in an orchestra pit at the front of the stage. They may be on stage, or even in a separate room off-stage, but the cast still need to be able to follow the conductor.

Prompt desks come in a variety of different forms, from portable to built-in consoles. They can be very simple, just a series of switches which operate the cue lights, or incorporate a complete communications system including intercom, telephone, video tie-lines, buttons for operating special effects and so on. *Figures 6.5, 6.6 and 6.7* show examples of different types of prompt desk, cue lights and headsets.

a. Portable prompt desk

b. In the set-up below, the prompt copy is to the right, and the stage manager also operates sound using SFX software on a PC.

c. Console prompt desk.
This prompt desk is custom built, incorporating the communications system, back stage tannoy, a clock and stopwatch.

d. Close up of c. showing labelled switches

e. Console prompt desk with Softcue

f. Close up of Softcue desk (e.)

In e & f the Softcue unit is set into a custom built desk beneath a communications control.
The desk also has back stage paging and communications, telephone and working light controls built in and provision for a monitor.

Figure 6.5 Prompt desks

The basic prompt desk in the UK consists of two rows of switches, one red and one green, and corresponding lights (see *Figure 6.6*). The red buttons are used to warn operators of an impending cue or to place them on 'stand by', and the green to tell them when to execute the cue or 'go'. The red light may flash until a button on the remote cue light box is pressed or stabilised. Some more recent prompt desks and cue lights have amber lights as well, which come on when the red light is stabilised. In the US and some European countries, cueing systems consist solely of red lights, which are switched on for the 'warn' and off for the 'go'.

The cueing system consists of the prompt desk and a set of remote cue lights, which may be either soft- or hard-patched into the system. With a simple portable system the cue lights are attached by cables to the rear of the desk and placed at appropriate points in the theatre. More sophisticated systems utilise permanent outstations at key points in the theatre to which individual cue lights are attached. Each outstation may either be associated with a particular switch on the desk, in which case the system is hard-patched, or it can be soft-patched to link to any of the switches according to the needs of the stage manager.

Most prompt desks have a 'master' switch. Each cue light switch will have three rather than two positions; in the 'up' position the cue light links to the master. This enables several cues to be given at the same time using one button and is extremely useful if a lot of cue lights are being used (see *Figure 6.7*). The latest generation of prompt desks are programmable, incorporating one or two button operation or touch-screen technology. These enable the stage manager to record cues while still maintaining control and make it easier to call complex sequences.

If any extra cue lights are needed, for entrances, off-stage effects, scene changes, etc, these should be organised as early as possible, as should any specific working–light requirements.

a. Facilty panel with headsets & cue light

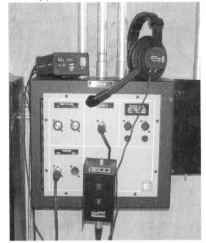

b. Close up of cue light with 2 lights

This panel also has provision for video tie-lines for monitors, sockets for blue working lights and two 'ring' options for the communications system

c. Simple facility panel with headset and cue lights only

d. Close up of cue light with 3 lights – red/amber/green

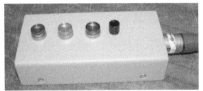

Figure 6.6 Cue lights and headsets

THE TECHNICAL PERIOD

The company should be called to arrive in good time for the technical rehearsal. They will need to find and settle in to their dressings rooms, meet their dressers if appropriate and generally find their way around the theatre. A member of stage management should make themselves available to answer any questions and make sure that company members know where everything is and have everything they need.

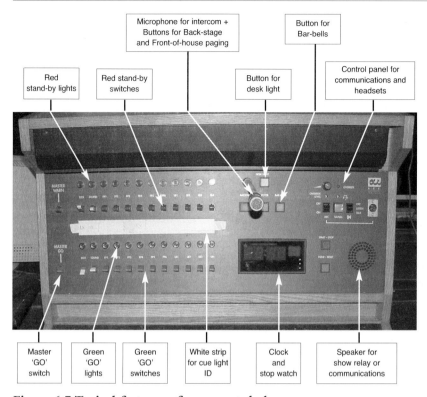

Figure 6.7 Typical features of a prompt desk

If possible time should be scheduled on stage before the technical rehearsal commences for the cast to find their way around. They will need to find the way from their dressing rooms onto each side of the stage, which is not always straightforward. Many theatres will have a 'crossover', a corridor behind the rear wall of the stage which allows quick access from up stage right to left, but this is not always the case; the route can be circuitous and may even involve crossing under the stage. When touring, the different layout and sizes of each theatre's stage area will make a difference. In one theatre there may be enough room for there to be a crossover directly up-stage of the set, in a different one the route may involve a trip outside. Sometimes there may appear to be enough room on the stage for a crossover, yet this cannot be used – someone passing up stage might cast an unwelcome shadow or cause the cyclorama to ripple. In this case physical barriers and signs will need to be installed to prevent passage.

Similarly, if members of the cast are to make entrances or exits via the auditorium, the quickest routes need to be found and the Front of House Manager informed. Many theatres have a 'Pass Door' which leads directly from back stage to the front of house but this is not always the best route as it may lead directly into the auditorium.

The Technical Rehearsal will be the first time that the cast have worked on the three-dimensional set. They will need to find out how much room there actually is, how doors and windows work, and so on. The cast will invariably think that the set is smaller than the way it was marked up in the rehearsal room, as discussed in Chapter 4.

Where the set involves moving scenery and complex scene changes the cast, and stage management, should be shown these before they actually start to work on the stage. Risk assessments concerning the cast should be made available at the Stage Door so that company members can find out what safety measures have been put in place to protect them. Any special effects involving cast members, such as flying, should be demonstrated under working lights before the technical rehearsal and the performers involved given time to practice and become confident, both in and out of costume. Steeply raked stages may also cause problems, particularly through the course of a long technical rehearsal, and the company should be given advice by an expert on how best to move around on them. If members of the cast will be required to lift or move heavy items they must be instructed in correct manual handling techniques.

In the UK the Theatre Safety Committee, a cross-industry body which monitors developments and disseminates information relating to health and safety in the theatre industry, has developed a Code of Practice for Health and Safety Demonstrations for Performers and Stage Management (see Appendix B).

THE TECHNICAL REHEARSAL

The technical rehearsal is the point at which all elements of the production come together for the first time. This is the culmination of everyone's hard work and creative endeavour. It is an exciting time demanding full concentration and a steady pace.

Many theatre practitioners believe that the 'tech' is just for the technical aspects of the production. This is true up to a point, but the technical aspects will inevitably include some re-staging as they are integral to achieving the artistic goals of a production. The act of opening a door or a letter, or walking across the stage to be in exactly the right place at exactly the right moment, is as technical as the lighting, sound and movement of scenic elements. Having the actual props in rehearsal for the cast to practise with as early as possible will minimise the likelihood of rethinks, but some glitches are unavoidable. If an actor discovers hazards on the set that were not evident in the rehearsal room, or cannot be seen by half the audience, or is masked by another actor, then it is entirely appropriate for the director to re-block the scene. This should be discovered and solved during the 'tech' rather than after a dress rehearsal.

Technical rehearsals may last several days, depending on the complexity of the production, and the days themselves may be long and intensive. The aim of the 'tech' is to rehearse all technical elements thoroughly, to develop and refine them so that they work together artistically. There is no point in rushing. Each member of the technical team must be confident that they can repeat their actions to the satisfaction of the creative team. The next time the production is run from start to finish will be at the first dress rehearsal, which may be several days later and should be approached as if it was an actual performance.

Very occasionally a director may suggest a 'cue to cue' or 'cut to cue' tech. This involves rehearsing only the cues, leaving out most of the dialogue in-between. This may be an effective use of time on a two-hander with a single set, but on anything larger it can be a false economy. Some of the more technical acting sections will inevitably be left out and the first dress will shudder to a halt as an actor finds that they can't open the door and carry the tea tray at the same time. This can be solved by following the 'cue to cue' with a 'Tech Dress' where problems can be ironed out and polished, a flawless run is not expected.

RUNNING THE 'TECH'

The 'tech' can only start when all technical elements are ready. This includes costume, furniture and all props including consumables. The cast must be able to rehearse with the actual props they will be using in performance, and the lighting designer, designer and director must be able to see everything under show conditions. If for any reason this is not possible – sometimes furniture is delivered late or a prop introduced at the last minute has still to be found – it may be acceptable to start the 'tech' as scheduled, particularly if the items are not used at the start. If there are likely to be any delays, or bits of costume or props are missing or not working properly, the director must be informed, with an estimate of when the problem will be solved. If they are crucial, however, then the tech must be delayed until they arrive. If such a delay seems likely, the stage manager must inform the director and agree a new schedule with the rest of the production team as soon as the problem is identified. Hoping it will all be all right is simply not an option.

For a simple 'tech' the stage manager will have overall authority, but will need to liaise closely with the person on the book, the director and lighting designer. With a stage management team of four, one member of the team will normally take responsibility for each side of the stage, one will run the corner, and the fourth will run the tech, acting as the link between the stage and the creative team in the auditorium. On a more complex production the stage manager will share responsibility with the technical and production managers.

Before the 'tech' can start, the stage manager must make sure that all work on stage has been completed, that everything is working and that all departments are ready. There is often a lot of pressure on technicians to continue sorting out technical issues right up to the last minute. If these are critical, rather than cosmetic, then the start may have to be delayed, otherwise the stage manager should ask for the stage to be cleared and made ready for the start. Back-stage calls may be made in the same way as with a normal performance (see Chapter 7), but it is often better to make appropriate calls giving information out to the cast as necessary. This will prevent them from having to hang around for too long should a last-minute delay become necessary.

When the stage is ready and the cast and crew have been called to the stage, the stage manager should ask for quiet, stand everybody by and then hand over to whoever is on the book, who will take over responsibility for initiating the opening sequence of the production. This is frequently the sequence that takes the longest to get right; it will be the audience's first experience of the show and therefore the way that it looks and sounds is critical.

Throughout the 'tech' it is important that nobody hesitates to ask to stop and go back over things that need working on. The director will certainly do this; in some cases they will request a microphone, or 'God mic.', so that they can be heard easily, or even a set of headphones.

The 'tech' may stop often and for many reasons. It may be because the timing of a particular sequence of cues needs changing, or is difficult to get right and needs practising. The stage manager on the book must use their judgement about whether they need to go back over a sequence or whether they can simply note any changes that need to be made and put them into action at the dress. This may be because technical problems are encountered that need solving or more practice, or for safety reasons. These will include things that the cast have to do on-stage, quick changes, and so on. It may be because the lighting needs to be adjusted and this cannot be done during the action.

If the 'tech' stops for no obvious reason the stage manager must find out the reason as quickly as possible and then inform everyone. It is far better to say that the cause of the problem is being investigated than to wait to find out. The creative team will feel cut off and get restless if they do not know what is happening and why. If the pause looks like it may be a few minutes, then the cast and crew should be asked to stand down but not to leave the stage area. If possible the stage manager should try to get an estimate of the time needed to solve the problem. They should check regularly on progress, but with tact, as their interruption may cause further delay.

When ready to start again the stage manager should liaise with the person on the book to find out a suitable point to go from and then give clear instructions to the actors where to start. This point is often earlier than expected, as stand-bys have to be given, though it must also be a suitable point for the cast. The stage must then be set back to the right point, as continuity is vital. Stage management cannot expect members of the cast to reset their props (though some may) and must be prepared to do so swiftly and accurately.

Before starting again the stage manager must check that everyone is ready, including the person calling the show. They can then ask for quiet, stand everyone by and hand over to the cast by saying something like: 'OK. Take it from [*insert line*]. In your own time. Thank you.'

It is important to remember that the director, designer and lighting designer are seeing the realisation of their visual concepts for the first time and that this is generally the first opportunity that the technical departments have to rehearse together. When the director yells that something is all wrong, when it has been done exactly as plotted, they may have changed their mind for a good reason, though without telling anyone yet. The stage manager on the book must grit their teeth, re-mark the cues and continue.

Unless the changes are minor it is a good idea to mark them on a clean sheet of paper that can be inserted in the book. Previous versions of cue sequences should always be kept and marked as to which version they are. The director may change their mind back again; if the previous sequence has been erased it will have to be set up again and time will be lost.

The stage manager on the book, the LX board operator and other technicians may be able to make a considerable creative contribution to the production during the tech. If a cue is not quite working they may be able to see a solution associated with the way it is executed. It is totally acceptable to make these suggestions. If a cue would work better if it is given one word earlier, then that can be suggested. Something simple like that does not even necessarily need to be rehearsed but can be tried at the dress.

During the 'tech' the lighting designer will adjust and add lighting cues and may even be lighting the show virtually from scratch. This can take time and may require frequent pauses. It will inevitably involve a great deal of talking over headsets. For the stage manager on the book it can be very distracting and they should have no hesitation in asking for quiet when a cueing sequence is coming up. A word at the wrong moment can mean that a cue is missed and the sequence has to start again. They may also have to insert extra cues as they are added by the lighting designer, sometimes even after the cue has been given. They will need to use their judgement, or consult the lighting designer and board operator, to decide whether they need to go back on the cue.

Scene changes will need to be rehearsed thoroughly and may need to be directed or choreographed if they are to be seen by the audience. If they have not been worked out in advance and individual roles assigned, then the 'tech' must pause while this is done. Any other technical aspects that involve the cast on stage and are associated with a certain amount of risk should be practised under working light conditions before the 'tech' continues. The cast and crew must be confident that they can make it all work before moving on to the next bit.

Quick costume changes must also be practised in real time to see whether they are possible. If they take place during a scene change, then it is wise to rehearse the scene change a few times first before adding in the quick change. If the 'tech' is called to a halt during a quick change, the change will need to be halted, the actor got back into the original costume and then started again from scratch. It is not possible to pick up from the point where it stopped, unlike lighting and sound.

The 'tech' can be a long, drawn out and potentially tedious exercise, particularly for the actors, who have been rehearsing the production for weeks. Sensitive handling is essential, as nerves can get frayed. Breaks must be scheduled and adhered to, with extra time allowed for the cast to get in and out of costume. If it looks like a problem is going to take longer to solve than originally predicted, it may be prudent to call an unscheduled break while it is being solved. Towards the end of each day the pace may begin to slow down as people get tired and lose concentration. Stage management need to find a way of maintaining their own pace, drawing on reserves of energy at the end of the day, so that they can keep the impetus going.

At the end of the 'tech', stage management must make sure that all master cue sheets and plots are updated and then circulated, and all changes confirmed.

CUES AND THE PROMPT COPY

The Prompt Copy acts as a set of instructions which should allow any stage manager using it to control the show in a set way.

The stage manager on the book is responsible for controlling most technical aspects of the production by giving cues. These must be designed to make everything happen at exactly the right time and in exactly the right order at every performance. They must be marked in the book in such a way that it is infallible. There can be no room for misinterpretation; the cue point must be described exactly and without ambiguity. This is not always easy.

The categories of cue points can be identified as follows (see *Figure 6.8*):
a. Word cue – on a word in the text
b. Timed cues – delayed by seconds, or beats, after a word or action
c. Action cues – on a piece of action, when something happens, or has happened
d. Visual cues – taken by the operator on an action, given S/By by SM but not the Go
e. Follow-ons – taken by operator as soon as previous cue is complete.
f. Word cue and cued follow-on
g. Simultaneous Word Cues
h. Word cue followed by action cue

Each cue exists to make something happen at a specific point or in a specific way. The point at which the cue is given will often be a couple of seconds before the action itself becomes evident. The 'tech' should be used to experiment with this. Often the moment that the cue becomes noticeable is not the same as its starting point; a flying piece may need to start to move some time before the audience becomes aware of it, a black-out called fractionally before the moment

a.   Word cue - on a word in the text

> If music be the food of love, play on   LXQ 2 GO (build DS)
>
> Give me excess of it, that, surfeiting,
>
> The appetite may sicken, and so die.

b.   Timed cues - delayed by seconds, or beats, after a word or action

> X - 1 Beat
>
> If music be the food of love, play on X   LXQ2 GO (build DS)
>
> Give me excess of it, that, surfeiting,
>
> The appetite may sicken, and so die.

c.   Action cues - on a piece of action, when something happens, or has happened

> As ORS turns DS
>
> If music be the food of love, play on   LXQ 2 GO (build DS)
>
> Give me excess of it, that, surfeiting,
>
> The appetite may sicken, and so die.

d.   Visual cues - taken by the operator on an action, given S/by by SM but not the Go

> As ORS turns DS
>
> If music be the food of love, play on   LXQ 2 Vis GO (build DS)
>
> Give me excess of it, that, surfeiting,
>
> The appetite may sicken, and so die.

e.   Follow-ons - taken by operator as soon as previous cue is complete.

> If music be the food of love, play on   LXQ 2 & F/on GO (build DS, f/on Ors spt↑)
>
> Give me excess of it, that, surfeiting,
>
> The appetite may sicken, and so die.

f.   Word cue and cued follow-on

> If music be the food of love, play on   LXQ 2 GO   (build DS)
>
> Give me excess of it, that, surfeiting,   F/on
>
> The appetite may sicken, and so die.   Sound Q 2 GO   (waves ↓)

g.   Simultaneous word cues

> If music be the food of love, play on   LXQ 2   GO   (build DS)
>
> Give me excess of it, that, surfeiting,   Sound Q 2.   (waves ↓)
>
> The appetite may sicken, and so die.

h.   Word cue followed by action cue

> If music be the food of love, play on   LXQ 2 GO   (build DS)
>
> Give me excess of it, that, surfeiting,   as ORS turns DS
>
> The appetite may sicken, and so die.   Sound Q 2 GO   (waves ↓)

Figure 6.8 Types of cue points

it needs to register as such. This may be due to the time it takes for something to happen, the reactions of the operator or the perception of the audience. Whoever is calling a show must be sensitive to this, and use their intuition and experiment as necessary. They must, however, be able to record what they did exactly so that they can repeat it and, more crucially, so that someone else can take over from them.

Each cue should be preceded by a stand-by. This should be long enough to enable the technician or actor to stabilise the cue light, if used, to check their cue sheet or console, and prepare to execute the cue: usually no more than a minute. The operators concerned will be able to advise about the length of stand-by that they require or prefer. If the sequence involves several actions, each technical department should be stood by at the same time. If there are a series of cues over a short period, technicians can be stood by for the whole series. The person on the book must use their discretion in this; they do not want to compromise their own ability to give the cues by cramming in stand-bys when they should be listening to the text, watching the action or giving other cues. On a very complex show with cues every few seconds, some technicians may be put on stand-by for a whole scene. This can be discussed and agreed during the 'tech' and noted on cue sheets. If any call or warning turns out to be unnecessarily long, the stage manager must liaise with the person concerned before deciding to change it.

If the gap between cues is long, the technical departments involved may need to be given back-stage calls, usually allowing them about five minutes to get to the stage (see Chapter 7). Lighting and sound desk operators would be expected to remain with their equipment throughout the performance, however, and would not need calling.

Cues can be given using cue lights, headsets or a combination of both. This may depend on the system being used, the preferences of the operators or practical considerations.

The illustration (see *Figure 6.9*) shows two pages of a prompt copy, with stand-bys, cues, calls and other instructions that enable the production to be called repeatedly in exactly the same way.

Verbal cues, given over headsets, must be given clearly and in the same form each time. The word 'Go' must be said after the cue it refers to, e.g. 'LX Q 9 Go' and not 'Go LX Q 9'. It is the word 'Go' that initiates the cue; in a complex sequence, saying 'Go' first would not tell the technicians to whom it refers, and they would either all go at once or nothing would happen. A gap of about two beats should be inserted between the cue number and the 'Go'. This enables the operator to check that they are ready and the stage manager to listen or watch out for the cue point.

If there is a chance of verbal cues being heard by the audience or on stage, e.g. from headsets in the flies, they should be kept short and quiet. In a studio

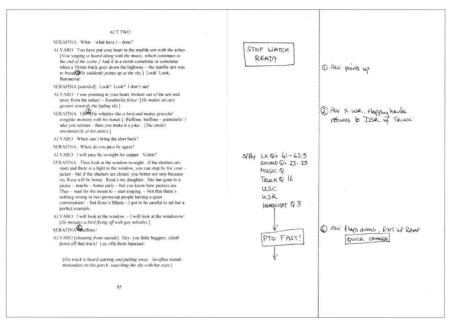

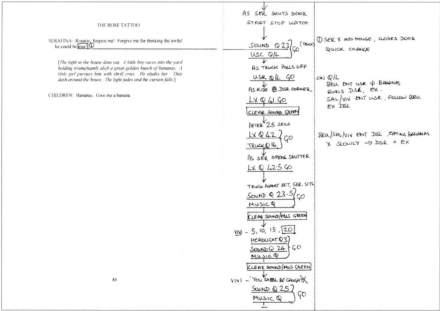

Figure 6.9 Cues in a prompt copy

theatre, where the stage manager is seated in the auditorium, it may be impossible to use headsets without distracting the audience and cast. Some sound operators will refuse to use headsets as they need to listen with both ears.

Cue lights are particularly useful for giving several cues at the same time or one after another. For instance the sequence 'LX Q 6, Sound Q 3, Fly Q 2, Truck Q 1, SL Winch Q 1, SR Winch Q 1 Go' would take about ten seconds to speak. The person cueing it would need to start speaking at least ten seconds before the cue point, which might be difficult to time accurately, particularly if relying on an action on stage. To make it work, the pause before saying 'Go' would need to be quite long. They would also need to take their eyes off the stage to read out the cues, or else learn the sequence by heart. Using cue lights, the master can be set up and one switch used at the precise moment. If the SL and SR Winch cues followed on immediately after the others, the sequence would be even more difficult to cue verbally.

When giving cues using cue lights, the stage manager should leave their finger on the 'Go' Switch (green) until they are sure that the cue has started. This will ensure that the green is not left on by mistake and the operator at the other end will not think they have been given the next cue. It should also rule out the possibility of a flashed green. Some desks have sprung switches which automatically return to the off position, while others will remain on until switched off.

Prompt desks that can be soft-patched can be set up so that the switches on the desk relate to cue lights in a logical and convenient order. The switches that relate to cue lights that are always given together can be set next to each other for ease of operation.

If a programmable desk is being used, each stand-by and go sequence becomes a new event for the stage manager, the events being numbered sequentially by the desk itself. In *Figure 6.9* the first event would be the stand-bys and these are designated as 'S/by 36', the first go (Sound Q 23 & USC Q/L) is 'Go 37', the next (USR Q/L) 'Go 38' and so on. These correspond to either the red or green master button on the desk, each event being programmed to operate the relevant cue lights. The actual cues still need to be marked in the prompt copy, as the stage manager needs to know what each event will be doing, and cue numbers should still be assigned to each technical operation.

DRESS REHEARSALS

Once the technical rehearsal has been completed the production can be rehearsed in real time. Most companies will try to schedule two to three dress rehearsals, but time will need to be allowed for any necessary technical work to be completed and for the director to give notes and rehearse specific bits of the production with the company.

Dress rehearsals should be treated as far as possible like actual performances.

Calls should be given as normal (see Chapter 7). Everyone will need to be extra alert, as the first dress rehearsal will be the first time that the technicians and cast have had the chance to experience the whole production at full pace, and it may come as a surprise. The interval between rehearsing the opening sequence and the first dress may be several days.

Stage management and crew are normally required to dress from head to toe in black when working back-stage. They may start to wear 'blacks' during the 'tech', though it isn't strictly necessary, but they must do so for the first dress onwards.

Dress rehearsals will be used to refine the production and may involve both additions and cuts. Whole scenes may be cut from new plays, including the associated scenery, props and costumes. Lighting cues may be added and cue points changed.

At the end of each dress the director and designer will normally give notes to the cast and technical staff, sometimes together, sometimes separately. The stage manager on the book should always be present at these sessions so that they too can take notes. Other members of the team may also be present. A good stage manager will be able to tell the director and designer what went wrong, what could be done better and what still needs attention. The notes session will generate a list of jobs for the next day and identify any sections that will need specific rehearsal. This will then be turned into a schedule and communicated to the relevant technicians.

PRESS AND PHOTO CALLS

A photographer is often invited to attend one of the dress rehearsals to take production photos for publicity and the programme. Many photographers specialise in production photography; they may chose to attend a prior rehearsal so that they can decide what will make the best shots. They normally try not to be intrusive, but some like to get on-stage with the cast to take close-ups. The cast and crew must always be warned that the photographer will be in attendance. The stage manager will need to liaise with them in advance, particularly if the schedule is likely to change. Sometimes production shots will be set up so that the photographer can take static images under enhanced lighting conditions, though these inevitably look staged.

Many productions will invite the press to take photographs. For this a staged photo call will need to be planned, normally prior to a dress rehearsal. This should not last much longer than half-an-hour, and the stage manager will need to work out a schedule of four to five scenes which will include all members of the cast at some point. It is often a good idea to work backwards so that the actors end up in the right costumes for the start of the dress rehearsal. Press photographers will invariably ask for the lighting to be enhanced so that they can get the shots they want that are suitable for printing in the papers.

PREVIEWS AND THE FIRST NIGHT

By the point that the production is scheduled to be performed in front of an audience, it is the actors who are all important. They are the ones who have to face the audience who have paid to see the play. Stage management must bear with them patiently and helpfully. It helps to find time to wash and look presentable. It may even be appropriate to wear evening dress (this will be expected in some situations, e.g. opera), and in any event a tidy appearance helps to give the impression that everything is under control. This also applies to the back-stage area, the prompt copy, cue sheets etc., which should be neat and tidy at all times. If possible, time spent re-writing cue sheets neatly and tidying up the prompt copy will actually make them easier to follow and make the show easier to run.

The stage manager may need to exercise tactful control over the excesses of an over-excitable director or designer. Five minutes before the curtain is scheduled to rise is not the time to give notes to actors, nor is it helpful if they come storming through the pass-door during the performance while something that has gone wrong is being sorted out. Their reaction is understandable; their reputation may rest on the success of the production and they don't want anything to mar it. A firm, but soft, confident word should turn away wrath. If things do go wrong during the performance, post-mortems should always wait until after the show.

Sometimes the production will be performed to an audience several times before the press are allowed in to review it on the opening night. These previews will allow the creative team to gauge the audience's response and to make adjustments as necessary.

THE PERFORMANCE AND BEYOND

Once the first performance has been achieved, the main focus for stage management is to manage the production. This involves running each performance, and monitoring and maintaining the quality of the production both artistically and technically. The stage manager is responsible overall for discipline both on- and off-stage.

MANAGING PERFORMANCE

In theory every performance should be the same and it is the responsibility of stage management to make sure that this is the case; in fact this is of course impossible and arguably not always even desirable. In order to minimise the risk of preventable mistakes occurring, however, each performance should be approached in exactly the same way. A number of protocols have been developed over the years and these should normally be followed by stage management and the rest of the company.

The cast, stage management and technicians should follow a routine that allows them to undertake their roles efficiently. This routine will differ, depending on the production and theatre and in response to particular requirements, but will always take the scheduled 'curtain' or 'lights' up' time as its basis.

Shown here (see *Figure 7.1*) is a summary of the procedures associated with a production on a daily basis. These are explained in more detail in the following sections.

BEFORE THE PERFORMANCE
THE RE-SET

The stage has to be re-set for every performance. On a large-scale production involving multiple settings this can be time-consuming and complex, sometimes involving as much of a shuffle backstage as on-stage. If this is not done correctly it can seriously affect the running of the performance. A piece of scenery set in the wrong place off-stage may cause problems during the show.

The re-set may take place in the morning or just prior to the performance. This will depend on the scale of the production and on the working practice of individual theatres. In the West End the theatre staff will normally be called for the re-set in the morning. This allows for rehearsals to be called for the afternoon, and for any maintenance or repairs to take place. The stage re-set is unlikely to involve stage management, though they may be required to be present at the end to check that everything is in the right place.

ACTIVITY		UK	US
Re-set and maintenance	Stage re-set for performance Maintenance undertaken Stage swept and cleaned (may wait until pre-set)		May be am or pm
Pre-set	Stage management or crew set props etc. Doors, windows, flown scenery, set in correct position Lighting and sound checked	1 hour or more After pre-set before performance	
Checks	Stage management double-check pre-set		
HALF-HOUR	Back stage call All cast and stage management must be present in the theatre unless agreed in advance Each cast member visited in dressing room Valuable property collected Personal props distributed Final stage check Blackout check Lighting and sound pre-set	7:25	7:30
House open	House curtain (if used) must be in Pre-sets must be up In some theatres a whistle is blown to open the house Backstage call to warn cast and crew not to enter the stage area until called, essential if no curtain	At an agreed time and/or when ready.	
Quarter-hour	Back stage call Any cast not present should have been contacted, or understudy placed on stand-by	7:40	7:45
Five minutes (UK)	Backstage call	7:50	
Beginners (UK) Five minutes (US)	Backstage call All members of the cast and crew involved in the opening few pages of the production called to the stage	7:55	
Front-of-house clearance	Front-of-house manager informs stage manager that the performance can commence	When all audience in	
Stand-by (UK) Places (US)	All 'Beginners' – cast, technicians and stage management on stand-by.	On FoH Clearance	
CURTAIN UP	Performance commences	8:00	
Interval	Stage set for second part Safety curtain demonstrated to audience (if appropriate) Beginners (Five in US) call only needs to be given unless scheduled interval is longer than twenty minutes		
CURTAIN DOWN	Cast and crew informed of next performance time and of any rehearsal call Valuable props etc. locked away Valuable property re-distributed to cast FoH inform SM when last audience member leaves auditorium Safety curtain brought in Performance report generated and circulated – forms basis for next day's maintenance programme.		

Figure 7.1 Summary of performance procedures (8:00 pm performance)

THE PRE-SET

For stage management the pre-set involves setting all the props and furniture in the right place both on and off-stage. As props are sometimes fragile or valuable the stage management pre-set is normally done close to the performance time. The exact timing will vary according to how long is needed, and should allow time for any last-minute repairs or adjustments to be made. It is difficult to re-set props whilst the stage staff are undertaking their re-set, as props can easily get damaged.

The props setting list should form the basis for setting props (see Chapter 8). It must be comprehensive and easy to follow, enabling stage management to set props in an efficient and methodical manner. Props must be set in exactly the same way for every performance.

Props that end up in dressing rooms, or obscure parts of the set or theatre, should be retrieved after the previous performance. Similarly, valuable or fragile props need to be stored somewhere safe, and anything that needs cleaning or adjusting retrieved and dealt with.

Small details are important; for example, audience members sitting in the front stalls will see the stage from low down, so stage management should regularly take a look from this angle to check for things like webbing hanging down under chairs. Practical objects such as cigarette lighters sometimes fail. Matches should always be set as a standby, with two or three matches sticking out of the box so that the actor doesn't actually have to open it. Soda siphons squirt very forcefully when new; with a new siphon, the pressure should be reduced by pressing the lever while holding the siphon upside down.

The lighting and sound technicians will carry out a 'rig' check and sound check before each performance, leaving themselves enough time to sort out any problems that may be revealed.

PRE-SHOW CHECKS

The stage setting and props should be checked before the 'half-hour' (see below) and again just before the house is opened, in case anything has been moved or is missing. 'Helpful' people have been known to close windows that should have been pre-set open and so on. It is important to stick to a routine so that nothing is overlooked. The stage manager must have a comprehensive checklist detailing everything that has to be checked. Nothing should be left to chance; relying on memory is certain to result in mistakes being made at some stage. Everything, and anything, that needs to be double-checked should be added to this list – nothing is too trivial.

The stage manager should check that the scenery, as well as the props and furniture, is set in the right place. This includes doors, windows and shutters which can be set open, closed or somewhere in-between. If house tabs are being used these can be brought in at this point.

The person on the book will need to check that all cue lights and headsets are working properly. This may involve the co-operation of another member of the team or other technicians.

The props setting list should form the basis for checking as well as setting props. If the props checklist is a long one, it can be covered it with clear plastic and each item ticked off with a water-based marker pen. It is also useful to carry out a 'shout check' with another member of the team, one calls out the prop and its setting, while the other checks and confirms that it is there.

At this point, as close as possible to curtain up, practical props such as lit candles, hot pots of tea or ice cubes in a bucket should be set.

If it is crucial to an actor's performance that certain props are set in a very particular way, it is helpful to encourage them to double-check this as well. Many performers will do this anyway.

THE HALF

In the United Kingdom a 'half-hour call' is giving thirty-five minutes before the performance is scheduled to start (in the US it is thirty minutes). The period from the half-hour call to curtain (or lights) up is referred to as the 'Half'.

The 'half' is generally sacrosanct – all members of the company, including stage management, should be in the theatre from the 'Half' onwards. Occasionally concessions are made, particularly if members of the cast are not required until after the interval, but this must be agreed in advance. In some theatres the technical staff will not be called for the show until five minutes before curtain-up, but there should always be someone available from the 'half' onward, in case any problems are encountered with the pre-set.

On some productions members of the cast may be called earlier for make-up, wigs or a warm-up on stage. Where this is compulsory, it constitutes an official and contractual call. The ramifications of one person being late for their wig call can be serious, even resulting in the curtain having to be delayed.

If the cast are all on-stage from the moment the audience are let into the auditorium, then the 'half' can be called thirty-five minutes before they have to be on stage. If only some cast members are pre-set on stage, two 'half-hour' calls may be given as appropriate.

At the 'half' the following back-stage announcement is made:

'Good evening (afternoon) Ladies and Gentlemen. This is your half-hour call. Half an hour please. Thank you.'

This is a generally accepted convention, though exceptions may occasionally be encountered.

If the production is in repertoire and/or the theatre is in a multi-venue complex the call might be:

'Good evening Ladies and Gentlemen of the [*insert name of play*] company. This is your half-hour call. Half an hour please. Thank you.'

or:

'Good evening Ladies and Gentlemen. This is the half-hour call for the performance of [*insert name of play*] in the [*insert name of theatre*]. Half an hour please. Thank you.'

This is the first of a series of back-stage announcements made during the 'half' that warn the company how much time they have left to get ready.

MAKING ANNOUNCEMENTS

Theatre PA (public announcement) systems are normally extremely sensitive and can pick up a whisper. Each dressing room, and other important areas, will have a speaker. As well as the PA, there may also be a show relay system which relays the show to the dressing room speakers via a microphone suspended above the stage. A volume control on each speaker will enable the show relay volume to be adjusted, but not the PA. This ensures that announcements can always be heard. When an announcement is made it overrides the show relay. In a multi-venue complex there will usually be a system whereby an announcement being made automatically takes precedence. This ensures that announcements do not get interrupted.

Calls over the PA system are usually given by the person on the book, except where this is impossible or would be distracting. It is advisable to write announcements down and then read them out. Standard calls should be written in the prompt copy, in full if necessary.

When making calls from the prompt corner it is essential to try not to be heard on stage or in the auditorium. If a call has to be made during a very quiet part of the show, a whisper should suffice. On the other hand, when making a call during a loud section it is tempting to shout, in order to be heard over the noise on stage; this is entirely unnecessary, the microphone will be sensitive enough to pick up a whisper close to it.

Calls must not be garbled or rushed; they are giving out important pieces of information and should be clear and to the point. Each piece of information should be repeated and the announcement finished off with 'Thank you'. This is particularly important when making Front of House announcements. The audience will not be expecting this and may be in a busy, noisy bar. The announcement must first attract their attention – 'Ladies & Gentlemen', allow a short pause for them to start listening and then give out the piece of information.

It is important to remember to substitute 'afternoon' for matinée performances. If understudies are performing, their names must be substituted for those of the principals.

The PA is a formal means of communication and should not to be used for private messages or by anyone else without authority. The correct protocol should be followed unless otherwise agreed.

CHECKING THE PRESENCE OF THE CAST

After the 'half' has been called the stage manager, or the designated member of stage management, should check that all members of the cast, and staff, are present in the theatre. This may be done in several ways:

1. A 'signing-in book' at the stage door. This is usually more appropriate with large casts and in large multi-venue complexes. It is often felt to be very impersonal.
2. A personal check around the dressing rooms. This should be done anyway, but with a large cast it may take half-an-hour, by which time it is too late to discover that someone is absent.
3. The cast check in with stage management at the half, say in the prompt corner. This is particularly appropriate in a small venue with a small staff.

If anyone is absent they should be contacted to find out if they are on they way. If they cannot be contacted, the next step is to warn the understudy (if there is one). The wardrobe, wig and make-up departments will also need to be informed, as will the dance captain and musical director if applicable. There may be a knock-on effect, with several members of the company having to take on different roles. If the production involves people being flown in harnesses, then the technical manger will also need to be informed. The front of house manager will also need to be informed, so that they can prepare slips for the programme, if there is time, and warn the ushers. If the missing artiste is a 'star', some of the audience may ask for their money to be refunded, although this is not actually a requirement.

The decision to place an understudy on stand-by can usually be delayed for ten to fifteen minute after the 'half' unless complex costumes, wigs or make-up are involved. The stage manager must use their discretion before making this decision, as there may be contractual implications involved in standing-by an understudy. Once on stand-by, the understudy will be due an extra payment, even if they are not required to perform, and can expect to go on. The principal, arriving late, can be required not to perform and may lose a percentage of their salary.

In the event of an understudy having to go on, the audience must be informed, either by an announcement or a slip in the programme or both. The decision must be made before the performance starts, even if the character does not appear until later in the play. Once the decision has been made, the rest of the cast must be informed via a back-stage call.

COMPANY WELFARE, PERSONAL PROPS, VALUABLES

It is customary for stage management to visit each member of the company during the 'half'. This is all part of keeping a company happy and is largely social, but it is a useful time to find out about any problems and tensions. It is also appropriate to say hello to the crew.

Any personal props should be issued to the cast individually in their dressing rooms and valuable personal possessions collected for safe keeping. These can be locked in a safe, if one is available, or kept by the stage manager in the prompt corner.

OPENING THE HOUSE

The 'house' is generally opened, and the audience allowed into the auditorium, from five to twenty minutes after the 'half'. In some theatres this will be a rigidly set time, at others it will be negotiable; always check what is expected. Whatever the system, the house should never be opened until the stage manager is satisfied that everything is ready.

FINAL STAGE CHECK

Before the audience can be let in, all props and practical aspects of the set, such as doors and anything else that seems appropriate, should be re-checked quickly. Things do get tampered with at the last minute, usually with the best of intentions.

AUDITORIUM CHECK

The stage manager should check that the auditorium is clear; sometimes a technician may have left a piece of equipment there. If necessary the technical manager or front of house staff should be asked to clear it.

LIGHTING CHECK AND PRE-SET

The lighting board operator may do a final rig check, bringing all the lights that are being used up to half their possible intensity. Some operators like to do a 'blackout' check, which involves taking all of the stage and auditorium to blackout. They can then bring up the lighting preset, including the house lights. This is good practice as it allows the stage manager to see whether any extraneous working lights have been left on, and to rectify this. The stage manager may have to ask for the pre-set to be brought up.

The sound operator should also be asked to start any pre-show music or sound effects.

HOUSE OPEN

When the stage manager is entirely satisfied that all is as it should be, they need to liaise with the front-of-house manager regarding opening the house. The front-of-house manager will generally have carried out an evacuation procedure drill with the ushers by this stage. In some instances stage management may be asked to give one long FoH bell, or even to make an announcement over the PA system; in this case the manager will usually supply any specific wording. The announcement may include a request not to use flash photography, take food or drink into the auditorium and to check that mobile phones are switched off.

It is traditional, in some theatres, for a whistle to be blown when the house is about to open.

Once the house has been opened by the FoH manager, the company need to be informed so that they know to avoid the stage area, particularly if it is an open stage. Even if a House Curtain is being used, any noise behind it will be audible in the auditorium.

The following back-stage call can be made:

'Ladies and gentlemen, the House is now open, please keep clear of the stage (or please do not cross the stage). Thank you.'

The wording should be appropriate to the situation, and will vary according to whether the theatre is a studio in the round, or a proscenium theatre using house tabs. The name of the venue may be mentioned as before if appropriate.

THE QUARTER

Fifteen minutes after the 'half' the following back-stage call should be made:

'Ladies and gentlemen, this is your quarter-hour call. Quarter of an hour (or fifteen minutes) please. Thank you.'

Many people are strict about this wording. It is tempting to call it as the 'fifteen-minute' call, yet this might upset some traditionalists.

THE FIVE (UK)

Twenty-five minutes after the 'half' (ten minutes before curtain-up), the following call should be made:

'Ladies and gentlemen, this is your five minutes call. Five minutes please. Thank you.'

BEGINNERS (UK)

'Beginners' (the 'Five' in the US) is five minutes before the show is scheduled to start and is the point at which all personnel involved in the opening few minutes of the production should assemble.

'Beginners' is announced with the following call back-stage:

'Ladies and gentlemen, this is the beginners' call for Act/Part One. Your calls please [list alphabetically using the actors' real names, women first, all members of the company involved in the first scene and subsequent scenes if need be].' Repeat.

If the full company is involved in the first scene, then call should be:

'Ladies and gentlemen, this is the beginners' call for Act/Part One. Full Company stand-by for Act/Part One please.' Repeat.

If it is the full company less a couple, then the second part can be:

'Full Company except/less [Miss..., Mr...,] stand by, etc.'

If the production is a musical or involves live musicians they should be addressed as:

'Ladies and gentlemen of the Orchestra…'

Call the technical departments:

'Stage management, lighting, sound, stage, fly, wardrobe departments [list all appropriate departments] stand by for Curtain/Lights up on Act/Part One.' Repeat

Finish off with:

'This is the beginners call for Act/Part One. Thank you.'

FRONT-OF-HOUSE CALLS AND BAR BELLS

Front-of-house calls and bar bells are designed to get the audience into the auditorium in time for curtain-up, and in order to achieve this are generally given one or two minutes early. Different theatres will have different conventions, however, and the stage manager should always check what these are.

Front-of-house calls are generally given at three, two and one minutes before curtain-up. Some theatres may require a five-minute, or even a ten-minute, call to be given. Calls warning stragglers that the performance is 'about to start' may also be given at the stage manager's discretion.

The wording of these may vary and may include a reminder to the audience not to smoke, drink or take flash photography and to turn off mobile phones. They may even be reminded to order their interval drinks in advance; if a theatre management has particular requirements, then these should give these to the stage manager in advance. In some theatres, the front-of-house manager will make all the calls and operate bar bells; the announcements may even be recorded. In small venues, however, the stage manager should be prepared to make live announcements in person.

It is important to remember that these are formal calls and are the public face that the company presents to the audience. They must be clear, precise and, above all, audible.

The three-minute warning is given either before or following the beginners' call, approximately five minutes before curtain-up. The two-minute and one-minute warnings are given at one minute intervals after this.

Three, two or one bells are rung as appropriate followed by:

'Good evening, ladies and gentlemen, would you please (kindly) take your seats (in the [insert name of] theatre), this evening's performance (of [insert name of play]) will begin (commence) in three/two/one minutes. This evening's performance will begin in three/two/one minutes. Thank you.'

The 'about to begin' warning is given one minute before curtain-up, preceded by one bar bell, and repeated at one-minute intervals until clearance is received:

'Ladies and gentlemen, would you please take your seats, this evening's performance is about to begin. This evening's performance is about to begin.

Thank you.'

During 'beginners' the stage management should check that all members of the cast and crew are present.

FRONT-OF-HOUSE CLEARANCE

Front-of-house clearance will be given to the stage manager once all the audience are seated in the auditorium, and will usually be given by the front-of-house manager. This may be done by personal contact, by telephone or any other agreed means, and is the signal that the performance can start. It may often be given directly to the member of stage management in the prompt corner, but the curtain-up procedure should not start until the stage manager gives the go-ahead.

On clearance the stage manager should inform the person on the book who should then stand by all technical departments.

STAND-BY (UK)/PLACES (USA)

The stage manager will then make some final checks. Where the team consists of three or more stage managers, it is usual to have one with responsibility for each side of stage, in which case they will liaise directly with whoever is on the book.

1. All beginners are in place, including any crew at stage level. They should be asked to 'Stand by please' ('Places, please' in the US).
2. Doors etc. on the set are preset correctly.
3. The lighting preset is correct, and all unnecessary workers are off.

Once the stage manager is confident that all beginners are standing by, including all technical departments, then they can give the go-ahead to the prompt corner and the performance can start. In order to speed up the process, and with spies in the auditorium such as a sound operator, it is sometimes possible to pre-empt clearance so that technicians and cast can be put on stand-by earlier. But it is important to remember that a long stand-by will make people lose concentration.

CURTAIN-UP

When all technical departments have acknowledged their stand-by and the cast are set the stage manager on the book can give the first cues. The time at which the show started should be noted at this point.

DURING THE PERFORMANCE

Once the performance has started the following back-stage call may be made:
'Curtain/lights up on Act/Part One.' Repeat.
Sometimes this call can be made to the front of house.

LATECOMERS

It is inevitable that some members of the audience will arrive late. If a large number are obviously late, the house may be 'held' for a few minutes until the majority have taken their seats. It is very distracting for both the cast and audience, however, if people continue to enter the auditorium every few minutes for the first half-hour or so of a performance. Instead, an appropriate moment needs to be agreed with the director at which latecomers can be allowed in to take their seats. This is usually between five and twenty minutes into the performance, and should is possible be timed to coincide with a noisy piece of action or a song or a scene change. It is not uncommon for latecomers not to be allowed in until the end of the first scene or act. The front-of-house staff will need to be warned that the moment is approaching in good time, either by giving a bell or making an announcement such as:

'This is the call for latecomers.'

It is important to be aware that bells or announcements may both be audible in the auditorium, in which case the ushers should be asked to listen out for the appropriate point themselves. If possible, latecomers should only be admitted using doors at the rear of the auditorium. If there is no appropriate moment in the first part of the show, the theatre management should be informed in advance so that they can inform the box office and post a notice in the foyer.

BACK-STAGE CALLS

Throughout the performance, calls should be given back-stage to summon members of the company and crew for their entrances or cues. These are courtesy calls but they should be written in the prompt copy during the technical rehearsal and adhered to thereafter. They must allow the actors enough time to get from their dressing room to the stage and to stand-by. As a guide this is generally about five minutes, although factors such as the layout of the theatre may make it necessary to vary. If there is less than five minutes between an actor's exit and entrance, or between cues, a call is probably not necessary; they are unlikely to go back to their dressing room or the crew room. Once calls have become established during the production period, however, the same routine should be followed at every performance. The actors and technicians must be called at the same point in the play, even if they are already in the wings – someone else may rely on that particular call as a warning before their own call. Changes are acceptable during dress rehearsals and previews, but the whole company should be made aware of this.

It is important for all concerned, however, to remember that calls are a courtesy and not a right; PA systems can break down, emergencies can happen, large chunks of dialogue can be skipped. It is the duty of every actor and technician to be aware of the progress of the play and not to rely on calls; not having heard the call is not a valid excuse for a missed entrance or cue.

Calls should take the following form:

'Miss/Mr [*insert names*] this is your call. Your call(s) please, Miss/Mr [*insert names*].'

or:

'Stage crew stand by for the change into Scene Two.' Repeat.

OTHER CALLS

There are many other circumstances where calls have to be made. Any information that needs to be communicated to the company during a performance should be given out over the PA. For example, the company made need to know if a prop or piece of scenery has broken or if a large section of the text has been missed.

If a member of the cast or crew is not standing by ready to make an entrance at the usual time, then a call for them to stand by, or to come to the stage, may be put out.

'Miss/Mr [*insert name*] stand by (to the stage) please.' Repeat.

If they still do not appear, then they should be called to stand by, or come to the stage, immediately.

'Miss/Mr [*insert name*] stand by (to the stage) immediately please.' Repeat.

If a member of the cast misses an entrance, then the following call should be made:

'Miss/Mr [*insert name*] you are off.' Repeat.

LIVE ANNOUNCEMENTS

Sometimes a stage manager may have to make a live announcement to the audience. Circumstances where such an announcement have to be made may include an understudy being put on at the last minute, a delay to the curtain going up or evacuation of the building.

A sample announcement might be:

'Ladies and gentlemen, owing to the indisposition of Miss/Mr [*insert principal's name*], at this evening's performance the part of [*insert name of character*] will be played by Miss/Mr [*insert understudy's name*]. Thank you.'

Where there is a knock-on effect, with the understudy's role having to be taken over by someone else, these should all be detailed. An understudy announcement would only need to be made when a principal player has become unable to perform during the half. With advance warning, notices can otherwise be displayed prominently in the foyer and slips placed in the programme.

An announcement of this nature would have to be made once clearance has been given and just before curtain-up. This can be a nerve-racking experience, as the audience are not expecting it and may be disappointed, and the response can sometimes be negative; groans and boos, followed by the sound of disgruntled people vacating their seats to ask for a refund. It is far worse for the understudy, who is waiting nervously back-stage listening to this response.

When making a live announcement to the audience, the stage manager should walk to DSC, then pause to attract the audience's attention. Once the noise has died down, and after a deep breath, the announcement can be made clearly, slowly and loudly. If the information is complicated it should be written down and referred to.

Occasionally the stage manager will have to delay the curtain-up because of technical or other problems. In this case the audience must be kept fully and regularly informed; there is nothing worse than sitting in an auditorium staring at a curtain while nothing happens. The audience will become disaffected, and when the show does eventually start it will be far more difficult for the cast to stimulate them. Sharing the problem with them will make them more sympathetic. If it seems possible that it will take a while to rectify the problem, then they should be given the option to return to the foyer, even to ask for a refund. With a long show, a delay of as little as fifteen minutes may mean that some audience members have to leave before the final curtain in order to catch their train home.

Very occasionally the stage manager will have to bring a performance to a halt because there has been a technical hitch, accident or fire alert. The last is the most difficult, as the cast will also be unaware of the situation and their performance will have to be interrupted. Evacuation procedures are covered in more detail in Appendix C, but the following announcement would have to be made:

'Ladies and gentlemen, I'm afraid that we have to evacuate the theatre. Please leave by the nearest exit as indicated by the ushers. Thank you.'

THE INTERVAL

Front-of-house, technical staff and cast need to be alerted approximately five minutes before the interval. The bar staff will need to get interval drinks ready, the ushers prepare to open doors to the auditorium and the stage staff prepare for any interval change. Front-of-house may be warned using one bar bell, a short call or a telephone call. Care should be taken to make sure that the bell or call cannot be heard in the auditorium.

The following announcement can be made back-stage:

'Stand by for the interval please. Stage staff, etc., stand by for the interval change.' Repeat.

In a proscenium arch theatre with a safety curtain, the curtain must be demonstrated to the audience at some point. Customarily this is done during the interval but it may also be before curtain-up or after curtain-down. It only needs to be dropped and then raised but is often conveniently used to mask noise back-stage. When the safety curtain is down for any length of time, the house tabs should be raised as a reminder. This also prevents members of the crew from banging into it through the curtains.

Interval procedures are similar to the pre-show routine.

Only the beginners' call for Act/Part Two need be given back-stage (unless the interval is very long):

'Ladies and gentlemen, this is the beginners' call for Act/Part Two.'

Front-of-house calls use the same pre-show sequence:

'Ladies and gentlemen, would you kindly return to your seats. This evening's performance will continue in three/two/one minutes/is about to continue.'

The start and finish times of the interval should be noted down by the stage manager on the book.

CURTAIN DOWN

Five minutes before the end of the performance the cast, back-stage and front-of-house staff should be warned as for the interval. The following call may be made back-stage:

'Full Company stand by for curtain down on Act/Part Two and curtain calls.' Repeat.

The curtain-down time should also be noted. This is usually taken as the final cue of the performance itself rather than the end of the curtain calls. Curtain calls themselves may be rigidly choreographed or may rely on the stage manager and principal actors judging the level of the audience's appreciation. If the latter, it is always preferable to err on the side of caution and leave the audience wanting more.

AFTER THE PERFORMANCE

The cast should be allowed enough time to return to their dressing rooms before the following back-stage call is given:

'Ladies and gentlemen, the next performance (of [*insert name of play and venue*]) will be at [*insert time, day and date*]. Repeat. Thank you and good night.'

At this point any company announcements can be made. These might include rehearsal calls, notes with the director, travel arrangements to the next venue, etc. It is really important to remind the company after the evening performance when there is a matinée the following day.

Any props left on or off-stage or in dressing rooms that might be valuable, fragile or easy to mislay should be retrieved and kept somewhere safe. If dishes or glasses need to be washed up, this should be done at the end of the show, and any table linen washed, if possible. The valuable property that has been kept safe by stage management will need to be re-distributed to cast.

The show experience is not complete for the audience until they have left the auditorium. The house-lights and any lighting state should be left up until they have all left. An open stage should be kept clear until the auditorium is clear, even on a matinée day, when the re-set time is reduced, as members of the technical staff starting their re-set can affect the audience's enjoyment. The front-of-house staff should inform stage management when the last audience member has left the auditorium by calling out 'House clear'. If house tabs are not being used, however, they can be brought in to allow the re-set to start if time is tight. It is not unheard of for the curtain-down on a matinée to happen after the 'half' has been called for the evening performance. Once the auditorium is clear, working lights can be turned on, the house tabs taken out if they are used, and the safety curtain dropped.

PERFORMANCE REPORT

A performance or show report should normally be compiled at the end of each performance. Copies should be circulated daily to the director, production manager, management and other key people; this may be the only way for them to keep in touch with the production. The report should be completed and circulated immediately after a performance so that anything that needs attention can be acted on the next day. The performance report forms a record of each performance and is the most effective way of monitoring the production.

A performance report should contain the following information:

- The name of the production
- The name of the venue
- The date of the performance
- The number of the performance from the opening night
- Whether it is a matinée or evening performance
- Timings
- Notes detailing anything different that happened and general comments
- Changes in technical staffing or cast

It is useful to the management, and cast, for stage management to monitor the duration of a performance, which can vary considerably over a run and may be an indication that quality is being compromised. The simplest timing is between curtain-up and down and the interval but it may also be useful to time each scene separately. This will make it easier to diagnose where exactly time is being lost or gained.

The running time of a performance is its total duration from curtain-up to curtain-down, including intervals, though not usually including curtain calls. The playing time is the time that the cast are actually on stage; that is, the running time excluding intervals. Both should be recorded. *Figure 7.2* shows how to work these out.

The stage manager calling the show should note down anything that happens during a performance that affects the smooth running of the show as directed by the director, designed by the designer, lit by the lighting designer, etc. All of

	LIGHTS UP	LIGHTS DOWN	PLAYING TIME	INTERVAL TIME
PART ONE	a	b	A = b − a	
INTERVAL				D = c − b
PART TWO	c	d	B = d − c	
INTERVAL				E = e − d
PART THREE	e	f	C = f − e	
TOTAL PLAYING TIME				A + B + C
TOTAL INTERVAL TIME				D + E
TOTAL RUNNING TIME				A+B+C+D+E (or f − a)

Figure 7.2 Timing a performance

these must be included in the performance report (see *Figure 7.3*). This includes understudies going on as well as any other special happenings, both artistic and technical. The stage manager should try to get to the bottom of any technical problems, find out the cause (at a suitable moment) and note it down. If it is operator error, that should be stated, including any mistakes made by the person on the book.

PERFORMANCE REPORT				
Production:	*The Rose Tattoo*			
Venue:	**Royal Theatre**			
Performance No: 6	Date: Saturday 24th April 2004		(matinée/evening) delete as applicable	
	LIGHTS UP	**LIGHTS DOWN**	**PLAYING TIME**	**INTERVAL TIME**
PART ONE	8:05 pm	8:56 pm	51 mins	
INTERVAL				18 mins
PART TWO	9:14 pm	10:32 pm	78 mins	
			TOTAL PLAYING TIME	147 mins
			TOTAL INTERVAL TIME	18 mins
			TOTAL RUNNING TIME	129 mins

NOTES

1. Miss Appleby said the offstage lines for Miss White as her voice was going
2. The novelty failed to explode
3. Mr Scott's voice was going during this evening's performance
4. The mirror got turned to face DS in the fight in Act 3 Sc. 1. It was reset during Act 3 Sc. 2.
5. Miss Watling missed the 'Guatemala' orgasm
6. The pig broke in Miss Oregano's hand just before she was to smash it to the ground
7. One set of fluorescent lights were turned off late in the final blackout – operator error
8. Miss Watling's quick change into Act 3 Sc.1 is getting longer

Comments

LX Operator: Dave Boston	Sound Operator: Rik Green

A full and very receptive house.

Signed: Karen Peterson	(DSM)	P. Smith	(SM)

CC. Director/Stage Manager/Prompt Copy/Management/Production Manager/Designers/Wardrobe/Notice Board

Figure 7.3 A performance report

A brief summary of the action being taken to solve any technical problems should be included. If something broke during the show this should be noted and the circumstances detailed. The report can then form the basis for next day's maintenance programme, and repairs can be made or replacements bought before the next performance. If something was missed out in the pre-set this should be noted, and why, including such things as sweeping or mopping the stage.

The performance report should not just note technical problems. If a performer dries, needs a prompt, misses out a section of the text, or an entrance, or paraphrases the text, these should also be included. If the problem is persistent, then a rehearsal may have to be called. It is also important to note if a performer decides to cut, or insert, a piece of action, a prop or a costume.

The stage manager should try to be sensitive and sensible, however; the odd word here or there is not a problem, unless it has an adverse affect on another performer, or on any cues.

No matter how inconsequential some of these points may seem, it is not inconceivable that they might become an issue later and it is important to keep a record. A technician constantly missing the same cue, or an actor their lines, may be subject to some form of disciplinary action. A prop or piece of scenery that breaks regularly may need to be re-made; it may even indicate a safety issue that will need correcting.

It is sometimes appropriate to note down variations in the curtain calls. Some productions may have shortened calls for matinées, but often the calls will vary in response to the audience's applause.

Changes in key personnel, particularly stage management, technical crew, lighting or sound operators and dressers, should be noted. If staff alternate on shows, a note should be made of who is doing what at each performance. This will help to identify and solve any anomalies that can be attributed to a particular person. If any members of the cast are off, that should be recorded, together with which understudy is playing their role.

The report may also include a brief comment on the show in general: how well it went, the size of the audience and how they responded. If it was a good, tight show, that is as important to note as any anomalies. If the show involves dancers, the temperature should be recorded, and it can sometimes be appropriate to record additional external factors such as weather conditions if these have affected the performance.

Accidents on or off stage should be recorded in the report but must also be entered in a special Accident Book that would normally be kept at the stage door.

THE PROMPT COPY

The member of stage management who runs the prompt corner should take personal responsibility for the prompt copy. This should never be delegated to another member of the team. When not in use, the prompt copy should be left somewhere known to other members of the stage management team, preferably locked in the stage management office. It is not advisable to leave it on the prompt desk as it could get damaged during the re-set, tampered with or even removed. The prompt copy should never, under any circumstances, be allowed to be removed from the theatre, except, of course, when the production is touring.

On a long run it is always desirable to have a duplicate prompt copy. This can be prepared by a different member of the stage management team, and may be used when relieving the person who normally runs the corner. It must be an exact duplicate in every respect and be kept up-to-date.

Sometimes stage management are required to produce a 'Bible' copy of the prompt book for archival purposes. This should contain all information concerning the production, the blocking, the cues, calls, cue and setting sheets, lighting plots, etc. It is particularly important when a long running production is to be re-cast, or an old production revived.

It is helpful to make such a copy up in coloured ink, with red for stand-by, green for go, blue for notes and black for calls and anything else. The stage manager on the book may be encouraged to ink in their own prompt copy once the production has opened and cues are unlikely to change further, although coloured inks often do not show up particularly clearly under the subdued blue light associated with a prompt desk.

Copies of lighting and sound plots and all cue sheets and setting lists should be kept with the prompt copy. The lighting master plots can be referred to if there are any errors in cues, blown lamps, etc., and discrepancies should be mentioned tactfully to the board operator. They may already know, but will be grateful if a blown lamp can be identified that cannot be seen from the lighting box. Lamps should be referred to by their circuit numbers.

When an actor says 'The lighting looks different', they are invariably right, so it is important to investigate the cause. This is particularly the case when the production is playing in repertoire or on tour, where the lighting rig will be re-focused regularly.

MAINTAINING STANDARDS

Productions are organic entities developed over a number of months and they will continue to develop until they finish. They involve a large number of people, including an audience, interacting to achieve a coherent whole. External factors will affect these interactions and the production will adjust accordingly. Personal circumstances, character, the weather, the time of year, familiarity with the production, the part of the country or world it is being performed in, are just some of a range of factors that will affect a performance.

Productions often involve complex and interacting technical effects which may also depend on the consistency of the cast's performance. A small change here, a dropped line there, may have a significant knock-on effect.

When something goes wrong it can cause an actor to dry – in which case they may need a prompt – or to 'corpse'. 'Corpsing' refers to a spontaneous fit of giggling which renders the actor, and sometimes the whole cast, unable to deliver their lines. There is little that the stage manager can do when this happens, beyond looking disapproving from the wings and telling them off afterwards.

The complexity of a production, combined with these external factors, means that things will occasionally go wrong or mistakes will be made. It is the role of stage management to minimise the potential for error and to respond swiftly and appropriately when errors do occur. They are responsible for ensuring that the show remains fresh throughout a long run. They should keep looking at scenery, props and costumes with a critical eye and arrange for any cleaning, repainting and repairs when necessary.

The performers themselves are susceptible to change, either by design or unconsciously; playing off one another, they will continue to develop beyond the first night. Sometimes this is for the better; sometimes it can be pure self-indulgence or lack of discipline. They will also respond to circumstance. A comedy may last ten to fifteen minutes longer on a Saturday night than on a mid-week matinée. When an audience laughs loud and long, an experienced actor may wait for the laughter to die down before interjecting the next line.

During a long run, familiarity with the production and the boredom that this can generate is the main challenge facing the company. The stage manager must maintain company morale while not letting standards slip. Bored performers may be tempted to alter their performance, to try out new 'business', even to try to put their fellow artistes off, causing them to 'corpse'. This is rarely acceptable, even when the production is a pantomime or comedy, and can sometimes be dangerous. Such behaviour can create tension within the company; one person's idea of fun may not be agreeable to the recipient. An exception might be when a production has been devised and involves a certain amount of improvisation.

Keeping the artistes' performance fresh is probably the most difficult part of the stage manager's job and depends on two basic requirements:
1. Becoming thoroughly familiar with the production during rehearsals as the director and cast develop it.
2. Retaining a fresh eye during the run, to detect and correct any changes for the worse that creep in to performances before they become established. If an actor disagrees that a change is 'for the worse' the problem must be referred to the director.

On long-running productions, the company or stage manager should try to watch the production regularly from the auditorium in order to monitor its consistency. This will also be one of the responsibilities of a staff director.

For the stage management team themselves, boredom can be alleviated on long runs by rotating roles. Even on a small-scale production and with a small team this can be useful, as it means that sickness can be covered and holidays taken. Learning a complicated book can be tricky, requiring familiarity with the production and clearly marked cues in the script, but it is better to plan for a member of the team to learn the book in advance rather than during the 'half' in response to illness.

FIGHT CALLS, WARM-UPS AND LINE RUNS

When a production involves any form of stage fighting, the fight should be rehearsed daily before the 'half'. A risk assessment concerning a stage fight should identify this as one of the ways of minimising risk, together with thorough rehearsal directed by an experienced fight director. If the fight involves swords or knives, these should be inspected daily and the blades changed regularly; the fight director can advise on this. If the fight involves special effects or lighting, these should be included in the rehearsal.

Stage fighting requires immense concentration on the part of the performers and is potentially very dangerous; the slightest alteration to the timing or the spatial relationship between the performers could prove nasty. The risk is not just to those actually involved in the fight. Other members of the cast who are on stage at the same time and even the audience could also be put in danger.

Many performers like to do a warm-up on stage before each performance and some companies will make this a requirement. This is particularly important when the production involves dance or is very physical. On a musical, the musical director may require the cast to participate in a vocal warm-up before the 'half'. This may be mandatory or voluntary, and it is worth noting that many performers have their own tried and tested way of warming up vocally and may resist compulsion. This should be treated with respect; they know their own voice and how to get the best out of it. Many actors will want to do a vocal warm-up even when the production does not involve singing. If they request access to the stage they should be allowed it, so long as it does not interfere with the pre-set and opening the house.

When a production is playing in repertoire or on tour and there is a gap of more than a couple of days between performances and no time for a rehearsal on stage, it may be necessary to call the cast for a line run. This can be in real time or a 'speed' run, where the objective is to say the lines as rapidly as possible. Some actors find the latter difficult, while it can help others to refresh their memories. The stage manager on the book should run this and correct any diversions from the written text.

UNDERSTUDIES

Ideally the understudies should be fully rehearsed and ready to go on by the first night, but in reality there is seldom time. It is the company or stage manager's responsibility to rehearse the understudies, unless there is an assistant director, but it is encouraging for them if the director takes some of the rehearsals. Rehearsals should be called daily until the understudies are fully rehearsed, and then once a week to keep up to scratch. Stage management will need to check with the theatre's technical staff before calling daytime rehearsals on stage during the run.

There is no established system for the principals to rehearse with the understudies and this is rarely done, although it does make sense. Understudies may well find themselves performing with the principals for the first time when they are called on to cover at a performance, which can be fairly stressful for the principals themselves. If enough warning is given before an understudy has to go on, a rehearsal with the principals can be called.

REHEARSAL CALLS
Rehearsals may be called at any point in a run, and particularly in response to problematic sections of the production identified through the performance reports. All rehearsal calls must be posted on the notice board at the stage door but it is courteous, and also saves embarrassing absences, if stage management also tell those concerned personally.

On a long run members of the cast may be replaced regularly through 'put-in' rehearsals. These may involve the whole company if there are a lot of replacements.

ADMINISTRATION
Throughout the course of a run, a certain amount of administration needs to be kept up-to-date. A petty cash float will need to be maintained so that running props can be bought and breakages replaced. Time sheets will still need to be kept to make sure that any overtime due is paid. Each member of the company will be required to take any holidays due to them during their engagement rather than at the end, and this will need careful planning to ensure that there is sufficient cover. On tour each member of the company will need to be paid the correct subsistence allowance and travelling expenses. On a foreign tour these would normally be paid in cash.

Many of these administrative tasks will be undertaken by the company manager, though other members of the team may help.

POST-PRODUCTION
Stage management's job does not finish once the final curtain has come down on the last performance.

All props and items of furniture will need to be returned to source and final bills settled. During the get-out the stage management team should concentrate on retrieving and packing up the props and furniture safely. Using the returns list created during the rehearsal phase (see Chapter 8), a returns schedule can be worked out and props should be packed in a logical manner to facilitate this.

Transport will need to be hired as appropriate and should have been included in the budget. The returns should be accompanied by a member of stage management so that proof of return can be acquired, particularly if props have been borrowed. Any breakages should be identified and paid for.

Once the props have been packed away and the cast have left, the stage management team should check each dressing room to make sure that no personal belongings have been left behind. The dressing rooms themselves and any office space should be left tidy. Before themselves leaving the building, stage management should make a final check of all areas to ensure that nothing has been overlooked. This is particularly important when on tour.

On a touring production the company manager will be expected to confirm box office receipts with the theatre manager and settle the 'Contra'. This refers to any expenses that are not included in the contract, such as telephone calls and faxes. The company manager may also have to negotiate the 'get-out' with the technical manager. Officially the crew are paid for the hours worked on the get-out, but the old tradition of negotiating a get-out fee still persists. This is now in terms of agreed hours rather than an actual price. It is also traditional for the company manager to tip the technical staff at the end of a run, to thank them for working hard and to ensure that they give a good service the next time the company visits. They are now more likely to provide refreshments for the get-out, however, for which a receipt can be obtained.

TOURING

Touring productions require a bit more organisation than others, but otherwise the main difference is that the get-in and get-out are repeated at each venue. Even this is similar to playing in a repertoire system.

Stage management need to plan to take everything that they need with them. This might include computers and printers, stationery, and all the things that would be taken for granted in a permanent base. If there are a lot of consumables, sources for these may have to be identified in advance.

If the tour is going overseas then a customs 'carnet' may have to be prepared. This identifies, and places a value on, every single item that is being transported. It may be checked off by customs officers when the containers are unloaded.

In the UK most touring theatres carry a stock of masking and lighting and sound equipment and it is usually possible to arrange to have this rigged appropriately in advance of the get-in. In the United States most theatres exist as an empty shell; each production will have to provide its own complete lighting rig and all necessary masking. Larger touring productions in the UK may also tour the whole rig with them and may use their own specialist technicians.

SUPERSTITIONS

A number of superstitions exist that stage managers should be aware of. These may seem old-fashioned but they should be respected, as many people will get upset if they are not taken seriously. Some of the superstitions originally had a practical basis.

- Do not whistle in a theatre either on-stage or backstage, unless required by the production. This has a practical history, as the flies used to be worked by sailors, who were experts at rigging and rope work. At sea they would have communicated using whistles and this continued into their theatre work; communication with the fly floor is still by means of whistles. A whistle in the wrong place and a piece of scenery might land on an actor's head.
- Do not wish a performer 'Good luck' before a show; 'Break a leg' is the accepted alternative. Opera singers may use the phrase *'voco lupe'*, Italian for 'voice of a wolf'.
- Never mention the name 'Macbeth' in a theatre, unless required to in a performance. The play itself is associated with bad luck and a number of disasters have been attributed to its staging.
- Never say the last line of a play except during a performance.
- Never use a peacock's tail feathers on stage.
- Never eat oranges or fish and chips backstage, the smell will pervade the whole theatre including the auditorium.

Transgressing any these rules may result in a forfeit, typically, leaving the stage or dressing-room, turning round three times, cursing, and not being allowed back in until invited.

STAGE PROPERTIES

Stage management are traditionally responsible for acquiring and managing stage properties (props) and furniture. This acquisition of props is referred to as 'propping'. The level of this responsibility will vary according to several factors, from the scale of the production and size of the production team to the individual skills of the stage management team. In small-scale theatre, stage management can expect to both source and make the props, often working very closely with the designer.

At the opposite end of the spectrum, in large companies, specialist 'props buyers' and makers may be employed and crew members may be detailed to set and move props on and off stage and even in the rehearsal room. In this situation the role of stage management will largely be that of a conduit for communication, relaying information from the rehearsal room to the relevant people and back again. This will include notes about changes and progress and also setting and cues. Even in this situation, however, stage management should be prepared to get involved with finding, making, preparing and setting props.

In any case stage management can expect to take an important role in deciding how to prop a show, drawing on their in-depth knowledge of the text and the requirements of the director, designer and performers.

WHAT IS A PROP?

'Furnishings, set dressings, and all items large and small which cannot be classified as scenery, electrics or wardrobe.'

- Francis Reid, *The ABC of Theatre Jargon*

This definition is less obvious than it seems and can lead to misunderstanding and, at the very worst, props failing to be acquired. The very simplest definition would be items that are neither built pieces of scenery (i.e. incorporated into the set) nor costume. There are many exceptions to this rule, however, often depending on the person whose responsibility it falls on to decide where they are to come from (usually the production manager). For instance, a garden bench built into a set as part of a wall would obviously be classed as a part of the scenery, whereas the same bench free-standing in the middle of the stage would be a piece of furniture.

Fundamentally the purpose of props is to enhance the performance, helping to set the scene and to give the characters a more rounded and personal identity. They are used by performers, referred to by performers, and form part of the environment of performance. Directors and designers will use props to establish location, character, social background, etc., when staging a production. This should always be kept in mind by anyone involved in propping a show.

It is therefore essential that stage management know what is needed throughout the process and whose responsibility it is to provide it.

TYPES OF PROP

It is useful to classify props into types; this helps to set priorities and to identify sources and setting. Before doing so, the function of each prop should be considered.

The terminology usually depends on the function of the props in question, including how or where they are set on stage. This may vary from production to production, even of the same play, and therefore should be seen as descriptive rather than definitive.

REHEARSAL PROPS OR STAND-INS

Anything used in the action should be available for the cast to use from the first rehearsal onwards, or as soon as possible after it is mentioned in notes; it is important to provide the performers, and director, with objects to 'play' with. By this process they, and the stage management, will find out exactly what props will eventually be required for the production. This is particularly important when a production is being created through the devising process. On the other hand, a director may occasionally request that props are not introduced into the rehearsal process until a later stage, as they can be distracting.

Rehearsal props should be as representative as possible; performers and directors need to experiment with the props to see how they can use them. Thus size and function are very important, particularly with furniture. A plastic chair is not the same as a comfortable upholstered armchair; it takes up less space, is sat on a different way and is usually easier to get up from. Similarly a plastic cup from a vending machine is not a suitable substitute for a glass – its function is nominally the same but it behaves differently; it is lighter, more flexible and less breakable. All of these may be important factors in the development of a performance.

It is often tempting to launch straight into searching for the actual prop but the time spent putting a stand-in into rehearsals is invariably time, and budget, saved. Nonetheless, rehearsal props should not be allowed to eat too far into the budget or time.

ACTUAL PROPS (ACTUALS)

These are the real objects that have been acquired and are actually going to be used on stage. They should be introduced into rehearsal as soon as possible, as otherwise performers may get used to the wrong item and then complain or change their minds. It is not unknown for a director to reject, or even cut, props during the technical rehearsal on the grounds that they haven't had time to rehearse with them. Anything particularly valuable, fragile, or expensive can be substituted for longer. Thus it is essential to keep the way the props are to be used in mind when introducing them to the rehearsal room.

Nevertheless the trying out, rejecting and altering of prop requirements is an essential part of the development of a production through the rehearsal process, and should be expected and allowed for. Props will be cut at the last minute, or changed, simply because they do not work artistically in the context of the performance space. The prepared 'propper' will be able to take this in their stride, even to have alternatives ready as a stand-by.

All props must be ready for the technical rehearsal. The way that the performers interact with their props on stage is as important a technical element as the lighting and sound. If props have been introduced earlier in the rehearsal process, the performers will be used to using them and this will save time.

Actual props can be broken down into the following sub-sets:

HAND PROPS
This term is used to describe any props referred to in the text, or added during the rehearsal process, which are used by the performers or are integral to their characterisation, the action or the plot. Without these, it is difficult for the director to develop the staging and the performers their characterisations. Hand props will be added, and subtracted, throughout a rehearsal period as the staging develops.

PERSONAL PROPS (PERSONALS)
Commonly confused with hand props, personals are props that are set in a performer's dressing room or costume prior to a performance. Personals are likely to change from production to production, and even during the course of the production period, as performers find out where they need to have their props set. Decisions concerning which props are personal must be made in consultation with the individual performer concerned. For instance, one performer in a production may prefer a pen to be set on a props table, while another prefers it to be set in a jacket pocket in their dressing room.

Personal props often go astray. It is prudent to collect them at the end of each performance and to reset them for the following one.

COSTUME PROPS
Some props, such as jewellery, are integral to a performer's costume and are referred to as 'costume props'. It is usual for these to be the responsibility of the costume supervisor, although items such as wallets, handbags, handkerchiefs, umbrellas, even watches, while obviously helping to define character, may be considered either costume or hand props (or both). It is important to establish whose responsibility it is to find these. A useful guide is that if the prop needs

to co-ordinate closely with the costume, for instance matching colour or style, then it can be considered costume.

Sometimes it is necessary to negotiate who takes responsibility for these ambiguous areas, particularly when working to a tight budget, or when either costume or stage management have a particularly heavy work load.

Sometimes costumes themselves have an element of the 'prop' about them, requiring the skills of the prop-maker in their construction as well as that of the costume constructor. Animal costumes, for instance, might require this level of collaboration. Masks are also frequently considered to be 'costume props'.

SET DRESSING (DRESSING)

Production design often requires props and furniture that are neither mentioned in the text nor used by the cast. Such 'dressing' might include books on library bookshelves, pictures, clocks and other ornaments on a mantlepiece, bottles and glasses behind a bar, and even the bar tables and chairs themselves.

Set dressing is an integral part of design and helps to define an environment for the cast to inhabit on stage. It can be used to define location and period and to establish character. Every single item will be interpreted by the audience and needs to be chosen with care.

Designers will appreciate a stage management team which displays a deep knowledge of the play and understanding of the period and/or design concept when dressing a set. The potential for intelligent and informed input into this part of props finding is large, and often expected by a designer, and so it is important to try to engage fully with the designer's concept. This will enable the 'propper' to make informed choices and offer alternatives that are well considered.

However it is worth noting that many designers like dressing their sets. This is often more in line with their design concept than the props that are specific to the action. Stage management should try not to let them get too carried away and to neglect making design decisions concerning the props needed for the actors to work with.

Dressing should be given a slightly lower priority than the hand props when propping a show, though it is no less important to the overall design. It is important not to devote too much time to looking for dressing items until the majority of the hand props that the actors will actually need to work with have been found. Nevertheless, dressing must not be neglected – a library with no books on its shelves ceases to be a library.

Dressing does not need to be introduced into the rehearsal process unless it is going to create a hazard or needs to be set precisely in order for the actors to find the props that they are actually going to use. Only one specific book may be taken off a shelf and used, but the others need to be there so that the actor can practise finding it and the stage management can record how it should be set.

PRACTICAL PROPS (PRACTICALS)

Any prop that has to fulfil a specific function, such as a gun that has to be fired, a candle that has to be lit, a table light that is switched on and off, is referred to as a 'practical'. The revolver that is fired is obviously 'practical' but so is the revolver that has to be cocked but not fired.

The function of a practical prop may often be in conflict with its actual everyday use. Plays are often, even usually, about unusual events, heightened emotions. Under these circumstances everyday objects may be expected to be used in an atypical way. A china cup may stand being slammed down on a table once in its lifetime, but not on a nightly basis.

Knowing that a prop is a 'practical' may affect the way that its source is identified; it may have to be made specially, or bought in large quantities.

CONSUMABLES

Consumable props are those that need to be replaced for each performance, such as food, objects that get broken within the action, blood, candles, matches, special effects. Consumables may be acquired in their entirety in advance, or bought on a daily or weekly basis as appropriate.

During the rehearsal period, consumables can be rationed and only introduced towards the end of rehearsals for runs or when specifically requested by the director. They are essential for the technical rehearsal.

RUNNING PROPS

Props, or other associated items such as batteries, that will need replenishing at regular intervals are referred to as running props. These may include consumables and some practicals, but they will not necessarily be running props as they can often be acquired in bulk for a whole run. Budget may affect this decision. Consumables that are also 'perishable', i.e. food that will go off, will inevitably be running props.

The frequency with which running props need to be replaced will vary with every production from daily, to weekly, to even longer intervals.

PROPPING: FIRST STEPS

Props can come from a range of sources, broadly divided into those that cost money and those that don't. How the stage management team approach the acquisition of props is predominantly dictated by budget, though a number of other factors will be involved.

BACKGROUND RESEARCH

Background research is essential. The more stage management know about the production, the easier it will be to make a contribution.

The text itself should be taken as the primary reference source. An in-depth knowledge of the text will help identify some of the factors that may influence the approach to finding the props. The text may identify any special or peculiar requirements, such as plates having to be smashed or blood needing to be splattered over the wall.

It is important also to research the period in which the play is set, including the art and design, clothing, music, associated with that time. Such research gives the 'propper' a clear idea about what things should look like. Photographs of more recent periods are an excellent source, as are old films and television programmes. For older periods, paintings are useful, as are museums and period buildings open to the public.

One of the main problems associated with period research is that ordinary artefacts, the things that people use from day to day, tend to be ephemeral and have not survived; they have either got broken or been discarded as they go out of fashion. Those objects that have survived are often associated with the wealthy or with ornament. Museums and houses are full of beautiful, and expensive, china but finding examples of the vessels that the servants or other members of the work force would have used to drink from is tricky. Paintings can be more helpful but even then the subjects are usually either wealthy or idealised in some way. This becomes more of a problem the earlier the period.

If the particular production is set in a different period from the one suggested by the text, number of anachronisms may well be identified. These will need to be resolved by the designer and director before any props can be acquired.

The historical events associated with the period of the play may be important influencing factors. These might be local, national or international. For instance, John Osborne's *Look Back in Anger* is set in London in 1956. At that time a Labour government which had introduced the welfare state system had just been superseded by a Conservative one. It was a time of austerity; food rationing had only ceased a couple of years earlier and cloth rationing less than a decade before. All of these factors form an important background to the plot and certainly influenced the playwright.

The location of the action is important, whether it is a particular region or country. Artefacts will look different; the furniture associated with New Orleans in the 1890s is significantly different from British furniture of the same period. There may also be a cultural aspect to the location that will make a difference. A play set in Amish country in Pennsylvania today would have very different props requirements from one set in Philadelphia.

Artefacts that are specific to a different country from the one in which the production is to be staged may be as difficult to acquire as those from an earlier period.

The social and economic background of the characters is important. They may be rich or poor, they may be proud of their heritage or ashamed of it, they may be trying to impress and to improve themselves, or pretending to be something that they aren't, they may be religious fundamentalists or liberal reformers, they may represent a minority or persecuted culture. All of these factors will have a bearing on the kinds of objects that are associated with them.

The play, or playwright, may be associated with a particular movement in art and design, literature or drama, such as Expressionism. The period in which the play is set, or was written, may also have an association with a particular style, such as the 1920s and Art Deco. The play itself may be of a particular genre, such as French farce, melodrama or pantomime. Understanding these associations is useful. The props associated with pantomime are generally larger than life, often two-dimensional, and painted in loud primary colours.

The playwright may be writing from a particular political or philosophical standpoint, or writing purely for entertainment. They may be influenced by a particular artistic movement and their work may be associated with a particular genre.

Ultimately it is the designer's artistic concept, in conjunction with the director's interpretation of the text and its staging, will be the biggest influence. Stage management should work very closely with the designer and should regard themselves as part of the creative team where props are concerned. Frequent discussion with the designer is essential. It is important to try to get inside their head, to find out what makes them tick. This requires more than simply gaining a precise visual picture of the design and all its associations, though that is essential in itself. Designers work in different ways. Some like to concentrate on the 'big' picture, leaving others (the stage management) to concentrate on the minutiae. They will happily let the stage management make decisions about how things will look, as long as this fits in with their overall concept. Other designers will wish to retain total control over every single item to be acquired. Knowing which kind of designer they are and how they like to work will save a lot of time and frustration.

SOURCING PROPS
DECIDING THE APPROPRIATE ACQUISITION METHOD
Props can be acquired from a range of different sources. They can be found, bought, borrowed, hired, made or adapted. A number of different factors will influence the appropriate approach for acquiring all the props on the props list. Background research and a detailed knowledge of the design will make some of these decisions more obvious. As with most other aspects of the production process, the initial decisions made may change later on.

BUDGET
Budget is probably the most important factor. A low budget will mean that most, if not all, of the props will have to be found for free. Even a decent budget can be stretched further by using free sources. Sometimes it is cheaper to make

a prop from scratch than to buy; at other times the opposite is the case.

AVAILABILITY

Not all props actually exist in the present or real world and it is essential to work out whether it is realistic to look for such items. Very old and very rare or unique objects will obviously be beyond any production's budget, unless good reproductions can be found. No museum or collector will lend the only example of a particular artefact to a theatre production.

Sometimes objects are no longer in fashion; last year's fad may be impossible to find the following year, nobody wants it any more, nobody is making it and nobody is selling it. Many goods are seasonal; Easter eggs are extremely hard to find in August.

Availability issues need to be identified early on. Time spent looking for things that no longer exist, are out of season or have been specifically designed for the production is time lost. If the object is old, rare or valuable, locating it is unlikely. An object that doesn't actually exist or will be impossible to find will have to be made.

DESIGN

Objects that have been specifically designed may not actually exist. This may be obvious, but isn't always. Sometimes a designer will design something that is either generic or an amalgam of several different influences and it is necessary to establish this. When a designer produces a picture, it is important to find out whether it is 'designed' or a reproduction of a real object. This should be ascertained early on; that is, whether the designs are to be used purely for guidance or whether exact copies are required. If the latter, the props will have to be made.

FUNCTION

It is a fact that theatre productions often require everyday objects to be used in an unusual way, or always to do exactly the same thing. This may be evident in the text but may also become clear during rehearsal. Props are often handled roughly, they may have to break on cue or not break at all when dropped. Performers tend to mishandle and break everyday objects that they would normally treat with care. Almost all props will suffer abnormal wear and tear. If the real thing is fragile or is used in a way for which it was not designed, it is usually better to have it made from scratch.

VALUE

Extremely valuable objects may be beyond most budgets, even to hire. If they are to be borrowed insurance may be an issue.

TIMESCALE

The amount of time available will also influence the approach to props acquisition. A short rehearsal period will mean that stage management and the designer have to be less choosy and make quick decisions. Deadlines should always be set and different alternatives explored.

Props-making takes time and this must be taken into account, particularly when props are added towards the end of the rehearsal period. Some prop-making requires an amount of experimentation, making it difficult to predict the time needed. If there is not enough time left for a new prop to be made, then an alternative solution will have to be found.

TRANSPORT

The size of furniture to be acquired should always be considered, together with the cost of transporting it. Similarly, transport must be taken into account when a particular prop is found from a source a considerable distance away. The apparent bargain may not actually be so good if transport costs are high.

QUANTITY

The quantity of a particular prop required will have an effect on the way it is acquired, particularly if individual items are liable to get broken. A beautiful bone china dinner service would have to be replaced in its entirety if just one item got broken and no spares are available. Spares, or a source for them, must always be found at the same time, particularly for a long run.

PRACTICALITY

Stage managers are rarely experienced prop makers, who can make large, complex or highly detailed objects. Prop-making is a specialist craft that takes time and is costly. If a company cannot afford to employ a specialist maker, and stage management do not have the skills, alternative options will need to be explored.

BUYING PROPS

Useful sources from which props can be bought cheaply include markets, auctions, specialist suppliers, charity shops, department stores, car boot sales, junk shops, in fact almost anywhere. The experienced 'propper' will keep a database of useful sources, including shops that have never been visited but that looked interesting when passing. No prop-shopping trip is a waste of time, even if the shopper returns empty-handed. Contacts are made, future sources are identified, and even unhelpful traders can be noted down.

However it helps to do a bit of research first. The Yellow Pages and other directories are essential reference points, both paper and on the internet. Specialist magazines are also useful, sometimes if only to identify an expert who might be able to help. It may also be necessary to identify manufacturers, suppliers or wholesalers, as they may be the only people who will be able to solve a particular problem.

When embarking on a prop-shopping outing, it is worth noting that retailers who sell the same goods tend to congregate in the same area. Most towns will have a concentration of antique shops in a particular area and it is worth finding our where this area is in advance.

It is always worth asking for a discount or the 'trade' price on antiques. Traders will often give discounts for cash and will sometimes look kindly on impoverished theatre companies. This is more likely in smaller towns where the theatre is part of the local community.

BUDGET

Props can be bought in a number of ways, depending on the size or type of organisation. It is possible to use cash, cheques, credit cards, accounts, order forms or purchase orders.

Whichever methods are used, it is essential to keep within the agreed budget which will have been established early on in the process (sometimes well before stage management become involved). It is therefore important to keep a spreadsheet with a running breakdown of the money that is being spent.

PETTY CASH

It is in the nature of props-buying that cash is often used – many props are bought on the spur of the moment, especially in markets and such like, and deals can often be done for cash payments. It is therefore necessary for stage management to raise a petty cash float against their budget. This is a sum of money which can be replenished as it is spent but which has to be accounted for at the end. On a large show this can be a considerable amount of cash.

One of the problems of petty cash floats is keeping track of spending. Twenty or thirty small purchases might be made in a day, which together total up to a significant amount of money. For accounting purposes, it is obligatory to obtain a receipt and to enter each amount onto the spreadsheet at the end of each shopping day.

RECEIPTS

Many theatre companies are registered charities and can claim back the Value Added Tax (VAT) so it is important to obtain a receipt with a VAT number, where relevant. 17.5% of a budget is a large amount to lose because someone didn't bother to make sure the VAT number was on the receipts.

The following information should be on the receipt given by the retailer; if it isn't, it should be written on:

- the name of the supplier

- the total cost of the goods
- the VAT number – the retailer should be able to supply this if it is not already on it
- what the item is
- the date
- the name of the production

Of course some traders are too small to have a VAT number, particularly in markets, where they may even be reluctant to issue a receipt. In that case a petty cash claim form can be filled out with as many of the above details as possible. It is useful to have a book of these to hand so that the trader can be asked to sign it there and then.

Production receipts should be kept separate from personal ones. A separate wallet is a good way of doing this.

During the production week, stage management will be busy setting up, running the tech and so forth, but may still have to rush out and buy last-minute props. It is very easy to forget to ask for a receipt when under pressure and they can go astray. It is also easy to lose track of petty cash spending at this stage.

Many theatre companies stick to the iron rule 'No receipt, no money'.

For accounting purposes it is not unusual for a further float to be released only up to the balance of receipts that are returned, that is, before extra cash can be raised the receipts must be returned. It is best to be realistic about the amount requested in the first place, and efficient about the way spending is accounted for. The raising or topping-up of a petty cash float is not an instant process, like going to the bank. The money has to be accounted for, cheques have to be signed and then cashed, and the process can take up to a week, so it is important to plan ahead.

Another thing to remember about petty cash is that any surplus not used is returned to the overall budget. The overall budget manager, usually the production manager, will allow only the balance, after petty cash is allowed for, to be used for other methods of payment.

At regular intervals, and at the end of a production, the petty cash float will need to be reconciled; that is, the receipts and any cash remaining are balanced against the total amount raised. If they don't add up, then the individual stage manager involved will be expected to make up the difference themselves. If a receipt has genuinely been lost, a petty cash claim form may be accepted, but too many of these and the individual's efficiency will be questioned and, at worst, they may even be under suspicion.

PURCHASE ORDERS AND COMPANY CHEQUES
Another common method of paying for props, particularly in larger organisations, is through raising a purchase order. An order form is filled in and

sent or given to the supplier, who then supplies the goods and sends out an invoice (or 'bill') which is then paid. This is particularly useful for expensive items and when dealing with large companies and it makes accounting easier too. Each order will have a number, which can be related to a production or department. Usually a company will hand over the goods on receipt of an order and then send an invoice. Sometimes payment has to accompany an order, in which case a company cheque can be raised. In this case it is essential to obtain a receipt.

As with petty cash purchases, it is important to record the amount being spent using purchase orders on the budget sheet. It is also important to beware of the 'VAT' trap here; many large suppliers will quote their prices excluding VAT. This is a bit of a shock if it hasn't been spotted, as 17.5% extra can send the props-buying over budget.

The raising of a purchase order, like a petty cash float, is not instant and has to be accounted for. It can be useful to think of a petty cash float as a purchase order for cash (this is often how it will be raised by the budget manager) except that, rather than receiving one invoice or receipt, there will be many receipts and change.

ACCOUNTS

Many long-standing theatre companies will have accounts with regular suppliers. This is usually beneficial, as the terms are often better for account holders. Occasionally a new supplier will insist that an account is opened but this should not be done without consulting the budget manager. Accounts work in exactly the same way as purchase orders; an order has to be raised and sent to the supplier, who will bill the company on a regular basis rather than sending an individual invoice. With a large production company with several productions on the go at the same time, it is essential that it is clear from the order number which costs refer to which production.

CREDIT CARDS, PERSONAL CHEQUES OR CASH

Very occasionally a company will have a company credit card which can be used. It can also be tempting to use personal money, and then ask for recompense at the end. In an emergency that is acceptable but the individual will need to be very disciplined about keeping track of spending, and the gap between spending the money and reimbursement may be quite long. In exceptional cases a company may refuse to reimburse an individual, on the grounds that the the spending was not authorised; it is best to avoid this method unless there really is no alternative.

HIRING PROPS

A surprisingly large number of props hire companies exist, particularly in London, where they tend to service mainly the TV and film companies. Hire companies can prove expensive for theatre budgets, however, and hiring is never suitable for long runs; it is often cheaper to buy an item than to hire it for a long period.

Each company tends to specialise in a particular period or types of props or furniture, so it is worth shopping around to get to know their stock. They often have original items, but are increasingly making their own reproductions to order. The range and quantity of stock is usually huge and thus it is essential to know exactly what is needed; when faced with several thousand chairs it is important to be able to describe or point out a range of possibilities. Some companies have begun to put their catalogue online so that items can be chosen and booked over the internet.

Hire companies generally charge a percentage of the value of the items per week and this percentage decreases the longer the period of hire. They will sometimes offer preferential rates for theatre companies, or will come to some arrangement. Hire companies can be useful for obtaining very rare, expensive or specialist items but, because of their cost, are normally a last resort for theatre companies.

It is useful for stage managers to keep a detailed record of every hire company visited, the sort of stock they carry and their terms. Even if they don't have what is needed for one production they may be useful for another.

MAKING AND ADAPTING PROPS

A number of factors need to be considered when deciding whether or not a prop should be made. These factors can change during a rehearsal period, so that a found prop will suddenly need to become a make. Made props are still part of the props list and as such should still be under the overall supervision of stage management, who will need to check on progress regularly. Liaison between stage management and prop-makers is therefore crucial; prop-makers are part of the same team, working toward the same end. The actors too may need to interact with a prop, have body casts made, be fitted or be instructed in how it works.

There will always be a certain number of props that can be made by stage management, whether they are skilled makers or not. Letters and documents, for instance, do not need the services of a professional prop-maker, yet they must look authentic. If an actor has to read from a document, it will normally need to contain the exact text, legibly written. The actor involved can be asked to write it in their handwriting but that is not always appropriate, particularly when dealing with period script. While calligraphy is a useful skill to have, it is now possible to download convincing handwritten fonts over the internet. If the actor does not need to read aloud, the writing should still be coherent and legible, but never distracting. It is always best to involve the actor in choosing their own text.

When deciding who should make a prop, it is important not to take on something that is beyond the individual stage manager's abilities. This will take up too much time, diverting a valuable member of the team away from more fruitful duties, and will certainly result in a sub-standard product. On a smallscale production, where the budget precludes the services of a prop-maker, the designer can always be asked to be involved in any making, or a compromise found.

Food that has to be eaten will often need to be prepared by stage management. This is rarely straightforward, as it must be easy to eat on-stage while actors are delivering their lines, yet look convincingly like the real thing. Anything that is difficult to chew or is very cloying is not practicable; equally, performers may be vegetarian, have strict religious requirements or food allergies, all of which must be taken into account. A convincing steak can be made from dark rye bread, bacon from thinly sliced banana with red food colouring.

Stage drinks may also need careful consideration. Alcohol cannot be consumed on-stage and non-alcoholic alternatives are not always appropriate. Fruit cordials, cold tea, burnt sugar (available from some pharmacists), gravy browning and food colourings can all be used instead; experiment will be needed and a formula noted down. The most important factor to consider is that they must be palatable but it is also worth noting that a drink that looks convincing in the props room may look less so under stage lighting. Burnt sugar and cold tea have a tendency to go cloudy and will need to be replaced regularly. Some champagne houses will supply 'stage champagne', usually ginger ale. This has roughly the same effervescent effect as real champagne but tends to lose its fizz quite quickly and also to go off if kept too long.

It may be appropriate to find or buy an item and then to adapt it to suit the design; this is often the case when objects have to be made to look older than they are, or much used. This process is called 'breaking down' and will often be carried out by stage management. Adapting may involve close collaboration between stage management, who will be doing the finding, and the makers, who will be responsible for the adaptation.

PROPS FOR FREE

The first thing to realise is that there really is 'No such thing as a free lunch'. Obtaining props for nothing takes time and money, telephone calls (hundreds of them sometimes), bus fares, insurance and so on. This has traditionally been the main approach used by stage management to acquire props; it is amazing how a limited budget can be eked out and how much can actually be obtained for little or no cost.

The main drawback is that choice is likely to be limited. When the budget is very tight, or non-existent, and finding props for nothing is the only option, it is essential to make sure that the director and designer are aware that they are unlikely to get exactly what they want.

FINDING

Many theatre companies will have a props and furniture store and there may be hidden wonders tucked away at the back. With a bit of adaptation and refurbishment, old items can be made to look as good as new. The props store should always be the first place to look, not least for the rehearsal props.

Municipal tips and skips can be a useful source but it is actually illegal to remove anything from them; the contents of a skip are legally the property of the owners of the skip. It is important to always ask permission of the foreman at a tip.

DONATIONS AND LOANS

Many suppliers and manufacturers, both big and small, and individuals will donate or lend props for theatre productions. It is always worth a try, although this usually requires a lot of detective work with directories and a lot of telephone calls. Local contacts are good to nurture, but large companies can also be helpful. It is usually better to try to find the main distributor, or the manufacturer or head office of the parent company, rather than a small retailer.

When trying to borrow a prop or asking for a donation, it is essential to be polite and businesslike; this is, after all, a business transaction. When making contact, it is wise to try to establish that the person contacted can actually authorise the loan or gift. It is frustrating to waste hours buttering up the warehouseman only to find that the foreman holds the veto. Appealing to their vanity and sense of community is a useful approach; most people like to think that they are helping to sponsor the arts, or are putting something back into their local community. In the case of a large company, the Public Relations or Marketing department will normally be able to help; in effect it is smallscale sponsorship that is being sought and many large companies will have a budget for this kind of sponsorship. Supermarket chains will often donate vouchers for food. Some people, however, will just not take the bait.

Once contact has been made, it is important to get the name of the person being dealt with and to have precise details of the props being requested; giving the model name and number of the object required is much better than just asking to borrow a generic one.

The supplier must be made fully aware that, theatre being what it is, their item may not actually get used. They must also be told what the item is to be used for; it is essential to be honest. Sometimes the item that arrives will be the wrong one, particularly if the deal is done by telephone or letter.

If approaches over the telephone or in person are successful, they must always be followed up with a covering letter. This is a business letter and must be coherent and spelt correctly. Many companies will ask for a request to be made in writing on official notepaper in order to establish that it is legitimate.

The value of any item to be borrowed must be checked and also whether or not they are covered by the theatre's insurance. If goods borrowed are not covered, a special insurance policy may have to be taken out. Some companies will ask for proof that their items are covered.

If a supplier is reluctant to lend a prop, they may agree to sale or return. This is, in effect, the same as putting down a deposit, which is returned at the end if the object is in the same condition as the beginning. If it is likely to get damaged, or even subject to excessive wear and tear, then the loan or sale or return routes are not viable options; they will cost more in the end both financially and in loss of goodwill.

It is imperative to keep track of where borrowed props have come from. A 'master borrows list' or 'borrows book' should be kept and a returns list drawn up. This is particularly important if more than one person is involved in props finding.

Even if the right items cannot be borrowed, the contacts made will always be useful. Many theatre companies will keep an up-to-date contacts book so that stage management can use the appropriate sources for future productions. The props list is a good starting point, with sources marked against each item. It is essential to keep an up-to-date list of all contacts made for each prop, particularly if several members of the team are engaged in propping. This will ensure that the same ground does not get covered twice, which is embarrassing as well as time-wasting, and also covers the team if one member falls ill.

Some productions may have an industrial sponsor who will supply items rather than funding. This is generally arranged well in advance and is out of the hands of stage management, though they need to know about it.

WHAT IS IN IT FOR THE DONORS?

Most people will expect something in return, and there are a number of things that can be offered. There are also a number of things that they may ask for that stage management cannot authorise. To avoid embarrassment, stage management must not make any promises that cannot be kept.

It is important to always write a thank-you letter and send a copy of the programme to the supplier. These are business transactions; if a supplier is upset, they may never be able to be used again and the contact will have been spoiled for any future stage management.

A credit in the programme can always be offered, but it is important to check that the deadline for credits has not passed, particularly with last-minute additions to the props list. If the deadline has been reached, the situation must be explained to the supplier; it is usually appropriate to offer to put up a notice or display in the foyer. This is often a good tactic anyway, as more of the audience are likely to see it.

The wording of credits is important. Stage management should check how the company wishes to be credited and double-check any spelling. Some companies may have a logo that they would like to go in the programme, if that is possible. A 'credits' list should be compiled that can be checked and updated at a glance and handed over to the people in charge of the programme at the right time.

Advertising is rarely something that stage management can offer; if a company asks for advertising space they must be referred to whoever is responsible for marketing. Advertising, whether in a programme or elsewhere, is a major source of income and space in the programme will have been sold well in advance. This is not a decision that the stage management can make.

It is sometimes appropriate to offer complementary tickets. Many theatre companies will have a policy regarding the issuing of comps which must be checked before they can be offered. There is rarely an unlimited supply for every performance and they are often restricted to certain days. However it is worth knowing that a number of 'House Seats' will be kept free until the evening of a performance. These are specifically for production personnel and VIP's, but can sometimes be used for last minute comps.

As a general rule comps should not be sent out; it is better to have tickets collected from the box office. Surprisingly, free tickets are often not used, and empty theatre seats that could have been sold do not endear stage management to the box office staff and management. When offering comps, it should always be emphasised that tickets are subject to demand and that if they are not collected by a certain time they are likely to be resold.

Before offering comps, it is wise also to consider the cost price of the items compared with the price of two tickets. If the tickets cost more, no saving has been made, but it may still be worth it to keep a regular, or potentially useful, supplier happy. If a donor asks for comps, they should be given them.

RETURNS

The date of return of hired or loaned items must be arranged with the supplier at the time of the initial transaction and must be honoured. This information should be recorded in the 'master borrows list' which can be used to organise returns logically. A realistic amount of time should be allowed; a large number of returns spread over a wide area may take a couple of days or may need to involve several people in different vans. The route should be planned in advance and the schedule adhered to.

If something cannot be returned at the arranged time, this may cause embarrassment and lose a good contact. Hire companies may charge an extra week's hire; if, for some reason, a return cannot be made at the agreed time or even on the agreed day, the supplier must be contacted as soon as possible.

Unfortunately accidents do happen and things do get broken, damaged through constant use and lost. It is important to be honest, informing the supplier as soon the damage is noticed and offering to pay for replacement or repairs. This may also be covered by the theatre company's insurance.

It is always necessary to get whoever receives the returned prop to sign a piece of paper saying that the items have been returned in good order. This is the only source of proof if the return is disputed later. It is not unknown for an item to go missing from reception areas and, without a receipt, there is no proof that it was returned. Some theatre companies will have a standard form for use when borrowing and returning props, which can be kept in a loose-leaf file as the master Borrows list.

WORKING WITH THE DESIGNER, DIRECTOR AND CAST

The designer is the main point of reference for the way props should look; stage management should work closely with the designer, consulting them regularly and involving them in all decisions. They should aim to build up a relationship of trust by putting forward suggestions regarding props that fit in with the designer's vision. This is where thorough background research pays dividends; an engaged and informed stage manager can make a considerable creative contribution to the process of props finding, and designer who trusts the stage manager's understanding of the design concept may give them a lot of leeway in making decisions about props. This will only work if the stage manager is seen to be striving at all times to find the perfect objects to complement the design.

A prop should never be acquired without first consulting the designer, unless it is very clear what is needed. If the 'perfect' item will be lost unless it is bought immediately and there is no time to consult the designer, then the stage manager should explain the situation to the trader, buy it and make sure that it can be returned if it is not right. Digital cameras are a very useful tool here as they enable the stage manager to photograph an item, with permission, and then show a copy to the designer the same day, either personally or via the internet. This means that meetings can be less frequent and decisions can be made quickly. The new generation of mobile phones with built-in cameras has made it possible for almost instant decisions to be made.

When a prop is added or changed during rehearsals, the designer must always be consulted before it can be acquired; if they disagree with the change, it is for them to liaise with the director and/or performer. If the designer decides to change a prop, they should always do this in consultation with the director. If stage management detect that this has not been the case, then they must, tactfully, make sure that it happens.

The cast are the people who have to use the props and furniture, so their involvement is important and they must always be given the option to try out and veto any prop that they have to use. A prop may need to have a specific function or be used in a particular way; the performers need to be able to practise with this and, if they are unable to make it work properly, it may need to be changed. It is far better that this happens during the rehearsal period than during the tech.

Props may add to an actor's characterisation; they may say something like 'I would like my character to smoke a pipe'. This should not be ignored; the director should be consulted first and then a rehearsal pipe provided.

Performers may also have particular preferences or needs, such as wanting to smoke a particular brand of cigarette, dietary requirements, ethical or religious considerations. These must be taken seriously and it is always a good tactic to ask individual members of the cast if they have any particular preferences.

Some actors will invent props to help them establish a character, and then jettison them later on in the rehearsal period. Directors may go along with this, but time should not be wasted trying to find 'actual' props that will never really be needed. If the issue is in doubt, it should be checked with the director and then confirmed with the designer.

REHEARSAL NOTES

Rehearsal notes are the best way of circulating information from the rehearsal room and should be generated on a daily basis even if there are only a few notes to circulate. They should include all additions to and subtractions from the props list, as well as any changes, and any further information and perceived problems should also be noted. Through the rehearsal process the exact quantity size or function of a prop may be confirmed or require changing. Anything that occurs with a prop in rehearsal that may later prove to be a problem needs to be aired as soon as it is identified, so that an appropriate solution can be found. Notes may also be used to make specific requests and to confirm something that was mentioned earlier (see *Figure 5.8*).

All rehearsal notes should be confirmed with the director before they are circulated and then double-checked with the designer. The designer needs to be clear about the director's intentions before the notes are acted on. If the designer disagrees, or wants to make a change, then they must discuss it with the director and agree on a decision before the props can be acquired.

The following set of consecutive notes demonstrates how these can affect the approach to the acquisition of a prop.
1. 'The sewing machine should be treadle-operated' – provides information about, or confirmation of, the type needed.
2. 'The treadle must be quiet' – specific request. The machine found may need adapting.
3. 'The sewing machine is being pushed aside in the fight' – it may get damaged, it can't be too heavy. This probably rules out hiring or borrowing.
4. 'The sound of the sewing machine will need to be amplified' – this will involve collaboration with the sound department: if a recording is used it will need careful cueing; if the sound is to be live a microphone and speaker may need to be hidden. As the machine is being pushed about in

the fight it may be difficult, and potentially dangerous, to conceal cables.

5. 'The sewing machine must look broken at the end of the fight, possibly the cable from the treadle can break' – a very specific requirement. The machine will need to be adapted. The cable for the treadle may become a running prop.

6. 'The blouse will not actually be sewn but must look as though it is. At the end of the scene it must look as though it has been completed. A partly finished blouse may have to be swapped with a finished one during the scene' – the machine will definitely need to be adapted so that it appears to be being used to sew the blouse. The costume department is now involved too, and a way of concealing a finished blouse may need to be found.

In this sequence, the sewing machine has moved from being quite a simple find to something with more exacting requirements. The timescale has changed, as the machine now needs to be adapted and may need to be worked on by sound, who will need to see the actual machine before they can make any decisions regarding speakers and a microphone.

THE PROPS LIST

The props list (see *Figures 3.3* and *4.2*) is the main source of reference for alterations coming out of rehearsal and communicated via the rehearsal notes. Only one version of the props list should be used at any one time, but it should be updated daily and circulated regularly.

The props list can be used to keep track of sources, that is, whether props are to be bought, donated, borrowed, hired, made or adapted. Specific information about the potential source of each item can be entered and updated as necessary. This may change throughout the process and so details of progress can also be entered, including whose responsibility each prop is, whether the source has been confirmed, and when they are being collected or delivered. Priorities may change as the needs of the actors and production change throughout the rehearsal period, and these can be noted on the list.

The list must be kept up-to-date with all this information and circulated to all relevant people, especially the director, designer, stage and production managers. This will enable all personnel to check that nothing has been missed, to identify problem areas and to check priorities.

Some stage management teams find it useful to enlarge the props list and stick it on the wall of their office for easy reference. This means that everyone will definitely be working from the same list and it is good for morale, as more ticks appear when props are acquired.

On a big show it can be useful to organise a 'props parade' with the designer and director before the end of the rehearsal period. All the actual props can be reviewed and anything that has been overlooked, or that is unsuitable, can be put right.

PROPS SETTING

The final aspect of props concerns their setting on stage and back-stage, and moving them during and between scenes. Throughout the rehearsal period, stage management will be able to note down how props are to be set. Where feasible they should try to set off-stage props in roughly the same position as they will be set in the theatre, which will help the cast get used to finding them. Toward the end of the rehearsal period this can be turned into a definitive setting list, which will be used to set the props on stage for the technical rehearsal. The only props that are likely to be missing will be set dressing that will be added by the designer once the set is on stage. The setting list is likely to change during the production week and should be updated accordingly.

Initially the props list can be used to note down settings, but the final setting list must be easy and logical to follow. It is usual to divide the list into areas of the stage, so that props can be set in a logical and efficient order; it will not be possible to do this using the props list unless it is very short. If the props list is a spreadsheet on a computer, however, an extra column can be included for the setting, and the props can be sorted by where they will be set rather than chronologically. The setting list must enable stage management, or props staff, to set props in exactly the right position for every performance. Nothing can be left to chance. The list must be detailed and unambiguous.

Diagrams and photographs can be included to help precise setting, together with measurements to help furniture setting as necessary (see *Figure 8.1i*)

i. Setting list

STAGE RIGHT PROPS TABLE		
Rag Doll (Vivi)		
Hoop (Salvatore)		
Basket	*containing*	White bags of herbs
Besom (Strega)		
Broken rope		
Piece of rose silk		
Paper bag, for rose silk		
Purse (Estell),	*containing*	Piece of paper with measurements written on it and pin attached to it
5 x rosaries		
Bunch of chrysanthemums		
Money		
Flat iron		
Rolling pin		
Shopping in bag (Peppina)		
Shopping in bag (Giuseppina)		
Brief case	*containing*	Novelty, practical
Dressing		

ii. Diagram showing props set on a table on stage

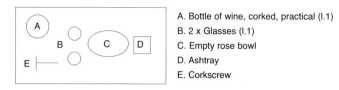

A. Bottle of wine, corked, practical (I.1)

B. 2 x Glasses (I.1)

C. Empty rose bowl

D. Ashtray

E. Corkscrew

iii. Diagram showing props set on a props table off stage

STAGE RIGHT PROPS TABLE

Basket containing bag of herbs		Shopping bag – Peppina		Shopping bag – Guiseppina		Briefcase containing Novelty & dressing		
Rag doll (V.vi)	Broken rope	Paper bag	Rosaries x 5	Chrysanth-emums		Rolling pin		
		Rose	Estelle's purse			Flat iron	Money

Hoop (Salvatore) – leaning against L end

Besom (Strega) – leaning against L end

Estelle's purse cont: Piece of paper with measurements on it and pin attached

Figure 8.1 Props setting

Props tables off-stage should always be set in the same way. To make this easier to set, the props table itself can be marked up with tape and labelled so that the right props can be set in exactly the right position and the cast will always be able to find them (*see Figure 8.1ii*). On tour a piece of black cloth can be marked and set on any table.

The props setting list should include the personal props, and it can be helpful to note where they will be found at the end of a show so that they can be retrieved. A list of running props is also useful, noting how often they need to be replaced and how they should appear on stage. This is particularly important for bottles of drink which may not be full, or candles which may need to be unused at the start of each show or appear to be part used already.

SAFE PRACTICE

In the United Kingdom and European Union all employees have both rights and obligations under health and safety legislation. Stage management rarely have overall responsibility for Health and Safety on a production, but are nevertheless obliged to consider those aspects that may affect themselves and their colleagues.

From the first design meeting onwards, they should be on the lookout for potential safety hazards and suggest solutions. In the rehearsal room they are responsible for alerting the company to any hazards or potentially dangerous activities and ensuring that these are dealt with properly; this extends to any intended activities on stage. These should be noted, assessed and the information passed on through rehearsal notes and production meetings.

Performers will often try out new moves themselves, or as suggested by the director, that may have implications for their health and safety. These may seem fine in the rehearsal room but may prove problematic when transferred to the set on stage over a long run. The stage management must have a detailed knowledge of the set so that they can offer advice and remind the cast and director of the potential hazards. A physical activity that seems fine on the flat rehearsal room floor may be very different on a steeply raked stage.

In the theatre, stage management must be aware of the potential hazards at all times. The cast must be alerted to these and precautions put in place to prevent accidents. The stage manager must be familiar with any safety precautions that have been put in place regarding the set and special effects; with the fire and evacuation procedures; and with the identity and whereabouts of designated First Aiders. Appendix D is a guidance note drawn up by the ABTT (Association of British Theatre Technicians) which outlines common areas of potential risk associated with stages and productions and suggests suitable precautions.

The key to the successful management of health and safety is through risk assessment. Stage management should become familiar with risk assessment procedures and carry out assessments of any hazards that they identify during the rehearsal process. These would include obvious hazards such as smoking and the use of live flame, but might also include some physical activities, difficult exits or entrances, and so forth. If there is a potential risk associated with an activity, it should be assessed. To put this in context, however, it is not necessary to assess every activity, only those that have an obvious danger associated with them, are unusual, or take place under unusual circumstances. Safe practice is above all about thinking and behaving responsibly at all times. Each individual should consider their own safety and that of others wherever they are working.

LEGAL REQUIREMENTS
REGULATIONS

The theatre industry is subject to the same regulations as any other. The regulations that apply to safe practice are laws approved by Parliament and are usually made under the Health and Safety at Work Act 1974, following proposals from the Health and Safety Commission (HSC). They may also be based on EC directives.

The Health and Safety at Work Act, and general duties set out in the Management of Health and Safety at Work Regulations 1992, are goal-setting and leave employers freedom to decide how to control risks which they themselves identify. Advice may be given through Guidance Notes and Approved Codes of Practice, but employers are free to take other measures provided they do what is reasonably practicable. However some risks are either so great, or the proper control measures so costly, that it is not thought to be appropriate to give employers discretion in deciding what to do about them. The regulations identify these risks and specify the arrangements that must be put in place. The requirements may be absolute; the arrangements must be made without qualification whether they are reasonably practicable or not.

Some regulations apply to all industries; for example, Manual Handling Regulations apply wherever objects are moved by hand or physical effort. Other regulations may be specific to certain industries or specialist activities.

The Health and Safety at Work Act applies to every work activity, setting out the general responsibilities which employers have towards employees and members of the public, and which employees have to themselves and to each other. These are qualified by the principle of 'so far as is reasonably practicable'; the degree of risk in a particular activity needs to be balanced against the time, trouble, cost and physical difficulty that may be associated with the measures needed to avoid or reduce the risk.

The Management of Health and Safety at Work Regulations 1992 sets out to make the employer's responsibilities for managing health and safety more explicit. Under these Management Regulations, employers are required to carry out *risk assessments*. If five or more people are employed, any significant findings of the risk assessments must be recorded.

Employers must control the risks to health and safety that arise from the work activity, and make provision for the welfare of their employees. They must take account of who does the work, what training and supervision may be needed, what equipment and materials will be used, where the work is taking place and so on. They must ensure that the arrangements required are put in place. The employer is also responsible for the health and safety of others who may be affected by the work – such as the audience.

In a theatre company the producer, artistic director or theatre manager will have overall responsibility for ensuring health and safety. Under the

Construction, Design and Management (CDM) regulations which came into force in 1995, a clear 'duty of care' is placed upon the artistic and design aspect as well as upon the way this is realised. Although there is still debate about how this applies to theatre, it is arguable that designers and directors should be responsible for health and safety on their particular productions. Normally, however, responsibility for risk assessment will be delegated to their representatives with the relevant experience, including the production manager, technical manager and stage management. Experts may be called in to advise on the health and safety aspects of specific activities.

Individual employees have a duty to co-operate with their employers, to take care of themselves and their colleagues and anybody else who may be affected by their work. Once proper arrangements for health, safety and welfare have been put in place, it is up to the employees to take these seriously.

Recognised trade unions, such as Equity and BECTU, may appoint safety representatives to represent their members in dealing with employers but the transient nature of the theatre industry means that these representatives do not specifically have to be employees.

GUIDANCE
The Health and Safety Executive (HSE), the support and executive branch of the Health and Safety Commission (HSC) publishes a range of free leaflets and other publications offering guidance, some of which are relevant to the entertainments industry. These are readily obtainable from HSE Books and some can be found online.

The main purposes of guidance are:
1. To help people to interpret and understand the law. This may include how requirements based on EC directives fit with those under the Health and Safety at Work Act.
2. To help people work within with the law.
3. To offer technical advice.

It is not compulsory to follow guidance and employers are free to take other action, but following the guidance is normally enough to ensure compliance with the law.

The HSC/E try to keep guidance up-to-date because, as technologies change, risks, and the measures needed to address them, change too.

APPROVED CODES OF PRACTICE
Approved codes of practice offer advice on how to comply with the law by providing a guide to what is 'reasonably practicable', giving examples of good practice. For example, if regulations use words like 'suitable and sufficient', an

approved code of practice can illustrate what this requires in particular circumstances.

Approved codes of practice have a special legal status. If an employer is prosecuted for a breach of health and safety law and it can be proved that they did not follow the relevant approved code of practice, they can be found at fault unless they show that they complied with the law in some other way.

Guidance and codes of practice are generally developed in conjunction with industry representatives and organisations such as the ABTT (Association of British Theatre Technicians) and Theatre Safety Committee, and are reviewed regularly.

RISK ASSESSMENT

The HSE defines a risk assessment as 'nothing more than a careful examination of what, in your work, could cause harm to people, so that you can weigh up whether you have taken enough precautions or should do more to prevent harm. The aim is to make sure that no one gets hurt or becomes ill'. Under normal circumstances risk assessments should be relatively straightforward.

Accidents and ill health can ruin lives, damage equipment, increase insurance costs and result in legal action. All this is likely to affect the progress and outcome of a project. The legal requirement to assess the risks in the workplace includes both the rehearsal room and the performance space. The important thing is to decide whether a hazard is significant, and whether satisfactory precautions are in place so that the risk is small. This must be checked when the risks are assessed. For instance, electricity can kill, but the risk of it doing so in most environments is remote provided that 'live' components are insulated and metal casings properly earthed. Current legislation requires all portable electrical appliances to be tested regularly and labelled accordingly. This 'PAT' testing applies to all equipment used in a theatre, including the hairdryers and music players that a performer may wish to use in their dressing room.

The HSE identify five easy steps that can be used to assess risks (see Appendix E):

Step 1: Identify the hazards.

Step 2: Decide who might be harmed and how.

Step 3: Evaluate the risks and decide whether existing precautions are
        adequate or whether more needs to be done.

Step 4: Record the findings.

Step 5: Review the assessment and revise if necessary.

There is no need for risk assessment to be over-complicated. In most work places the hazards are few and simple and checking them is common sense but necessary. The stage manager will probably already know whether, for example, the set involves a piece of moving scenery that could cause harm, or if there is an awkward entrance or stair where someone could be hurt. If so they should check that reasonable precautions have been taken to avoid injury.

Hazard and risk are emotive words, but that shouldn't be allowed to put anyone off. A *hazard* is anything that could cause harm (e.g. chemicals, electricity, working from ladders, running on a raked stage, moving scenery, pyrotechnics, live flame, stage fighting). A *risk* is the chance, high or low, that somebody will be harmed by the hazard.

IDENTIFYING HAZARDS

As the stage manager participates in design and production meetings or sits in the rehearsal room, they should try to identify what could reasonably be expected to cause harm. Ignoring the trivial, they should concentrate on significant hazards which could result in serious harm or affect several people.

There is absolutely nothing wrong with consulting colleagues or seeking advice; others may notice things that are not immediately obvious. Codes of practice, guidance notes and manufacturers' instructions or data sheets can also help the stage manager to spot hazards and put the risks in their true perspective, as can previous experience.

DECIDING WHO MIGHT BE HARMED, AND HOW

It is important to consider everybody who might come into contact with the production, whether on or off-stage or in the rehearsal room. Members of the public should be taken into account if there is a chance they could be hurt by any of the identified hazards. People who may not be involved in the rehearsal process, or in the workplace, all the time must be considered. This might include cleaners, visitors, understudies. Inexperienced members of the company, children, people with particular health needs, expectant mothers and elderly people, who may be at particular risk, must be included.

EVALUATING THE RISKS

The next step is to consider how likely it is that each hazard could cause harm. This will determine whether precautions need to be put in place to reduce the risk, although some risk will usually remain even after these precautions have been taken. For each significant hazard the remaining risk must be identified as high, medium or low.

Firstly it is important to identify whether any legal obligations have been met. For example, there are legal requirements regarding prevention of access to dangerous chemicals as laid out under COSHH legislation. Secondly any generally accepted industry standards can be checked and used if appropriate.

But risk assessment shouldn't stop there. The law also requires that the individual must do what is reasonably practicable to keep their working environment safe. The real aim is to make all risks minimal by adding to the precautions as necessary. If something needs to be done, it is useful to draw up an action list and give priority to any remaining risks which are high and/or those which could affect most people.

In identifying action that may need to be taken the following questions may be helpful:

1. Is it possible to get rid of the hazard altogether?
2. If not, what needs to be done to control the risks so that harm is unlikely?

The following principles may be applied to controlling risk:

1. Propose a less risky option.
2. Prevent access to the hazard (e.g. by providing secure storage or some form of a guard).
3. Organise work to reduce exposure to the hazard.
4. Ensure that adequate training, or rehearsal, is provided.
5. Issue personal protective equipment, such as safety boots or hard hats.
6. Ensure the provision of welfare facilities (e.g. washing facilities for the removal of materials that may cause an allergic reaction, fire fighting equipment and first aid).

Improving health and safety need not cost a lot in either money or time, or unduly affect the artistic integrity of a production. For instance, putting some non-slip material on slippery steps, rubber soles on shoes, calling a fight rehearsal before each performance, are all inexpensive precautions considering the risks. Failure to take simple precautions can cost a lot more if an accident does happen.

In theatre the nature of the work tends to vary a lot and move from one location to another. It is important to monitor the process constantly, identify any hazards that can reasonably be expected and to assess the risks from them. If any additional hazards are spotted when moving to a new venue, the local staff should be consulted and necessary action taken. Any risks that may be particular to the new venue must be checked and the company informed. Equally the local staff and any self-employed people at each venue must be informed about any risks associated with the production, and what precautions are in place.

Many of the hazards associated with the workplace will be common to other places or situations. For example the risks associated with flown scenery are generic and the precautions required to ensure safe practice may be assessed as standard. Once the 'hazard' has been assessed and the precautions needed to minimise risk identified, this can be checked off and applied to all productions that involve flown scenery.

RECORDING THE FINDINGS

Any significant findings of the risk assessment must be recorded by writing down the significant hazards and conclusions. These must be made available to all those concerned.

REVIEW

Risk assessments should be reviewed regularly. This is especially pertinent to long running productions and generic assessments associated with permanent equipment or stage machinery. If there are any significant changes, such as new or updated equipment, these should be added to the assessments to take account of any new hazards. Assessments do not need to be amended for every trivial change, or for each new job, but if a new job introduces significant new hazards of its own they should be considered in their own right and any potential risks minimised. As a general rule it is good practice to review assessments regularly to make sure that the precautions are still working effectively.

Risk assessments may be carried out by any competent person who is familiar with the requirements of the task to be assessed. A risk assessment is essentially a very simple operation; the purpose is to identify a hazard and to put precautions in place that will eliminate or reduce the associated risk. The outcome of risk assessment should be that anyone involved in the assessed activity is informed of the potential risk and made aware of any precautions to be taken to avoid or lessen the chances of injury.

RISK ASSESSMENT IN PRACTICE

The following is an example of a risk assessment for a common, yet potentially dangerous, feature of some theatres.

Many stages have an uncovered orchestra pit between the front of the stage and the auditorium. On the auditorium side the pit will certainly have a railing, but it is extremely unlikely to have one on the stage side. During a performance this would be impracticable, but as the cast and crew should have been sufficiently rehearsed on stage the risks to either would be considered minimal.

During a normal working day, however, there could be a considerable risk and no precautions in place to prevent this. The steps to risk assessment outlined above can be applied as follows:

Step 1. Identifying the hazard
In this case the hazard is falling into the orchestra pit.

Step 2. Deciding who is at risk
Anybody on stage or in the auditorium could be considered to be at risk. Many stage areas do not have totally restricted access, there will be performers, technicians, stage management and outside contractors, there may also be visitors, guided tours, administrators or office staff showing people around.

Step 3. Evaluating the risks
The first stage is to examine the likelihood of the hazard happening,

the second is to examine the severity of the hazard and the third is to assess existing precautions and propose any new ones that will minimise the risk.

This can be done using the following six point scale:

	Probability	Severity
1	Very unlikely	Very minor injury
2	Unlikely	Minor injury
3	May occur	Lost time to injury
4	Likely	Major injury
5	Very likely	Single fatality
6	Will occur	Multiple fatality

The risk factor for each hazard can be worked out by multiplying the probability by the severity, giving a range of one to thirty-six. This can be further divided into three:

0 – 6	Low risk factor	No further action required
7 – 17	Medium risk factor	Above 6: improve if possible
		Above 12: further action required
18 – 36	High risk factor	Above 17: immediate action required

In this case the likelihood of falling into the pit from the auditorium is minimal, as there is already a handrail provided, giving a score of 1. However the severity of an accident, should it occur, could be quite high. Most orchestra pits are two or more metres below the level of the auditorium, plus the height of the railing. A score of 4 might be a reasonable assessment, giving a risk factor of 4. This is considered low and no further precautions would need to be taken.

The risk of falling into the orchestra pit from stage level will be higher as there is no handrail, though this will depend on the circumstances. Although people who know the stage well should be aware of the edge of the stage, other people have been identified as potentially at risk who will be less well briefed. It is possible that somebody could fall into the orchestra pit and so a score of 3 can be given.

The depth of the orchestra pit from the stage is more than likely to be in excess of three metres and such a fall could cause death, thus giving a severity score of 5. The overall risk factor is 15 and this necessitates further action.

In this example the risks can be divided into two scenarios that relate to performance and normal working hours. During performance the risk can be reduced by ensuring proper briefing and training, in this case through time allocated during the production week for stage orientation and thorough rehearsal on the stage. The probability is reduced to 1 and the risk factor to an acceptable 5. During normal working hours the only option is to provide a temporary handrail. A physical barrier that is capable of stopping someone from falling into the pit could be provided, or a rail which functions purely as a warning. Under these circumstances the latter would appear to be sufficient, that is, ropes and posts that alert anyone, even those who are not familiar with the space, to the hazard.

Step 4. Recording the assessment

The risk assessment can be recorded on a form and these stored in a file for reference. Different formats for risk assessment forms exist. *Figure 9.1* is an example of a risk assessment for evacuating a theatre building using the Schwarz model. This shows exactly how the risks have been identified, the precautions that are to be put in place, and how these change the risk factor.

Risk assessments must be suitable and sufficient; they are not expected to be perfect. They should demonstrate that a serious effort has been made to consider all possible health and safety issues. The management will need to show that:
- A proper check has been made;
- All those who might be affected have been considered;
- All the obvious significant hazards have been dealt with, taking into account the number of people who could be involved;
- The precautions are reasonable, and the remaining risk is low.

Written records should be kept for future reference or use. This will help if an inspector asks what precautions have been taken, or if the company becomes involved in any action for civil liability. It will help to show that the company has done what the law requires. The records can also act as a reminder to keep an eye on particular hazards and precautions.

LICENSING

Under the Theatres Act 1968 and the Licensing Act 2003, all premises used for public entertainment must obtain a licence from the local authority. Theatres may apply for an annual licence or individual productions for an occasional licence, if the premises are not normally used for public entertainment or do not fulfil the necessary requirements for an annual licence to be granted.

The regulations relating to annual licences are stringent and apply to all aspects of the building and the way it must be managed. Local authorities can impose conditions which have to be met before a licence can be granted. Until recently each local authority had its own set of licensing regulations (though usually based on a generic model). These were applied rather unevenly across the country, with some authorities acquiring a reputation for leniency, even slackness, whilst others were regarded as draconian. The intention is to standardise licensing regulations

VENUE Embassy Theatre	HEALTH & SAFETY Risk Assessment	AREA Stage & Auditorium

Activity	Emergency Evacuation

Description of operation

People leave the building as a result of an emergency evacuation

Who is affected by this operation?

Production Staff	x	Contractors	x	Cast		x	Public		x	Others		x

Description of hazards/risks	Likelihood	Severity	Risk Factor	Risk (before precautions have been taken)
1) Injury due to smoke inhalation or burns	3	6	18	High
2) Injury due to panic or confusion	4	6	24	High
3) Injury due to blocked escape routes	4	6	24	High

Recommended precautions

1) Ensure that a clear and simple evacuation takes place and that all involved leave the building immediately and do not stop to collect belongings.
2) Ensure all exit routes are clearly marked and that all students / staff are aware of the assembly point and that there are suitable exit routes to the assembly point and signage is in place. If public are present, ensure that sufficient ushers are present and briefed correctly.
3) Ensure all exit routes are free from obstruction.

Description of hazards/risks	Likelihood	Severity	Risk Factor	Risk
1) Injury due to smoke inhalation or burns	3	4	12	Medium
2) Injury due to panic or confusion	3	4	1	Medium
3) Injury due to blocked escape routes	2	1	8	Medium

Details of further action required

1) Re-assess the activity if an accident, near miss or change in operation takes place.

Assessed by (Print name)		Position		Signed		Date	
Approved (Print name)		Signed				Date	

Probability	1 Very unlikely	2 Unlikely	3 May occur	4 Likely	5 Very likely	6 Will occur
Severity	1 Very minor injury	2 Minor injury	3 Lost time to injury	4 Major injury	5 Single fatality	6 Multiple fatality

Risk Factor 0-6 Low Risk factor above 6 Improve if possible	Risk Factor 7-17 Medium Risk factor above 12 Further action required	Risk Factor 18-36 High Immediate action required

Multiply Probability x Severity to obtain Risk Factor

Figure 9.1 A typical risk assessment

across the UK, and eventually Europe. To that end the ABTT and the District Surveyor's Association, which represents Local Authority Building Control, have drawn up and published Technical Standards for Places of Entertainment (ABTT, 2001) and Model National Standard Conditions for Places of Entertainment and Associated Guidance (ABTT, 2001). The first outlines a set of guidelines concerning the technical requirements for a place of entertainment. This includes the stage space and scenery but also seating, emergency lighting, ventilation and so on. The second sets out to provide a uniform standard for the safe management of premises licensed for entertainment. The model standards have now been adopted by many authorities in the UK.

Once a building has obtained a licence, approval must be obtained for each 'change of use', that is each production to be staged. This normally entails sending details of the production, including a full set of risk assessments, to the licensing authority. Details should include any special effects that are being used, especially smoke, pyrotechnics and firearms and a 'smoking plot' if the production involves smoking. Though many will rubber stamp this, authorities reserve the right to make an inspection, to ensure that the company is not doing anything that would contravene the rules. They will then issue a 'change of use' authorisation, which will include permission to use the special effects as detailed. If an inspector does not approve, conditions will be imposed. This can mean that effects, even scenic elements, have to be cut.

Inspectors have the authority to make an inspection at any time, and to stop a production if it is in contravention of the terms of the licence; any conditions attached to a licence should therefore be taken seriously. The bottom line could be closure of the theatre and a hefty fine. If an addition to the production is made after the inspection, the authority should be informed immediately. It will often fall to stage management to enforce the terms of the licence.

An occasional licence is primarily intended for buildings that are not normally used for public entertainment. As the requirements are generally less strict than those for the annual Licence, most authorities impose a ceiling on the number of productions that can be mounted in a year, and on their duration; too many and the company should be applying for an annual licence. If the production is for a very short period inspectors may be more lenient, though that should not be relied on.

The ABTT have compiled a 'Model Technical Rider' for theatres which summarises a visiting theatre company's responsibilities for the well-being of its staff, the public and other visitors to the premises, as defined by the Health and Safety at Work Act 1974 and other legislation, including the requirements of the licensing authority. This is included in full in Appendix F. The intention is that this should be adopted by theatres and will help to standardise the approach to safety in theatre. Stage management should be familiar with these recommendations, though on larger productions their input to the licensing aspect may be quite narrow.

The standardisation of licensing regulations will hopefully make planning a lot easier. In the past a show could be taken to one town where it would pass the licensing inspection, and then move to another where it would fail. The regulations were too open to interpretation, even within the same authority, where different inspectors would interpret and enforce rules differently.

STAGE MANAGEMENT AND LICENSING

The main involvement that stage management will have with licensing will concern:

- furniture and props
- firearms, knives and other weapons or sharp objects
- smoking and the use of live flame including candles, matches, flaming torches (flambeaux) etc.
- pyrotechnics and other special effects
- stage fights and any other physical activity concerning the cast

While the licensing regulations are reasonably specific with respect to scenery and the degree to which it should be flame retardant, they are less so about furniture and props. Ordinary or antique furniture may be used when required, so long as it does not obstruct exits, stage equipment or fire appliances, particularly when pieces are stored off-stage. There is no specific definition of 'ordinary' furniture, however, which means that approval is at the discretion of the authority. As a general rule, new upholstered furniture should be maintained flame-retardant, as should curtains and drapes, but this may also be applied to antique upholstered furniture, particularly if the production involves smoking or other live flame. In these circumstances the authority may grant a licence on the condition that there is no smoking, often a problem for plays that require both antique furniture and smoking. The alternative would be to re-upholster the furniture, which may be a problem if it is on loan or hired. Any items of furniture that are specially made must comply with the same regulations that govern scenery. Carpets must always comply with the strict rules governing fire-retardant properties of stage floor coverings.

It is worth noting that if certification cannot be provided by the supplier for any of the above soft furnishings, drapes or floor coverings, the inspector may conduct a flame test. If this is negative not only will the item be badly damaged but it will also need to be appropriately treated or replaced. New upholstered furniture is normally labelled accordingly. It is a good idea to test samples of fabric in advance so that precautions can be taken or alternatives sought. Fabrics such as silk are inherently flame-proof; that is, they will not continue to burn when the flame is removed. However many fabrics sold as silk are actually a mix of silk and artificial fibres which negate this. Similarly, surface treatments can change the flame retardant properties of fabrics and other materials, rendering them flammable even though they are certified as flame-proof. If upholstered furniture does need to be treated, the stage manager concerned should be aware that some treatments may cause dermatitis or irritation to sensitive skins.

Generally props are not a problem unless they are exceptional items, in which case details should be supplied in advance. Hand-held props will normally be approved without any flame proofing treatment, even if they are plastic. Artificial flowers made of polythene should be avoided as they are flammable, though it is possible to treat them with a special lacquer. Larger props may have the same standards applied to them as to scenery. Bed linen will normally be allowed if it is to be used as such.

Smoking may be permitted so long as the licensing authority has been informed in advance and is confident that the proposed safety precautions are sufficient. The authority should be sent a risk assessment and 'smoking plot' which details exactly how much smoking will take place, the duration of each occurrence, where each cigarette/cigar will be lighted and extinguished and how. They will always require that ashtrays are provided on stage, even if this is not appropriate and they need to be disguised; that these are dampened in some way; and sometimes also that extra fire extinguishers are provided off-stage. They may demand that a fire-marshal is present in the wings whenever smoking takes place on-stage. On occasion, if they have allowed fabrics that are not flame retardant to be used on the set, they will not grant permission for smoking.

The licensing authority will make conditions about any proposals for using real flame on the stage, for using firearms, and for explosions. All of these must be shown on the application form and accompanied by risk assessments. Inspecting officers may ask to see a rehearsal of the effects in action on stage. They will reserve the right to refuse permission for the effect until they have seen it and if appropriate safety measures have not been put into effect they may either impose strict conditions or decide not to grant the licence.

In general, real flame will only be allowed if the action of the play definitely requires its use (e.g. burning documents using a candle) and then only under the most stringent conditions. In the first place, if at all possible, it is better to use imitations. A variety of electrical substitutes for candles, flambeaux, etc., can be obtained from theatrical suppliers. A real fire in a fireplace would be unlikely to be allowed. If the play demanded that something had to be cooked on stage then an alternative effect would have to be devised.

All firearms and other weapons used on stage are subject to scrutiny by the licensing authority. Real weapons may be used only under the supervision of a member of the production staff holding a firearms and/or shotgun certificate. The types of firearms allowed are restricted by law and their usage and storage is governed by stringent legislation. The licence holder must have complete control of the firearms at all times. They must be handed to the actors who will use them on stage, taken off them once they have been used and locked away in a proscribed secure location. The licence holder can have no other duties while the firearms are being used and must have sight of them at all times, even when they are on stage. This applies to all real firearms, whether or not they are used to fire blank rounds.

Firearms can also be obtained that are either real ones that have been deactivated or realistic replicas. Some of the latter are capable of firing blank shots. A firearms licence is not yet required for either of these, and there is no legal requirement to keep them locked away in a designated area when not being used. However, most licensing authorities will make the granting of the licence conditional on any weapons being kept locked up when not in use and being supervised when in use; a replica revolver cannot be left unattended on a props table.

When blanks are being fired, the recommended distance must be maintained between the firer and anyone else on stage. Blanks should never be fired in the direction of the audience. The calibre of blank may also be an issue and the inspector may use a decibel meter to determine whether it is at an acceptable level or demand that all involved wear suitable ear protection – not often practicable for performers.

Edged weapons such as swords should be blunt and made out of the correct steel if they are to be used in a stage fight. They should be checked for flaws and serviced regularly to prevent breakage. The licensing authority may need to see the staging of any stage fights before they agree to the licence. Any sharp props should be blunted, unless they are being used specifically for cutting things on stage, in which case the inspector may wish to be shown the activity.

Pyrotechnics for use in stage productions, such as maroons and flashes, can be obtained from specialist suppliers. These must be set up and operated according to the manufacturer's instructions and the recommended guidelines and codes of practice. As a general rule the firer, often the stage manager in the corner, must have a clear view of the effect before it is fired. If their view is obscured, or a member of the company is closer to the effect than the permitted distance, then the pyrotechnic must not be fired. As with other effects, the licensing authority will need to be informed in advance and may ask to see a demonstration.

OTHER REGULATIONS
Stage management should be aware of a number of other regulations that may affect them directly or indirectly.

Personal Protective Equipment (PPE) should be provided under certain circumstances and stage management may be required to wear hard hats and steel-toe-capped shoes when on-stage during the production period. Manual handling training may need to be provided if the cast or stage management are required to move heavy objects during a production. Electrical equipment, including electrical props, must be PAT-tested.

Special rules apply to children appearing in live performance, as detailed in the Model National Standards for Places of Entertainment, the Children and Young Persons Act 1963 and the Children (Performances) Regulations 1968, 1998 and 2000.

Stage management should make themselves aware of RIDDOR, the Reporting of Injuries, Diseases and Dangerous Occurrences Regulations. Any accident, however minor, should be recorded in an accident book, as well as in the performance report if it happened during a performance. Major incidents must be reported to HSE. Serious near-misses should also be reported, even if no injury resulted.

Stage management must be familiar with fire regulations and evacuation procedures and their own responsibility under those circumstances. Appendix C gives a sample Fire Evacuation Procedure.

CONTEMPORARY PRACTICE

The core job of the stage manager has not changed radically over the last 60 or so years. The stage manager today must still be a motivated, well-organised and creative individual, able to communicate effectively with everyone involved in a production, handle difficult challenges with sensitivity and adapt to new situations. The theatre industry itself has changed, however, and stage managers have had to respond accordingly. At times this has necessitated a change of approach or working practice.

TECHNOLOGY

The increasing use of complex technology within theatre production has had an impact on stage management, both in terms of the types of challenges that they may encounter within a production and in the way that they approach their job.

The digital age has made complex technology more affordable resulting, ironically, in the need for both a greater degree of specialisation and more generalised interdisciplinary skills. Many theatres now employ general technicians, able to turn their hands to almost anything, rather than specialist departments. When specialists are required they are brought in on a show-by-show basis.

The computerised automation of scenery, lighting, etc. has increased the creative and technical options open to designers, who have embraced this opportunity. Largescale productions are now more spectacular than ever, yet they can be operated by fewer people. In fact digital control systems have made it theoretically possible for one person alone to operate a complex production. The technology exists to control lighting, sound, flying, automated scenery and special effects from one control panel, though the industry has so far resisted this temptation. Once the control system has been programmed by an expert it is simply a matter of pressing one button each time something has to happen. Of course when it goes wrong a specialist will be needed to solve the problem, though high speed internet access means that this can sometimes be done remotely. A long-running debate is still taking place concerning whose responsibility it should be when this eventually happens; whether it should be a stage manager, an electrician, or a specialist computer operator. At present the need to engage with the artistic side of a production through attendance at all rehearsals is swinging the outcome in favour of stage management.

Multi-media has become easier to use and increasingly affordable, and projected images, both still and moving, are now a staple of many designers – they are often a cheap option. Experiments have been made with virtual scenery and this could become a real option for designers.

For stage management this increase in the use of technology has a number of implications. Advances in sound technology have enabled sound designers to create ever more complex soundscapes and effects, yet playback has become simpler. PC-based sound programmes enable complex editing to be undertaken on a computer and stored on the hard disc and for levels to be set and memorised. Playback can then be operated through the computer without the need to set up levels and raise faders manually each time. It has become feasible for the stage manager calling a show to operate sound with little technical knowledge or expertise. Whether this is right is another matter, though sound was operated by stage management in the days before magnetic tape was invented and often still is on smallscale shows.

The use of complex automated scenery often has a huge safety implication. Automation has allowed scenery to become bigger and heavier and to be moved in complex sequences using fewer people, but all of this has made it potentially more dangerous. The stage manager calling a show must be aware of this and may need to rely on a well defined communication pathway. Once a sequence has been initiated, the margin for error is very small and individual elements may be difficult to stop. Performers and stage management must be aware of these implications at all times.

As well as opening up new creative possibilities, the increased use of moving lights has made it possible to light productions with fewer lanterns but often at the expense of the traditional lighting rehearsal. Computerised lighting boards are quick to programme but the addition of moving lights adds to the complexity and time required. When changes need to be made they take longer to programme.

This increase in the use of complex technology has also added to the time required to rehearse it. Technical rehearsals of largescale productions last longer and the stage manager has to keep the cast and crew motivated over a longer period.

Technology does not only operate at production level; it has also enhanced the way stage management can approach their own tasks. Computers allow templates to be created and used to update and circulate information regularly and to store it centrally. The internet has introduced rapid global communication using e-mail and the worldwide web can be a fantastic research tool. Direct contact can be made with experts across the world and information that might have taken weeks to acquire can be accessed in seconds. Although the 'paperless office' is in fact an unrealistic fantasy, information can be circulated electronically, thus cutting back on postage and the use of fax machines. Rehearsal notes and show reports can be circulated rapidly and can be read by people on the other side of the world within seconds of publication. Broadband access has made video-conferencing a realistic option, allowing people to contribute to meetings without actually being present.

Digital cameras have the potential to revolutionise the work of stage management. Pictures of possible props can be taken and shown to directors and designers either in person or over the internet and are a cheaper and quicker option than a Polaroid or 35mm photography. It is not beyond the realms of feasibility for a designer to approve a prop from a different country using the internet. Complex settings can be recorded and the images downloaded straight into setting lists.

Mobile phones enable a stage manager to make contact with other members of a company whenever they need to without having to rely on messages left on answer-phones. Text messaging can be used to circulate rehearsal calls. The new generation of mobile phones incorporating a camera has made it possible for virtually instant decisions to be made.

Stage management should not be complacent when using this technology, however; it is only as good as its operator and, as it becomes more complex, it is more likely to fail. Computers crash, mobile phones lose their signal, the internet is a useful tool but is unregulated and not always accurate. Electronic communication should always be followed up with a phone call or physical meeting. Libraries, museums and experts are still the best source for reliable specialist information.

NEW THEATRE FORMS AND SPACES

The last few years have seen new forms of live theatre enter the mainstream of popular culture, all of which offer different challenges to stage management. Arena opera, circus theatre, large scale spectacle, have all become immensely popular and all employ stage management. While the core skills required are the same, the individual challenges may be radically different. An arena opera may employ several teams of stage management, each in charge of a particular area, who may never meet. Circus performers will have very different requirements and expectations from actors or opera singers. Puppetry, once thought of as the preserve of children's theatre or Eastern Europe, is now used in West End shows and by the national companies and can add an extra dimension to a production.

Devising, once the realm of smallscale fringe theatre companies, has entered the mainstream and many contemporary directors now work with their companies in a more collaborative way. Productions are developed from scratch through the rehearsal process, including design. Stage managers can expect themselves to be involved in this creative process, which can be both exciting and stressful. They may find themselves having to set deadlines and force decisions to be made as the time available for realising the scenery and finding props gets shorter. Usually, however, the sense of ownership and achievement more than compensates.

Non-text based or physical theatre is now commonplace and may sometimes be more akin to dance theatre. Companies are often made up of performers from different genres, dance, ballet, mime, classical acting, each with their own expectations and requirements. Directors and designers may push the performers to their physical limits as they experiment with new ideas.

Alongside this movement of alternative theatre forms from the fringe into popular culture, many theatre companies are moving away from the traditional playhouse into found spaces. Theatre can be made literally anywhere, including the open air, and many companies are doing just that. Productions may be traditional in nature, such as a Shakespeare production in the grounds of a castle, or site-specific, where a production is devised using the site as inspiration. Productions may also be promenade, where the cast and audience move from place to place for each scene. Community theatre has also become popular, where a director and sometimes designers and actors work with a local community to produce a piece of theatre that explores issues relevant to that community.

These are just some of the challenges and opportunities that present themselves to the stage manager today and in the future. The stage manager of today must be willing to embrace these new opportunities and adapt their practice accordingly.

LEGAL OBLIGATIONS

The individual's responsibility at work is defined by Health and Safety and EU regulations such as the Working Time Directive. This has had a significant impact on the responsibilities associated with stage management. What was once regarded as common sense is now enshrined in the law. Many people regard this as intrusive and anti-creative but in many ways it actually makes the stage manager's job easier. Risk assessments can be used to demonstrate that a certain activity is dangerous. If the risk cannot be reduced, for whatever reason, then the activity will not be allowed by a licensing authority. It is far better to predict this in advance than to find it out at the last minute, when it is often too late for alternatives to be put in place. The boundaries can still be stretched, so long as the constraints are recognised and safety is always considered. Stage management should always be aware of their legal obligations, however, particularly those that are contractual. It is not unheard-of for a production company to try to place responsibility for health and safety on the shoulders of the stage manager. If this happens, the stage manager must be clear that they have total authority and right of veto; if they decide that something is not safe, they must not be over-ridden.

The Working Time Directive sets out the maximum hours of work allowed per week, referenced over a period of four months. While some industries are exempt from this, theatre is not, though individuals can be asked to opt out. The directive also specifies the number and duration of breaks that must be taken and holidays. In the past it was possible to be paid in lieu of a holiday at the end of a contract. This is no longer allowed. All members of a company must take their holiday entitlement before the end of their contract. This has to be administered, often by the stage manager.

BECOMING A STAGE MANAGER

The traditional way of becoming a professional stage manager, through an apprenticeship as a student stage manager or acting ASM in a theatre company, has long since passed away. Some small companies will still take untrained people on as stage management but it is now generally considered essential to undertake a training course.

In Britain two organisations represent schools or colleges at Further or Higher Education level (post-16) that offer vocational courses to a professional standard. The Conference of Drama Schools (CDS) represents the schools themselves and exists 'to strengthen the voice of the member schools, to set and maintain the highest standards of training within the vocational drama sector'. CDS members aim to offer intensive full-time courses that are professionally orientated. Students are taught by staff with professional experience and by visiting professionals and have the opportunity to work in professional-standard theatres and studios. Although courses lead to academic qualifications, including graduate and masters degrees, they offer practical training for work. The National Council for Drama Training (NCDT) represents the theatre industry by offering accreditation to courses that meet a set of stringent criteria.

'The purpose of the NCDT is to promote, enhance and maintain the highest possible standards of vocational training and education for the professional actor and stage manager/technician and to provide a forum within which the various sides of the profession can discuss matters of common interest in relation to training. It is particularly concerned to promote the possible links between those engaged in training and those working in the profession.'

In the UK eleven schools offer accredited courses in stage management, technical theatre and associated disciplines. Traditionally stage management courses offered a general training in all backstage subjects and were the only way to train for a career in technical theatre. Some of these courses were diagnostic; students could specialise in an area that they wanted to pursue as a career, such as lighting, but most had stage management as the core subject. Stage managers were expected to have an understanding of all areas. Cynics might argue that this enabled the drama schools to mount productions for their acting students to a quasi-professional standard without having to employ expensive professionals; that stage management courses were set up to service acting courses.

As the technical theatre industry has become more specialised and the technical subjects have become recognised as legitimate professions, some schools have begun to offer more specialised courses. It is now possible to train as a specialist prop-maker or production electrician to degree level as well as in stage management. These students will work together in a way that emulates a professional theatre company and they are able to learn about each other's discipline through interaction.

One of the major developments in theatre education over the last 30 years has been the rise of drama, theatre studies and theatre production courses offered at secondary level. This has seen a rise in the number of students seeking to make a career backstage and the average applicant today will have studied theatre at school rather than experienced it as a hobby through amateur dramatics, extra-curricular drama societies at school or youth theatre, though these still represent an important stimulus. Outreach work by theatre companies has also contributed to this interest in, and recognition of, stage management and technical theatre as a possible career.

The university sector has also responded to this demand. Many offer theatre degree courses that include aspects of technical theatre or allow students to specialise. While these tend to have a more academic basis and are less vocational than NCDT accredited courses, many of their graduates are successful in their chosen field. The qualities offered by a student graduating with a good honours degree are exactly those valued by theatre employers. The ability to communicate effectively, analyse information, problem-solve, respond to new situations positively, be self-critical, carry out thorough and targeted research, in fact the ability and desire to learn, are as important as technical knowledge and proficiency. While these transferable skills are hugely valued, a good understanding of the process of creating a piece of live theatre is also essential.

A degree is not an essential requirement for a career in stage management, however, but training of some sort is now considered mandatory.

STAGE MANAGEMENT AS A CAREER

Many factors have affected the traditional career progression of a stage manager. Although there is still a hierarchical progression from Assistant through Deputy to Stage, and eventually Company, Manager, which is reflected in both status and salary, many stage managers will stay with the job that they are best at and enjoy the most. A stage manager who is good at props finding and management may have to stay at ASM level in order to specialise in this area and may find themselves the most experienced member of a team. Many stage managers do not want to progress to the role of Stage Manager yet may have to do so if the want to see their career and salary progress. Some companies will reward an individual's particular skills accordingly, rendering hierarchical progression less essential but pay scales in the industry still recognise and reward this traditional progression.

Changes within the theatre industry itself have had a profound effect on stage management as a longterm career. With fewer main-stream theatre companies producing their own work and when they do, producing less of it, it is now more difficult for a new stage manager to get a job with a company as an ASM, move up to DSM over a couple of years and then move on to a larger theatre or eventually become Stage Manager. Apart from the large national companies, many of the theatres that do make their own productions now tend to employ a small core team of stage management, and a range of freelancers as necessary. Their own productions are interspersed with visiting touring companies, with their own stage management teams, and it is simply not cost-effective to employ a full team year round. Those individuals who are lucky enough to find a full-time job in a producing theatre are more likely to hang on to it and so there is less movement and fewer opportunities to move on.

A career in stage management has never involved a linear progression; a fluctuation of roles is the norm. Many will start out working as a stage manager on a fringe theatre production, often unpaid or on a profit-share basis; move on to being an ASM with a small repertory company; move up to DSM, and then on to ASM, with a bigger company and so on. This will involve them in a wide range of productions and often with a large number of jobs over their career. Theatre is one of the few industries where it is seen as an advantage the more jobs someone has had.

One of the outcomes of an increasingly better trained and educated stage management work force has been the shortening of the career span. Before training became essential, a stage manager would have expected to work as an ASM for a number of years as they learnt 'on the job', before promotion to DSM and so on. The greater emphasis on education and the resultant 'professionalisation' of stage management has affected graduate expectations, as well as increased their understanding and experience of theatre production. Today's graduate stage manager can expect to move up the ranks over four or five years, as opposed to the ten or fifteen years of the past.

Changes in employment law, coupled with the diminishing influence of the unions on their industry, have also affected theatre. In the past, Equity imposed restrictions on the number of new members allowed each year, including stage management. To gain a job as an ASM on a commercial West End production, a stage manager had to have a full Equity card and at least three years professional experience. This is no longer the case and it is now possible for a graduate to move straight from drama school onto a West End show, without even being a union member.

For many stage managers this shortening of the career structure has made it a less attractive option. Reaching the top of the profession after five years leaves little room for progression, other than sideways. An increasing number of stage management personnel, on achieving the role of Stage Manager, decide to move on after a few years to a different career either in theatre or associated industries. In fact many students see stage management as a stepping-stone to a different role within theatre, as it gives them an all round experience of theatre-making. Stage managers will often progress to careers in company management, production management, theatre management, even as producers or directors. They may move on to the television, film or events industries.

OTHER OPPORTUNITIES

The potential areas of employment for theatre-trained stage management have both increased and changed over the years. Thirty years ago the most common route into floor management, or assistant directing, in television was through stage management in the theatre. Indeed the BBC, which operated a training scheme, would only take on people with theatre experience. Today, while the skills necessary for a successful career in theatre may still be valued within the television industry, the increase in media studies and specialist film courses at degree level has produced a generation of graduates who also have the requisite skills, together with a more specialist knowledge of television. Theatre experience is no longer essential to someone intent on a career on the television studio floor; there is more competition.

Similarly industrial theatre (sometimes referred to as the 'conference' or 'trade show' industry) can be a useful and lucrative source of employment for theatre stage managers. Large conferences may involve complex theatrical lighting, sound and staging, all of which needs to be co-ordinated. Show calling under these circumstances is ideally suited to someone with theatre experience. However the need for economy and the greater use of multi-media technology, including auto-cues, has meant that many conference producers are as likely to employ somebody with media experience as they are a stage manager.

Probably the most recent development in opportunities for theatre stage managers has arisen from the events industry. Largescale events such as music festivals and national celebrations require co-ordinating, and events producers are increasingly turning to the theatre industry for expertise in this area. It is no coincidence that an event such as the Queen's Golden Jubilee celebration in London in 2003 was co-ordinated by theatre stage managers with responsibility for ensuring that all elements of the celebration, including military bands and a fly-past by the air-force, happened at the right time. This is a growing, and attractive, area for theatre-trained stage managers to make their career.

BIBLIOGRAPHY

1. OFFICIAL PUBLICATIONS

HSE, *An introduction to health and safety* INDG259, HSE, 1997

HSE, *Essentials of health and safety at work* 3rd ed., 1994

HSE, *Five steps to risk assessment* INDG163 (rev), 1998

HSE, *Five steps to risk assessment: case studies* HSG183,1998

HSE, *Guide to fire precautions in existing places of entertainment and like premises*, 1990

2. OTHER PUBLICATIONS

ABTT/DSA, *Model National Standard Conditions for Places of Entertainment*, Entertainment Technology Press, Royston, 2002

ABTT/DSA, *Technical Standards for Places of Entertainment*, Entertainment Technology Press, Royston, 2002

Baker, H., *Stage Management and Theatrecraft*, J. Garnett Miller Ltd, London, 1968

Barker, A., *How to Manage Meetings*, Kogan Press, London, 2002

Baugh, C., *Risk Assessment in Practice*, Theatre Safety Seminar, www.abtt.org.uk/info/risk3.htm, 1996

Belbin, R., *Management Teams; Why They Succeed or Fail*, Heinemann, Oxford, 1997

Booth, M. R., *Theatre in the Victorian Age*, Cambridge University Press, Cambridge, 1991

Booth, M. R. (ed), *Victorian Theatrical Trades*, Society for Theatre Research, London, 1981

Copley, S., and Killner, P., *Stage Management: a Practical Guide*, Crowood Press, Marlborough, 2001

Covey, S., *The Seven Habits of Highly Effective People*, Simon & Schuster, 1999

Craig, E. G., *On the Art of Theatre*, Heinemann, London, 1911

Dean, P., *Production Management*, Crowood Press, Marlborough, 2002

Eyre, R., and Wright, N., *Changing Stages*, Bloomsbury, London, 2000

French, J.R.P., and Raven, B.H., 'The bases of social power', in *Studies in Social Power*, ed. Cartwright, D., University of Michigan Press, 1959

Goffin, P., *The Art and Science of Stage Management*, J. Garnet Miller Ltd, London, 1953

Granville-Barker, H., *The Exemplary Theatre*, Chatto and Windus, London, 1922

Gurr, A., and Ichikawa, M., *Staging in Shakespeare's Theatre*, Oxford University Press, Oxford, 2000

Handy, C., *Understanding Organisations*, Penguin, Harmondsworth, 1976

Ingham, R., *From Page to Stage*, Heinemann, Oxford, 1998

Jackson, R., *Victorian Theatre*, A. & C. Black, London, 1989

Kelly, T. A, *The Back Stage Guide to Stage Management*, 2nd edn, Back Stage Books, New York, 1999

Lilley, R., *Dealing with Difficult People*, Kogan Press, London, 2002

Mackintosh, I., *Architecture, Actor and Audience*, Routledge, London, 1993

Neutel, W.D., *The Dramaturgy Pages*, www.dramaturgy.net, 1995

Pallin, G., *Stage Management: The Essential Handbook*, 2nd edn, Nick Hern Books, London, 2003

Read, A., *Theatre and Everyday Life: An Ethics of Performance*, Routledge, London, 1993

Reid, F., *The ABC of Theatre Jargon*, Entertainment Technology Press, Royston, 2001

Reid, F., *The Staging Handbook*, 2nd edn, A & C Black, London, 1996

Rowell, G., *The Victorian Theatre: 1792–1914*, Cambridge University Press, Cambridge, 1978

Stanislavski, K. S., *An Actor Prepares*, Methuen, London, 1980

Stewart, H., *Stage Management*, Pitman, London, 1957

Stoker, B., *Personal Reminiscences of Henry Irving*, Heinemann, London, 1906

Taylor, J., *Communication at Work*, Kogan Press, London, 2001

Tuckman, B., *Development sequences in small groups*, Psychological Bulletin 63, 1965

Van Beek, M., *A Practical Guide to Health and Safety in the Entertainment Industry*, Entertainment Technology Press, Royston, 2000

Wickham, G., *A History of the Theatre*, Phaidon, London, 1992

3. USEFUL ORGANISATIONS: UK

Association of British Theatre Technicians (ABTT), http://www.abtt.org.uk

Equity, http://www.equity.org.uk

National Council for Drama Training (NCD), http://www.ncdt.co.ukStage Management Association (SMA), http://www.stagemanagementassociation.co.uk

4. USEFUL ORGANISATIONS: INTERNATIONAL

International Organisation of Scenographers, Theatre Architects and Technicians (OISTAT), http://www.oistat.org/

Stage Manager's Association (US), http://www.stagemanagers.org/

United States Institute for Theatre Technology (USITT), http://www.usitt.org/

APPENDIX A: Health and Safety Legislation

Besides the Health and Safety at Work Act itself, the following apply across the full range of workplaces:

1. *Management of Health and Safety at Work Regulations 1992*: require employers to carry out risk assessments, make arrangements to implement necessary measures, appoint competent people and arrange for appropriate information and training.
2. *Workplace (Health, Safety and Welfare) Regulations 1992*: cover a wide range of basic health, safety and welfare issues such as ventilation, heating, lighting, workstations, seating and welfare facilities.
3. *Health and Safety (Display Screen Equipment) Regulations 1992*: set out requirements for work with visual display units (VDUs).
4. *Personal Protective Equipment (PPE) Regulations 1992*: require employers to provide appropriate protective clothing and equipment for their employees.
5. *Provision and Use of Work Equipment Regulations (PUWER) 1992*: require that equipment provided for use at work, including machinery, is safe.
6. *Manual Handling Operations Regulations 1992*: cover the moving of objects by hand or physical effort.
7. *Health and Safety (First Aid) Regulations 1981*: cover requirements for first aid.
8. *Health and Safety Information for Employees Regulations 1989*: require employers to display a poster telling employees what they need to know about health and safety.
9. *Employers' Liability (Compulsory Insurance) Regulations 1969*: require employers to take out insurance against accidents and ill-health to their employees.
10. *Reporting of Injuries, Diseases and Dangerous Occurrences Regulations 1985 (RIDDOR)*: require employers to notify certain occupational injuries, diseases and dangerous events.
11. *Noise at Work Regulations 1989*: require employers to take action to protect employees from hearing damage.
12. *Electricity at Work Regulations 1989*: require people in control of electrical systems to ensure they are safe to use and maintained in a safe condition.
13. *Control of Substances Hazardous to Health Regulations 1994 (COSHH)*: require employers to assess the risks from hazardous substances and take appropriate precautions.

In addition, specific regulations cover particular areas, for example asbestos and lead:

1. *Chemicals (Hazard Information and Packaging for Supply) Regulations (CHIP 2) 1994*: require suppliers to classify, label and package dangerous chemicals and provide safety data sheets for them.
2. *Construction (Design and Management) Regulations 1994*: cover safe systems of work on construction sites.
3. *Gas Safety (Installation and Use) Regulations 1994*: cover safe installation, maintenance and use of gas systems and appliances in domestic and commercial premises.

APPENDIX B: Code of Practice for Health and Safety Demonstrations for Performers and Stage Management

Reproduced courtesy of the Theatre Safety Committee. The Theatre Safety Committee is a cross-industry body which monitors developments and disseminates information relating to health and safety in the theatre industry.

Procedures relating to health and safety vary considerably both in theatres and in opera houses. It is the aim of this code of practice to establish best practice in the industry, to improve communication and ultimately to reduce accidents and near-misses.

1. Risk assessment documentation should be made available to performers, if requested, before the first rehearsal on the stage set.
2. There should be a health and safety demonstration of the set by a technical representative of the management at the first rehearsal on the stage set, be that in the rehearsal studio or on stage, before any rehearsal activity takes place. All performers and stage management should attend and, at the conclusion of the demonstration, should be asked to identify any concerns they may have either individually or collectively.
3. If there are any changes to the set between the rehearsal studio and the first rehearsal on stage on the set, then a further health and safety demonstration should take place, as detailed above, before any work using the set gets under way.

4. There should be a further health and safety demonstration of the set when the performers are in costume.
5. Such demonstrations will form part of scheduled working time.
6. If the show transfers from one theatre to another and there is a substantive change to the set between the final performance in one venue and the next, a further health and safety demonstration should take place before the first rehearsal or performance using the set.
7. In the event of any change of performers, any

newcomers should witness a health and safety demonstration before they first use the set.
8. Should a performer be required to work on a steeply raked stage (one that is 1 in 12 or steeper), the Manager should provide an appropriately qualified individual to demonstrate how to work safely and without longterm injury on a raked surface and to provide such continued supervision and support as is considered appropriate by the qualified individual.

APPENDIX C: Fire and Evacuation Procedures

Safety is the prime concern of all members of a theatre's staff, both backstage and front of house. When an audience is present in a theatre space, it is the responsibility of the theatre to ensure their safety. For this reason it is important that all members of staff are aware of the procedures associated with the discovery of a fire, or any other potential hazard such as a bomb threat, which might result in the evacuation of the building.

The cardinal rule in dealing with such situations is not to cause panic, which may result in a greater danger to the audience than the original threat.

The words BOMB or FIRE must NEVER be used in the hearing of the public, and it is better not to use them at all. These words are bound to spread alarm and panic if heard by a member of an audience.

All theatres will have a code word, such as Mr Jet or Mr Sands, and it is this word that should be used when reporting a fire.

The Fire Brigade recommends the following procedure:

IF YOU DISCOVER A FIRE
1. Operate the nearest fire alarm.
   N.B. Most theatres will have a means of isolating the fire alarm system in the auditorium, thereby ensuing that the audience are not caused to panic.
MAKE SURE YOU KNOW WHOSE RESPONSIBILITY IT IS TO TURN THIS ON AND OFF.
2. Attack the fire, if possible, with the equipment provided, but do not take any personal risks.
   N.B. It is your responsibility to familiarise yourself with the location of all fire fighting equipment and alarm points.
3. Inform the stage manager and duty front-of-

house manager. This may be done by telephone, or using the back stage PA. Remember to use the code word. Your message must contain information that can be relayed to the Fire Brigade, in particular the location, for example: *'Mr Jet is in Dressing Room Two',* or *'Mr Jet is in the Ladies Cloakroom'.*

ON HEARING OR SEEING THE ALARM
1. The duty manager will call the Fire Brigade immediately.
2. In public areas light and buzzer units will actuate. All staff should proceed directly to their allocated stations. Act calmly and be ready for further instructions.
3. In non-public, i.e. back-stage, areas, the fire alarm will sound. Staff responsible for the evacuation of the public should proceed to their allotted stations. Those not involved with the evacuation should report to the assembly point.

EVACUATION PROCEDURE
1. The person in charge, generally the duty manager or stage manager, should decide whether to evacuate.
2. If the theatre is to be evacuated, the duty manager or stage manager should inform the prompt corner and ask for the house lights to be brought up. They will then make an announcement from the stage, such as:
   'Ladies and Gentlemen, I'm afraid that we have to evacuate the theatre. Please leave by the nearest exit as indicated by the ushers.'
   If it would be dangerous to use a particular exit, then it should be indicated which exits should be used, for example: .
   'Please leave by the exits on the right hand side of the auditorium ....'
3. The safety curtain should be activated by the delegated person once it is clear to do so, i.e. the

performers are clear. If a serious fire has been discovered in the stage area, then this should be done immediately.

4. If an evacuation announcement is made, ushers at exits should open curtains, indicate the exit and in a firm voice repeat:
   'This way out please.'
   If it has been indicated that certain exits are not to be used, then ushers should prevent the audience from using these.

5. Designated members of back-stage staff should check that all areas are clear, and that all electrical appliances have been switched off, reporting to the stage manager once this is done.

6. When the evacuation of the auditorium is complete, all exit doors should be closed, and all cloakrooms, toilets, etc., searched. Designated staff should report to the duty manager once

their section is clear.

7. All members of backstage and front-of-house staff, and performers, should proceed directly to the assembly point.

N.B.
Do not use lifts
Do not stop to collect personal belongings or to change
Do not re-enter the building
Always walk, never run
The public rely on you to get them out of danger quickly and safely
Keel calm, do not panic
Remember:
1. The code word
2. The assembly point

APPENDIX D: Risk Control – Managing the Stage

This Appendix, based on guidance issued by the Association of British Theatre Technicians (ABTT) is intended to be a practical guide to indicate some of the precautions that should be taken before the actors are allowed on stage.

Most accidents on stage occur during the production period of fit-up and technical rehearsal. Possibly the most dangerous time is when the fit-up is not complete but the actors want to get on to the set which is not quite finished; the electricians are focusing lights; and the director wants to start a technical rehearsal. The actors and many other people involved in the production are not yet familiar with the set and the potential for a disaster awaits.

Proper management of the stage is essential if accidents are to be avoided. Pre-planning and vigilance are equally necessary. With more

complicated productions there may be much to be said for adopting the principles set out in the Construction (Design & Management) Regulations as applied to the building.

First establish who is in charge: there should be no doubt as to who has the authority to permit strangers in to the workplace. During performance the stage manager will be in charge but during the fit-up someone else – the production or technical manager, or the stage carpenter or chief technician – will be in control. During a technical or dress rehearsal someone else again may be in charge. This changing responsibility can leave grey areas and lead to confusion. Actors and musicians (artistes) should not be let into the stage area without the authority of the person in charge. There are special rules if children are to appear on stage (see Model National Standard Conditions). The meeting or phone conversation to establish the schedule is a good time to agree the question of command.

1. Before the get-in or fit-up starts:

Incoming show staff	Venue staff
Full exchange of information with resident technical staff	Full exchange of information with incoming stage manager/chief technician
Visit venue if possible	View incoming set if possible
Pre-fit set if possible and examine for hazards and possible problems	Clear and clean the stage area and associated areas
Agree a schedule with resident technical team leader	Agree a schedule with incoming stage/production manager/chief technician

A typical chronology might be:
1. Hang lighting
2. Get in set
3. Hang cloths and borders
4. Fit up set
5. Focus lighting
6. Plot lighting and sound
7. Rehearse scene changes
8. Artistes on stage in working lights
9. Technical rehearsal
10. Dress rehearsal(s)
11. First performance
12. Meeting to clear snags

Risk	Confirm	Other points to consider
Tripping	There is sufficient light to see all obstacles and other hazards.	Particular care needed to ensure overhead and eye line hazards, such as ends of flying bars, are removed.
	All floor coverings in wings (carpets, drugget) are secured to the floor. Any cables on the floor are secured, protected from damage and will not cause a trip hazard.	Loose carpeting should be flame retardant. Wherever possible cables should be routed overhead.
	The floor is not slippery.	It may be necessary to use rosin to improve grip.
	Scenery tracks and similar holes do not present hazards.	As far as possible no gap should exceed 8mm, although wider gaps may be acceptable where the performers have appropriate footwear.
Cuts and bruises	There are no sharp edges or projections, especially in the wings and other constricted areas.	All edges of scenery should be smoothed (arrised) during construction. Check especially for protruding nails, screw bolts. Bars should be above head height.
	Textured surfaces are not abrasive.	This is particularly important for the floor surface.
	The floor is clean.	All screws, nails and any breakages should be removed. Check especially that there are no protruding nails or screws.
Falling	Edges of steps are clearly marked.	Where edge marking is inappropriate on-stage, temporary marking is desirable and frequent rehearsals needed.
	Any change of level is marked.	Any changes of level should be clearly indicated. This is essential in off-stage areas.
	The front edge of the stage is clearly defined.	If there is a drop exceeding 600mm, the downstage (front) edge of the stage should be clearly indicated. Possible methods include the use of marking tape, a contrasting finish to the auditorium or a lip on the floor about 300mm upstage of the front edge. Some indication of the edge of the stage, e.g. a rope barrier, may be desirable during rehearsal.
	Any hole in the floor is clearly marked.	Safe methods of working, e.g. guard rails and rehearsal to prevent falls, must be established before edge markings are removed.
Falling from a height	Practical upper levels are complete and safe to use.	Access should be barred to any incomplete upper levels.
	Upper levels should be guarded to prevent falls.	Wherever possible, balconies should have strong barriers. Hand rails may be omitted from scenery solely for artistic effect, in which case training by frequent rehearsal will ensure safety. Some form of edge marking is, however, essential in these cases. A grab wire may be appropriate. Be aware of 'blinding' problems from bright lighting
	Get-off stairs are complete.	Any get-offs should have strong hand rails (on both sides where the rise is more than 2m). Pitch must be constant and not excessive. A ladder may be preferable to a steep stair.

Electric shock	Any dangerous electrical equipment is isolated electrically or mechanically.	Incomplete wiring, such as open busbars or switch fuses, may be a serious hazard.
	Any necessary safety earths are in place.	If electrical equipment is to be mounted on exposed metalwork, the metalwork should be properly earthed. If there is risk of damage to electrical cables, either provide mechanical protection or ensure exposed metalwork is earthed.
Collapsing scenery/set	The set is complete and secure.	If it is not secure, access to any unsafe area must be prevented.

2. Before a technical or dress rehearsal or performance is allowed to begin, check all the above items and:

1. Clarify who is in charge and how the person in charge communicates instructions, especially in an emergency or in poor lighting or noisy conditions.
2. Check that all artistes, including any cast changes, have walked the set in costume in working light conditions.
3. Consider temporary marking of hazards. It is important that there is sufficient time for the cast to become familiar with the set.
4. Artistes should walk through any scene changes that involve actors in working lights.
5. Consider the effects of lighting blackouts. Decide how light can be restored quickly if needed.
6. Consider the effects of noise. Decide how noise, especially amplified sound, can be stopped quickly if necessary.

Risk	Confirm	Other points to consider
Fire	Ensure fire doors are closed.	Door 'silencers' must not prevent doors from closing fully.
	Fire escape routes are clear of obstructions.	Fire lanes are a good way of marking escape routes. Help to ensure they are kept clear.
		Cables over doorways must be adequately secured.
	Fire escape routes are clearly signed.	Consider additional temporary lighting and additional temporary escape route signs.
	The wings are not overcrowded.	
	Emergency equipment is in place and accessible.	Fire exits, fire extinguishers, safety curtain, drencher and lantern light/ventilator releases must be kept clear.
Falling objects	Scenery packs are properly secured.	
	Secondary suspensions are fitted.	Secondary suspension safety bonds/chains are recommended on all lanterns/luminaires and suspended sound equipment.
	Weapons/spear racks and the like are in place.	
	Counterweight systems are properly balanced.	Rope locks should not be used to secure out-of-balance loads.
Poor lighting	The wings are adequately lit.	Way-finding lighting 'blues' should be installed and working.
Moving scenery	Flying crews can see any moving, flown scenery.	Operators must be able to see. Where direct sightlines are not possible, CCTV or sighters are essential.

	Paths of moving scenery are clear.	Operators must be able to see. Where direct sightlines are not possible, CCTV or sighters are essential.
	Remotely controlled scenery has safety limits properly set.	Some means of stopping powered scenery is essential. Emergency stops should be in place and working.
Special effects	Bomb tanks are appropriately sited and warning notices posted.	Operators must be able to see. Where direct sightlines are not possible, CCTV or sighters are essential.
	Pyrotechnics are properly stored and located.	Operators must be able to see. Where direct sightlines are not possible, CCTV or sighters are essential.
	Dry ice is stored in an appropriate ventilated place.	Dry ice vapour is heavier than air and a potential asphyxiant.

3. Further guidance:
Further guidance on some of the issues raised in these notes may be found in:
ABTT Guidance Note: Risk Assessment:
Scenery; ABTT Codes of Practice, Firearms and Ammunition and Pyrotechnics; and in Model National Standard Conditions produced by ABTT, DSA and LGLF.

APPENDIX E: Summary of Four Steps to Risk Assessment (after HSC guidelines)

STEP 1	STEP 2	STEP 3
Hazard	Who might be harmed?	Is more needed to control the risk?
Look only for hazards which could reasonably be expected to result in significant harm under the conditions in the workplace. Use the following examples as a guide: • slipping/tripping hazards (e.g. shiny floor treatments, steep stairs, steps or loose carpets) • snagging or banging hazards (e.g. fixings such as nails or projecting pieces of scenery) • fire (e.g. from flammable materials, live flame or smoking) • chemicals (e.g. battery acid) • moving parts of machinery (e.g. automated scenery) • work at height (e.g. from ladders or mezzanine floors on a set) • electricity (e.g. poor wiring or proximity to liquid)	There is no need to list individuals by name – just think about groups of people doing similar work or who may be affected, e.g. • cast • stage management • technicians/operators • contractors • cleaners • members of the public Pay particular attention to people who may be more vulnerable: • staff with disabilities • visitors • inexperienced staff • children • lone workers	For the hazards listed, do the precautions already taken: • meet the standards set by a legal requirement? • comply with a recognised industry standard? • represent good practice? • reduce risk as far as reasonably practicable? Have the following been provided: • adequate information, instruction or training? • adequate systems or procedures? If so, then the risks are adequately controlled, but the precautions put in place need to be recorded

• stage fights • dust • fumes • manual handling • noise • poor lighting • low temperature		Where the risk is not adequately controlled further action must be identified.

STEP 4
Keep a record
The risk assessments relevant to the production should be kept in a file which can be shown to inspecting Health and Safety Officers and which should be made available to all members of the company.

APPENDIX F: Model Technical Rider

(Courtesy of the ABTT)

ABOUT THIS DOCUMENT

The ABTT is frequently consulted about the technical content of contracts.

Clearly many smaller venues would welcome a model to use when contracting touring companies or when hiring out their premises.

This Model Technical Rider is intended to fill this need. A technical rider is a corollary to a contract detailing technical requirements.

The Technical Rider should form a part of or be attached to the main Contract between the Theatre and the Visiting Company.

The issues covered in the Model Technical Rider all relate directly or indirectly to safety concerns and good practice. These matters affect all users of the premises whether amateur or professional.

The Model Technical Rider does not attempt to cover copyright or performing rights issues. The ABTT has observed that many technical riders include quite unreasonable conditions and also that large parts of them are simply ignored. To be enforceable any contract must be reasonable. Technical riders are most effective when worded to be as helpful and informative as possible. The language should be simple rather than legalistic.

This Model Technical Rider is based upon a number of models which have been found to work, modified in the light of good practice as set out in the Model National Conditions for Places of Entertainment and Associated Guidance.

The text may be freely adapted to suit local circumstances and inappropriate sections should be omitted, for example references to the safety curtain if there isn't one. Generic words should, where possible, be replaced by the particular, for example 'Production Manager' may replace 'Theatre' in some clauses. "Hirer" or even 'you' may replace 'Visiting Company'. However, in the interest of achieving a uniform approach, the ABTT would urge against totally rewriting clauses, except where unavoidable.

The text is the copyright of the Association of British Theatre Technicians but may be freely reproduced in the interest of achieving a uniform approach.

The ABTT welcomes suggestions for improvements or corrections.

Whilst all due care has been taken in the preparation of this document, the Association of British Theatre Technicians, together with its members, officers and employees, cannot be held responsible for any omissions or errors contained herein or for any damage or injury arising from any interpretations of its contents.

Foreword

The Theatre has responsibilities under the Health & Safety at Work Etc Act 1974 and other legislation for the wellbeing of its staff, the public and other visitors to the premises. It also has to meet the requirements of the Licensing Authority. For these reasons the Theatre has issued the following Technical Rules. These form part of the contract between the Theatre and the Visiting Company and in many cases reflect requirements of statutory regulations. The Visiting Company should ensure that all relevant company members and staff are fully aware of these Rules.

Theatre Technical Rules 2003

Definitions
In these Rules the following words have the indicated meaning:
The Theatre is the organisation engaging the Visiting Company or letting the Visiting Company use the premises. The Theatre is [*complete by inserting name*].
The Visiting Company is the organisation, group or individual intending to use the premises for the Production. The Visiting Company is [*complete by inserting name*].
The Licensing Authority is the authority having jurisdiction, this may be the local Council, the Fire Authority, the Health & Safety Executive (HSE), the Police, etc.
The Production is the event or performance intended to take place in the Theatre's premises. The Production is known as [*complete by inserting name*].
The Production Period starts at the beginning of the get in and ends at the finish of the get out.

Health & Safety, Fire and Licensing Regulations
1. The Theatre is subject to Health & Safety, and Licensing Regulations. The Theatre requires the Visiting Company and all persons associated directly or indirectly with the Visiting Company or the Production, whether or not they be members/ employees of the Visiting Company, to comply with the Theatre's Technical Rules and all legal and licensing requirements for the premises as detailed in this document. It is the Visiting Company's responsibility to inform all relevant members of its organisation, including any sub-contractors and helpers, of these rules. If there are any queries please contact the Theatre as soon as possible for clarification well before the Production Period.

Production file
2. It is strongly recommended that the Visiting Company create a Production File that carries full details of the Production. This will help the Theatre and the Licensing Authority satisfy themselves that all of the arrangements for the Production are in order and safe. The file should contain as appropriate:
    All licences required for the Production (as distinct from the premises)
    Detailed method statements for the Production's construction and operation including flying plot and ground plan

Certificates of flame-retardancy
Full details of any special effects including risk assessments (which may form part of the Production's general risk assessment)
    Assessments under the Control of Substance Hazardous to Health Regulations (COSHH) of substances used in the Production
Temporary Structure Inspection Certificates
    Insurance certificates for the Visiting Company's equipment, scenery, costumes, etc.
    Electrical safety, including Portable Appliance Testing (PAT), certificates
    Details of any special electrical power requirements and connection facilities
    A copy of the Production File should be sent to the Theatre at least two weeks before arrival of the Visiting Company.

Technical Meeting
3. A technical meeting must be arranged between the Visiting Company and the Theatre. The Visiting Company must contact the Theatre at least 6 weeks prior to the date of Production to schedule a meeting unless already contacted by the Theatre. The Theatre also strongly advises the Visiting Company to arrange for the Theatre's technical manager to visit a rehearsal in advance of the performance to make sure the planning is effective and efficient.

4. The Construction (Design and Management) Regulations (CDM) may apply to the Production although generally this is not the case. However it is sensible to apply the principles of CDM to ensure that the work is properly planned during construction, fit up, rehearsal, performance and get out. Records of decisions made should be kept in the Production File. The technical meeting with the Theatre forms part of the process of ensuring that all parties concerned understand what is intended and how it can be achieved safely and economically.
    As far as possible all technical issues should be resolved before the Production Period. Provision can be made for most production requirements but only following discussion and mutually agreed timetabling. All certification and testing of all equipment should be in hand or complete before the Production Period. The Theatre cannot be held responsible if lack of attention to these requirements causes production equipment to be withdrawn, delays or cancellation.

Technical Facilities
5. A list of what is supplied, what can be provided

at additional cost and arrangements for consumables such as colour, microphone batteries, etc., will found in Annex A. The Visiting Company will be asked to countersign a Contra Report detailing the consumable items used.

Permitted use

6. The Visiting Company has the exclusive use of the stage, dressing rooms, auditorium but only for the purpose of agreed rehearsals and performances, and basic lighting, sound and staging facilities for agreed rehearsals and performances. The Theatre will endeavour to provide but cannot guarantee access to any of its facilities except during the Production Period. It is not always possible to schedule rehearsal time in the premises prior to the Production Period.

7. Minor repairs and alterations to scenery, costumes, props and furniture may be carried out in designated areas in the premises with the prior consent of the Theatre. If significant use is made of the Theatre's spares, equipment or staff a charge will be made to the Visiting Company to recover these costs.

Access.

8. No unauthorised persons (including friends, parents and relatives) or animals are allowed backstage at any time. Authorisation may be gained only from the Theatre. Authorised personnel are allowed access only on the dates and during the hours mentioned in the Contract or as subsequently agreed with the Theatre. It is essential that only performers and crew are backstage after the half has been called.

9. No flammable items or packing of any kind may be left anywhere within the premises except as approved by the Theatre.

10. Smoking is not permitted anywhere in the premises except in the green room with the consent of other users.

11. Smoking or the use of incense is only permitted on stage as part of agreed rehearsals and performances. The Theatre must be informed at least 14 days in advance if the performance involves smoking or incense; additional fire fighting equipment may be required. It is essential that smoking does not otherwise occur in the stage area or in the auditorium, especially during fit ups and technical rehearsals.

Food and Drink

12. No eating or drinking is allowed on stage (except as part of agreed rehearsals and performances) or in the auditorium. Do not prepare hot food after the 'half' or during the show in the vicinity of the stage (except where required as part of the performance.)

13. No alcohol or illicit drugs are allowed backstage, in the pit, or in the auditorium at any time.

Children

14. All rehearsals or performances with children on stage or in the auditorium must have an adequate provision of licensed chaperones to keep order at all times, to take charge of the children in an emergency and to ensure their welfare at all times. Children under 16 must be supervised at all times. There must be at least one chaperone with every 10 children. This is the law; failure to comply may result in the performance being cancelled. The Theatre may assist in providing chaperones if required for which an administrative charge will be made. The licensing of children as defined in The Children (Performances) Amendment Regulations 2000 is the sole responsibility of the Visiting Company.

Technical Staff for Performances and Rehearsals

15. A 'Performance' is defined as the period from one hour before curtain up, until 30 minutes after curtain down. In the case of a single or the final performance, or one that is followed by a Get-Out, a 'Performance' is deemed to end at curtain down. In both cases, Performances should not exceed 5 hours, start earlier than 9am, or finish later than 11pm if overtime penalties are to be avoided. In effect, this means playing time should not exceed 3½ hours including interval(s). If these times are exceeded the Visiting Company will incur additional expenses as set out in Schedule 1. The Visiting Company will also be charged for taxi fares incurred if staff work after the end of public transport.

16. The Theatre provides two technical staff for a 'Performance', one in the control room, and the other at the prompt corner. They are there primarily to deal with emergencies. If they can perform a useful function from these positions they will do so, for example operating the lighting control, or house tabs. Additional staff such as sound operators, flymen, follow spot operators can be supplied and will be charged to the Visiting

Company as detailed in Schedule 1.

17. A 'Rehearsal' means any period when the venue is used to rehearse, get-in, fit-up, tech., dress, or any other non-performance use in connection with the Production. This includes any time taken by the Theatre staff working on the Production including preparing and setting up equipment and putting it away at the end.

18. The Theatre provides one technician for a Rehearsal. There are no restrictions on use of this member of staff who may not, however, be qualified or available to do all the jobs required. Additional staff can be supplied and will be charged to the Visiting Company as detailed in Schedule 1.

19. The Get-Out will start immediately after the final performance once the auditorium is clear, or sooner if practicable. The Get-Out will be charged to the Visiting Company as detailed in Schedule 1.

20. The Theatre reserves the right to set minimum staffing levels both for Rehearsals and Performances and any additional staff will be charged to the Visiting Company as detailed in Schedule 1. For example: shows that make use of flying may require a Stage Manager and a Flyman for the fit-up; work requiring the use of the Tallescope will require at least two and possibly more crew. The Visiting Company will be asked to countersign a Contra Report detailing the staff hours to be charged.

21. The Visiting Company may bring its own technical staff. However the Theatre reserves the right not to allow the Visiting Company's technical staff to use the premise's equipment or facilities if the Theatre deems them not competent so to do.

22. It is the Visiting Company's responsibility to ensure that the Theatre's staff get their required meal and overnight breaks as laid down in their contracts of employment. Any penalty payments will be recharged to the Visiting Company as detailed in Schedule 1. The Theatre will advise when breaks should be taken.

23. All staff provided by the Theatre remain under the control of the Theatre.

24. Any accident, dangerous occurrence or untoward incident, however it occurred, must be reported to the Theatre and be logged in the appropriate accident or incident book. Verbal or physical abuse of (or by) the Theatre's staff will not be tolerated.

Scenery

25. All scenery, decorations, borders, drapery, gauzes, cloths, curtains and similar decorative hangings must be made of material which is not readily inflammable, or of material which has been rendered and is maintained flame-retarded to the satisfaction of the Theatre and the Licensing Authority.

26. On a stage with a safety curtain scenery made of the following materials is acceptable, subject to any requirements of the Licensing Authority: all materials acceptable on an open stage (see below);

flame-retarded fabrics; any non-durably flame-retarded fabrics will be tested for flame-retardancy and may have to be re-treated if found unsatisfactory;

plywood, hardboard or similar boards; any boards under 6mm thick must be treated by a process of impregnation which meets at least class 2 when tested in accordance with BS 476-7.

Any scenery downstage of the safety curtain must meet open stage standards.

27. On an open stage without a safety curtain scenery made of the following materials is acceptable, subject to any requirements of the Licensing Authority:

non-combustible material;

inherently flame-retarded fabric;

durably-treated flame-retarded fabric;

fabrics rendered and maintained flame-retarded to the Licensing Authority's satisfaction by a non-durable process;

timber, hardboard or plywood treated by a process of impregnation which meets class 1 when tested in accordance with BS 476-7;

timber framing of minimum 22mm nominal thickness;

medium-density fibreboard (MDF), plywood or chipboard not less than 18mm in thickness;

plastics material subject to special consideration by the Licensing Authority;

any other materials approved by the Licensing Authority.

28. The use of plastics or expanded polystyrene must be avoided whenever possible. Decorative items such as statues made of expanded polystyrene must be enclosed by a non-combustible skin of,

for example, plastered scrim, Artex or Rosco Foamcoat, and care taken that this skin is maintained undamaged.

29. Plywood and similar boards must be branded with a recognised stamp to certify the standard of flame retardancy achieved. Where the stamp is not visible, certificates must be retained in the Production File. Certificates of the flame retardancy of other materials must be retained in the Production File.

30. The Theatre reserves the right to check and test where deemed necessary all scenery for compliance with the appropriate fire standard. The Theatre will remove, or render flame-retarded at the Visiting Company's expense, any items not conforming to the appropriate standard, since failure to comply may result in the performance being delayed or cancelled.

31. Where very large quantities of scenery are proposed the Visiting Company should consult the Theatre in case there are concerns about overcrowding the stage or an excessive increase in fire load. Whilst detailed calculations are unlikely to be required, the acceptable volume of flammable scenery depends upon consideration of a number of factors including the structure of the premises, the fire spread control provisions, the fire-fighting arrangements and the specific risks presented by the performance; all of these factors will determine the Licensing Authority's requirements in any particular case. Lower or less permanent standards of fire retardancy may be acceptable in premises provided with a separated stage, a sprinkler installation and a Duty Fire Officer than may be approved on an open stage.

32. The line of descent of any safety curtain must not be obstructed by objects such as scenery, furniture, luminaires, sound equipment or pianos without prior agreement from the Theatre who will need to consult the Licensing Authority; such consent is unlikely.

33. All scenery must be stable and not likely to collapse once erected other than as an intended effect. The Theatre may refuse to allow the erection of any scenery that it considers unsafe unless a certificate issued by an appropriately qualified person, for example a chartered engineer, is provided. This is desirable where the use of scaffolding or raised staging is proposed.

34. Whilst fastening fittings such as hinges or sheet materials to the stage floor by using screws or nails is permitted, no holes may be cut in the floor without the prior consent of the Theatre. No other fixings may be made to other parts of the premises without the prior consent of the Theatre. Any redecoration of the stage or auditorium must be approved by the Theatre who will normally require the previous decoration to be restored to its satisfaction at the end of the Production.

35. The stage must not be overcrowded with scenery or other items. All escape routes must be maintained clear and unobstructed at all times.

Weight

36. Individual items of scenery or other equipment exceeding 15kg must have their weight marked on them if they are to be manually handled by the Theatre's staff. Ideally the weight of each separate item should be marked on it. Where the decoration of double-sided pieces makes this impractical a note should be available in the Production File. The Visiting Company must provide the Theatre with the exact (or estimated if so agreed at the Technical Meeting see Clause 3) assembled weight of any pieces to be suspended or flown together with details of the distribution of the load. Likewise the Visiting Company must provide the Theatre with the assembled weights of any heavy items, including the point loads of any trucks or wheeled pieces.

37. Scenery must not be suspended other than from the venue's approved building anchor points or the flying system.

38. Any lifting equipment, including drift wires and other lifting accessories brought in by the Visiting Company must be accompanied by documentation of inspection as required by Lifting Operations & Lifting Equipment Regulations (LOLER). This should form part of the Production File.

39. The Theatre must approve all rigging and lifting operations before work commences.

Floors

40. Sheet materials such as hardboard or plywood laid in direct contact with a structural floor need not be treated flame-retarded. Any carpets and other textile floor coverings and under-lays when tested appropriately in accordance with BS 4790 must either not ignite or have the effects of

ignition limited to a radius of 35mm on both upper and under surfaces. Appropriate certificates must be retained in the Production File.

41. Where temporary floor surfaces such as sand, soil, turf, wood chippings, straw are to be used, certificates of treatment against fire, biohazard, toxicity as relevant, together with any special operating procedures must be retained in the Production File. A charge may be made for cleaning. Dusty materials such as Vermiculite or flour must not be used as floor coverings.

Props
42. Similar considerations of reducing the risk of fire apply to the use of properties and furnishings as to the use of scenery. Where the action does not involve the use of naked flame or smoking lesser standards may be appropriate.

As a general rule hand-held properties and antique furnishings will be approved without flame retardancy treatment. However the Theatre and the Licensing Authority will generally apply the same standards as apply to scenery to large properties, large quantities of furnishings and to items especially constructed for the presentation. Appropriate certificates must be retained in the

Production File
43. Items such as tablecloths, curtains and bedclothes must be flame retardant. Appropriate certificates must be retained in the Production File. Some flame retardancy treatments may cause dermatitis or irritation to sensitive skins; it may therefore be permissible for sheets in contact with naked skin not to be treated flame-retardant where hazards such as the use of real flame are not present.

44. The Theatre may require sight of the risk assessments for props and effects devices and, if deemed necessary, to see them in use under performance conditions before they are used in performance. The use of any substances (liquid or solid) or props with potential likely to permanently mark or damage in-house surfaces or to create substantial dust must be approved by the Theatre and, if deemed necessary, be tested under performance conditions.

Costumes
45. Where real flame is in use it may be necessary for flimsy costumes to be fireproofed in which case some form of recognised certification must be retained in the Production File.

46. Only designated dressing rooms or quick-change areas may be used for costume changes. Backstage toilets, corridors, stairwells, the green room and the stage door area must not be used; this is to ensure that all passageways are kept clear in case of an emergency.

47. Quick-change arrangements must not affect the means of escape or access to fire-fighting equipment.

Electrical equipment
48. If additional lighting or sound equipment is required, the Visiting Company must arrange for it to be provided and fixed at its own cost.

49. Any additional electrical equipment, including luminaires and sound equipment, must carry an indication of a valid PAT certificate. The PAT certificate, if not on the equipment, should be retained in the Production File.

A charge will be made if testing of uncertified equipment using either in-house equipment or staff is deemed necessary. The Theatre reserves the right to remove from the premises any electrical appliance deemed to be unsafe.

Temporary Wiring
50. All temporary electrical wiring must comply with recommendations of BS 7671 or where applicable BS 7909.

51. Luminaires may only be rigged to approved suspension points. All luminaires must be provided with secondary suspensions (safety bonds or safety chains.)

Blackouts
52. If essential to the Production, the low-intensity management lighting in the auditorium area may, with the consent of the Theatre, be reduced or extinguished subject to the requirements of the Licensing Authority but the escape route (exit) signs must remain illuminated at all times.

Access equipment
53. The Theatre's access equipment, including ladders, the Tallescope and any powered access equipment, may only be used with the consent of the Theatre and must be used in accordance with HSE regulations and guidance. Visiting Company personnel may only use access equipment if the Theatre is satisfied of their competence.

54. The Theatre will require evidence of thorough

examination and other appropriate certification before permitting the use of access equipment supplied for or on behalf of the Visiting Company. Any proposal to bring in powered access equipment must be approved by the Theatre.

Special Effects

55. Special effects include any device or effect that was not included in the original licensing risk assessment for the premises which, if not properly controlled, may present a hazard. Examples include the use of dry ice machines, cryogenic fogs, smoke machines, fog generators, pyrotechnics and fireworks, real flame (including smoking and the use of incense,) firearms, motor vehicles, strobe lighting, lasers and animals (including birds, fish and reptiles) as part of the performance. The Theatre has to obtain the consent of the Licensing Authority before special effects may be used. All special effects for a Production should be set up and thoroughly tested as far as reasonably practicable before the fit up at the Theatre. This testing should replicate performance levels and conditions as far as possible. The Licensing Authority may require the proposed effect(s) to be demonstrated in performance conditions before consent can be given and may refuse consent or make specific requirements. As much notice of any proposed effects should be given to the Theatre as possible but in any case no less than fourteen days. Failure to provide sufficient information will result in late or non-acceptance of the effect even though such non-approval may have a serious artistic implication.

After an effect has been demonstrated and approved it must not be altered.

56. Only a responsible person who has received appropriate training may operate special effects.

57. The warning notices required by clauses 59.3, 60.4, 61.7, 63.8 and 66.3 must be conspicuously displayed at all public entrances to the premises (or auditorium, where appropriate) so that the public may read them before entering.

Where practicable similar notices should also be printed in any programme.

58. Any proposal to use excessively loud sound effects or music or high-power audience lights must be discussed with the Theatre in advance who may require all programmes and pre-performance advertising literature to carry an appropriate warning. Failure to obtain approval from the Theatre may result in modification of the desired effect.

Dry ice machines and cryogenic fogs

59. Cryogenic (low temperature) fogs are produced using dry ice (solid carbon dioxide) or liquefied gas (generally liquid nitrogen or liquid synthetic air). The gases released by conversion from the solid or liquid form can displace the normal atmosphere, including the oxygen in the air, to become an asphyxiant (except liquid synthetic air, which includes oxygen). Good ventilation is essential to ensure that the gas disperses in order to prevent hazardous concentrations. This applies particularly to carbon dioxide from dry ice, which is heavier than air and can gather in low places. Particular care is necessary in respect of basements, under-stage areas, orchestra pits and auditorium stalls. Stores in which dry ice is kept should be well ventilated. If there is any doubt about the safety of the carbon dioxide vapour present, oxygen levels must be measured during a test of the effect before its use in performance. Meters to monitor oxygen levels should be provided if there is any doubt about the gas concentrations present. Specialist advice should be sought particularly on the siting and appropriate detection levels for oxygen meters.

Fog may cause irritation to those with respiratory sensitivity, including asthmatics. The Licensing Authority may require approval of the type of fog generator proposed.

59.1. Documentary evidence of the non-toxicity and non-flammability of the fog must be retained in the Production File.

59.2. The volume of fog must be limited so that it does not seriously affect means of escape or obscure escape route signs. The penetration of fog into public areas must be restricted as far as is possible. Ventilation plant must be running while the fog effects are in use.

59.3. Warning notices must be displayed stating that fog is used as part of the effects.

60. Smoke machines & fog generators
Smoke is the product of combustion and is made up of small, solid particles. Fog is composed of liquid droplets. This difference is important. Apart from as a by-product of the use of pyrotechnics, smoke is rarely used as an effect, whilst fog or vapour effects are relatively frequent. Most 'smoke machines' should more properly be known as 'fog generators'. Fog or smoke may cause irritation to those with respiratory sensitivity, including asthmatics. The Licensing Authority may require approval of the type of fog generator or smoke machine proposed. Some Licensing Authorities operate an approved list of smoke machines or fog

generators and will not consent to other machines unless adequate technical information is provided in sufficient time to enable them to determine whether the type of smoke machine or fog generator proposed is acceptable.

60.1. Documentary evidence of the non-toxicity and non-flammability of the fog or smoke must be retained in the Production File.

60.2. Smoke machines and fog generators must be sited and controlled so that they do not obstruct exit routes nor cause a hazard to surrounding curtains or fabrics.

60.3. The volume of smoke and/or fog must be limited so that it does not seriously affect means of escape or obscure escape route signs. The penetration of smoke and/or fog into public areas must be restricted as far as is possible. Ventilation plant must be running while the smoke and/or fog effects are in use.

60.4. Warning notices must be displayed stating that fog or smoke is used as part of the effects.

61. Pyrotechnics including fireworks
Specialist manufacturers supply pre-packed pyrotechnics, which enable strict control of the quantities of components and the easy safe repetition of pyrotechnic effects. Pyrotechnics supplied specifically for stage use must be used unless the entire effect including the operation is under the direct control of a specialist contractor.

61.1. All pyrotechnics must be used strictly in accordance with the manufacturer's instructions.

61.2. The Duty Fire Officer must be present on stage whenever pyrotechnics are used. Additional fire fighting equipment may be required.
61.3. Pyrotechnics must be confined to the stage area and not be taken into public areas.

61.4. Pyrotechnics must be fired from an approved key-protected control/firing box (and never directly from the mains electricity supply.) The key must be kept in the possession of the operator responsible for firing the devices. The control/firing box must only be energised immediately before firing the pyrotechnic devices.

61.5. The operator must have a clear view of the pyrotechnic device and its immediate vicinity from the firing point. This may be achieved by the use of an appropriate closed circuit television system.

61.6. The device must not be operated if there is any risk to anyone. In the event of a misfire the circuit must be switched off until after the performance.

61.7. Maroons must only be used in suitable bomb tanks in safe locations.

Warning notices must be displayed stating that maroons operate as part of the effects on the premises.

61.8. Only sufficient pyrotechnic supplies for one performance may be withdrawn from store. At the end of the performance any unused pyrotechnics must be returned to store. The storage arrangements must comply with Clause 68.

62. Real flame
Whenever possible an electrical or mechanical effect should be substituted for the use of real flame.

62.1. Real flame must be kept clear of costumes, curtains and drapes. Real flame must be kept out of the reach of the public and must not be taken into public areas.

62.2. The lighting and extinguishing of the flame must be supervised by the Duty Fire Officer who must remain where there is a clear view of the flame and easy access to it until it is extinguished. Additional fire-fighting equipment may be necessary.

62.3. Any candleholders and candelabra must be robustly constructed, not easily overturned and where practicable fixed in position.

62.4. Hand-held flaming torches must incorporate fail-safe devices so that if a torch is dropped the flame is automatically extinguished. Fail-safe devices must be tested prior to each performance and recorded in the fire log-book.

62.5. Only solid fuel or paraffin may be used. The amount of fuel in torches must limited to the minimum necessary for the effect. Storage arrangements for fuel must comply with Clause 68.

63. Firearms
Guns used on stage should generally either be replicas or deactivated firearms; both types may be capable of firing blanks (provided they are not readily convertible to fire live ammunition.) Firearms that have been deactivated to Home Office standard and certified by a Proof House and replica guns which are not readily convertible to fire live ammunition are not treated as firearms for legal purposes and do not at present require a licence. The same security arrangements must be applied to replica guns and deactivated firearms as apply to licensed weapons. The use of a working firearm, including a shotgun, would require the issue of a Firearms Licence or a Shotgun Certificate as appropriate by the police as well as the consent of the Council. Some firearms, notably automatic weapons and most pistols, are classified

as prohibited weapons. The use of any prohibited weapon would require the consent of the Home Secretary and the attendance of a registered firearms dealer whilst such firearms are on the premises as well as the consent of the Licensing Authority.

63.1. Any gun or ammunition must be under the direct control of the person holding the appropriate firearms certificate. Firearms and ammunition must not be left unattended by the responsible person. This does not preclude the use of the firearm by the performer provided it is returned immediately after use to the responsible person.

63.2. All ammunition and firearms including deactivated, replica and imitation firearms must be stored in a robust locked container in a room, which must be kept locked when not in use in a part of the premises to which the public do not have access. The storage arrangements must meet the requirements of the Licensing Authority, where applicable. See Clause 68.

63.3. Firearms must not contain any article or substance that could act as a missile. Blank ammunition must have crimped ends.

63.4. Firearms may only be removed from the store (together with the amount of ammunition necessary for the performance) immediately prior to the performance and must be returned to the store as soon as possible after use. Any unused ammunition must be returned to store. All discharged cartridges and percussion caps must also be accounted for at the end of the performance.

63.5. There must be sufficient rehearsal to ensure that any flame and hot gases are discharged safely.

63.6. Firing mechanisms and barrels must be cleaned and checked before use.

63.7. No firearm may be pointed directly at any person or at any readily combustible material.

63.8. Warning notices must be displayed stating that gunfire occurs as part of the effects.

64. Weapons

If the Production involves the use of weapons including firearms of any type, toy or replica, the Visiting Company must nominate an armourer, who will be responsible for the safe storage and maintenance of all weapons. The Theatre may require to see the weapons in use under performance conditions and reserves the right to refuse use if it deems them or the action unsafe.

65. Motor Vehicles

If a production-line motor vehicle is to be used on stage the following rules apply.

65.1. The fuel tank must be drained so as to retain only the minimum quantity of fuel necessary for the action.

65.2. The fuel cap must be (preferably locked) in place.

65.3. The fuel tank must not be replenished when the public are on the premises.

65.4. A drip tray must be provided under the engine when the vehicle is not in use.

65.5. Arrangements must be made to minimise the hazards of exhaust fumes.

65.6. A Duty Fire Officer must be present whilst the public are on the premises. Additional and appropriate fire-fighting equipment must be provided in the proximity of the vehicle. Foam extinguishers will usually be required.

65.7. The storage arrangements of any spare fuel must comply with Clause 68.

If a vintage motor vehicle or specially constructed engine is to be used the following additional precautions must be observed:

65.8. The quantity of flammable liquid in the engine must not exceed 0.3 litre and must be wholly taken up by a suitable absorbent material in a detachable container of an approved type.

65.9. A screen of metal gauze or other suitable means must be provided between the container and the inlet valve to the engine to prevent backfiring to the container.

65.10. The exhaust pipe must be carried well clear of the engine.

66. Stroboscopic lighting effects

Photosensitive people are particularly sensitive to light. Tests have shown that gazing at stroboscopic lighting may induce epileptic attacks in photosensitive individuals. For this reason stroboscopic lighting effects must operate at the lower frequencies which have been shown to be likely to affect only about 5% of the flicker sensitive population. The Licensing Authority may require approval of the type of stroboscopic lighting effects proposed.

66.1. Strobes must not be sited on escape routes, corridors or stairs or other changes of level.

66.2. Where stroboscopic effects are used in public areas, the sources must be synchronised and locked off to operate at a fixed frequency outside the band of 4 to 50 flashes per second. This rule may be relaxed for purely momentary effects on stage.

66.3. Warning notices must be displayed stating that stroboscopic lighting operates as part of the effects.

67. Lasers

Lasers produce very intense light beams, which could blind, cause skin burns or even start a fire if used improperly. Even reflected beams can be dangerous. This clause does not apply to Class 1 or Class 2 lasers (such as are used in CD players, bar-code readers, etc.)

67.1. Laser beams must be at least 3 metres above the highest affected floor level at all times and arranged so that they cannot scan onto any member of the public, performer or staff. Supporting structures must be rigid to avoid any accidental misalignment of the laser(s). Any mirrors must be securely fixed in position.

67.2. Laser equipment, including mirrors, must be placed out of reach of the public.

67.3. The alignment of the laser installation including any mirrors must be checked on a daily basis.

68. Storage of special effects & firearms

Special effects and firearms may only be kept in the Theatre's approved store. This includes pyrotechnics, maroons, blank ammunition, petrol, flammable gases and liquids.

68.1. The storage receptacle must be kept locked shut at all times except when withdrawing material from store. The key must be kept under the direct control of the person responsible for the safe storage.

68.2. Quantities must be limited to the practicable minimum necessary for the requirements of the presentation. No more than 0.6 litres of flammable liquid or 2.3kg gross weight of pyrotechnics will normally be allowed on the premises unless kept in a store licensed by the appropriate authority.

68.3. Smoking and naked flame is prohibited in areas where any explosives or highly flammable substances are stored and notices or signs must be displayed both in rooms and on containers to this effect.

68.4. Storage areas and containers must be indicated by the explosive or inflammable symbol as appropriate on the door or lid.

68.5. All ammunition and firearms including deactivated, replica and imitation firearms must be stored in a robust locked container in a room, which must be kept locked when not in use. The police will also require approval of the storage arrangements for any firearms and ammunition.

68.6. When not in use all pyrotechnics must be stored in a suitable container, which may be a metal or wooden trunk, box, cupboard or drawer. All exposed metalwork, including any nails or screws, must be non-ferrous, preferably of copper, brass or zinc, or be otherwise covered with a thick layer of non-ferrous metal, not-easily-ignitable material or paint at least 1mm in thickness. The opening face of the storage receptacle must carry the explosives symbol together with a sign reading 'Danger – No smoking – No naked flame' in letters no less than 25mm high. Storage receptacles must be resealed and replaced in the main storage receptacle and the main storage receptacle re-locked.

68.7. Only the minimum amount of any explosives or highly flammable substances may be withdrawn from store as is necessary for the particular performance.

Supply the following appendices with the Technical Rider (these may vary with the specific terms of the Theatre Contract for the Production and also should be regularly revised):

Annex A

Provide full technical specification of the premises and equipment supplied as part of the Contract.

Detail what can be supplied at extra costs and the arrangements for consumables such as colour filter or radio microphone batteries, flash charges, etc.

Schedule 1

Provide details of pay rates, overtime rates, 'extras' and any other charges as they affect the Technical Rider and the Theatre Contract.